A LOST CAUSE

A LOST CAUSE

*Bill Clinton's Campaign for
National Health Insurance*

NICHOLAS LAHAM

PRAEGER

Westport, Connecticut
London

Library of Congress Cataloging-in-Publication Data

Laham, Nicholas.
    A lost cause : Bill Clinton's campaign for national health
insurance / Nicholas Laham.
      p. cm.
    Includes bibliographical references and index.
    ISBN 0–275–95611–3 (alk. paper)
    1. National health insurance—United States. 2. National health
insurance—Law and legislation—United States. 3. Health care
reform—United States. I. Title.
RA395.A3L339   1996
368.4'2'00973—dc20   96–2197

British Library Cataloguing in Publication Data is available.

Library of Congress Catalog Card Number: 96–2197
ISBN: 0–275–95611–3

First published in 1996

Praeger Publishers, 88 Post Road West, Westport, CT 06881
An imprint of Greenwood Publishing Group, Inc.

Printed in the United States of America

The paper used in this book complies with the
Permanent Paper Standard issued by the National
Information Standards Organization (Z39.48–1984).

10 9 8 7 6 5 4 3 2 1

To my mother, Laure, and Martha,
with love and appreciation

Contents

Tables

Preface

"This health care system of ours is badly broken and it is time to fix it," President Bill Clinton declared in his address to a joint session of Congress on September 22, 1993, urging the establishment of national health insurance:

At long last, after decades of false starts, we must make this our most urgent priority, giving every American health security; health care that can never be taken away, health care that is always there. . . . So let us agree . . . before this Congress finishes its work next year, you will pass and I will sign legislation to guarantee this security to every citizen of this country.[1]

On October 27 Clinton went to Capitol Hill to personally introduce his national health insurance bill, the Health Security Act, to congressional leaders. In his speech formally introducing the Health Security Act, Clinton noted that the bill "guarantees every single American a comprehensive package of health benefits . . . that are always there and can never be taken away."[2]

However, the full 103rd Congress failed to take action on the Health Security Act, as well as every alternative health care bill introduced by lawmakers. True, in June 1994 modified versions of the Health Security Act were approved by three of the five congressional committees exercising jurisdiction over health care reform. On July 2 a fourth committee, Senate Finance, approved a health care reform bill which would have guaranteed 95 percent of the public health insurance by 2002.

Approval of health care reform legislation by the four congressional committees exercising jurisdiction over national health insurance cleared the way for bills to be introduced on the Senate and House floors. However, due to the existence of substantial congressional opposition to national health insurance, Democratic leaders failed in their efforts to bring a health care reform bill to a vote on either the Senate or House floor before the 103rd Congress adjourned in October.

Clinton's failure to secure passage of a national health insurance bill in the 103rd Congress dealt a fatal blow to his health care reform initiative. Clinton needed to have the 103rd Congress complete action on health care reform if there was any realistic hope of obtaining enactment of a national health insurance bill during his first, and possibly only, term as president. National health insurance legislation is only likely to be passed in a heavily Democratic and liberal Congress. The Democratic Party maintained overwhelming majorities in both houses of the 103rd Congress, which included dozens of liberal members. As a result, the partisan and ideological composition of the 103rd Congress favored passage of national health insurance legislation.

By contrast, the Republican Party won a landslide victory in the 1994 congressional elections, securing control of both houses of the legislative branch for the first time in forty years. The Republican majority in the 104th Congress was almost unanimously opposed to national health insurance and had no intention of granting serious consideration to, let alone passing, a comprehensive health care reform bill. As a result, the Republican Party's success in securing control of the 104th Congress dealt a fatal blow to prospects for passage of a national health insurance bill during the final two years of Clinton's first term as president. The best chance for Clinton to have secured the establishment of national health insurance, at least during his first term, was in the 103rd Congress. Clinton's failure to do so guaranteed that no national health insurance program would be established during his first term.

This book addresses a single, central, overriding question: Why did Clinton fail to secure passage of a national health insurance bill in the 103rd Congress? True, Clinton is not the first president to launch a campaign to institute such a program. Presidents Harry S. Truman, Richard Nixon, and Jimmy Carter spearheaded similar campaigns, which ended in failure.[3] However, it seemed that Clinton would succeed in his drive to establish national health insurance, in contrast to the failure of past presidential attempts to do so. Clinton himself was sure of this. In his 1994 State of the Union address, he confidently predicted that his campaign to establish national health insurance would turn out differently from similar efforts undertaken by his predecessors: "For sixty years this country has tried to reform health care. President Roosevelt tried. President Truman tried. President Nixon tried. President Carter tried. Every time the special interests were powerful enough to defeat them. But not this time."[4]

Clinton was more effective in publicizing his support for national health insurance than Truman, Nixon, and Carter had been. Clinton's three predecessors recommended passage of national health insurance bills in written messages to Congress which received scant public and media attention.[5] Unlike his three predecessors, Clinton chose perhaps the most highly publicized and closely watched political forum in which to recommend passage of national health insurance legislation: a prime-time televised address to a joint session of Congress.

In choosing such a highly visible forum in which to urge congressional action on national health insurance, Clinton made it clear that health care reform represented one of his top domestic policy priorities, if not the most important.

The messages to Congress delivered by Truman, Nixon, and Carter urging the establishment of national health insurance were short documents, designed exclusively for lawmakers, which contained sketchy and incomplete outlines of their health care reform plans. None of the three presidents produced lengthy and detailed documents outlining their plans to the public. By contrast, the Clinton administration produced two large and extensive documents on health care reform which contained a detailed summary of its national health insurance plan. The first document detailed the administration's case for health care reform; the second contained a summary of Clinton's national health insurance plan.[6] The administration disseminated the documents to the public in the form of three books, which were sold in retail stores throughout the United States. The books were designed to mobilize popular support for the Clinton plan.

Clinton did a better job of outlining his national health insurance plan to the public and building popular support for it than Truman, Nixon, and Carter had done. Rarely is an administration document on a policy issue widely disseminated to the public. The fact that the Clinton administration's documents on health care reform were designed for public review reflected the president's success in generating popular interest in this issue and is consistent with his decision to make national health insurance perhaps his most urgent domestic policy priority.

Clinton's address to Congress on health care reform marked the climax of a highly publicized and closely watched nine-month-long effort by his administration to develop a national health insurance bill, which ended on October 27, 1993, when the president sent his long-awaited health care reform measure to Capitol Hill. The public closely followed every major twist and turn in this effort, and gave its initial approval to Clinton's campaign to secure the establishment of national health insurance; though, as we shall see, popular opinion of the president's health care reform initiative soured once opponents of the Clinton plan organized their successful campaign to defeat it.

Given the existence of strong public interest in and initial support for health care reform, the media devoted extensive coverage to the issue in 1993 and 1994. During those two years, front-page headlines on health care reform in the nation's largest newspapers appeared almost daily. The nation's newsmagazines contained articles on health care reform almost weekly. During 1993–1994, the media provided more coverage on health care reform than any other single period in which the issue has been on the national agenda since the turn of the century. The existence of strong public interest in and support for health care reform coupled with extensive media coverage of the issue created the expectation that the 103rd Congress would pass a national health insurance bill before its adjournment in October 1994. However, this did not occur. Why the 103rd Congress ignored Clinton's pleas for swift passage of a national health insurance bill, despite strong public interest in and support for health care reform, remains a puzzle, which this book attempts to solve.

During the course of writing this book, I have accumulated substantial debts to a number of individuals, without whose support the book could not have been published. I am grateful for the editorial support and assistance received from James R. Dunton and Nicole M. Burke at Praeger Publishers. I am especially grateful to my mother, Nadia Laham, aunt, Laure Abu-Haydar, and sister, Martha Laham, for the moral and financial support they provided me during the course of the writing. I benefited greatly from the patience and understanding my family displayed in supporting this book. I hope that it proves worthy of their support.

Chapter 1

The Political Obstacles to Health Care Reform

The doctors don't like [national health insurance]. The hospitals don't like it. The drug companies don't like it, and the insurance companies don't like it.[1]

Representative Pete Stark of California

During 1993 and 1994, Clinton failed in his campaign to secure the establishment of national health insurance for four major reasons: first, the health care industry has traditionally opposed the program, and has the political resources to prevent its adoption; second, popular support for Clinton's national health insurance plan, while initially strong, faded as opponents of the president's program organized a successful public relations campaign to defeat it; third, the business community, with few exceptions, opposed the Clinton plan, depriving the president of a critically important constituency vital to the achievement of health care reform; and fourth, the Democratic Party was deeply divided over what kind of national health insurance program should be established, dealing a fatal blow to Clinton's ability to build a Democratic majority in the 103rd Congress behind any single health care reform plan. Opposition from the health care industry, business, and a plurality of the public, combined with deep division within the Democratic Party over the issue of national health insurance, collectively served to derail Clinton's medical reform initiative.

THE HEALTH CARE INDUSTRY'S OPPOSITION TO NATIONAL HEALTH INSURANCE

The single, central, overriding obstacle which has consistently prevented the establishment of national health insurance is the health care industry's strident, vociferous, and unwavering opposition to the program. The industry has had a rational interest in opposing the program. National health insurance poses a threat to the financial interests of the politically powerful medical industry. By reducing financial barriers impeding public access to health care, universal health insurance coverage would raise patient utilization of health care services, particularly among the poor and those currently uninsured, driving up medical costs and the overall inflation rate. To the extent that universal coverage is achieved through the public sector, the program would raise the already swollen federal budget deficit.

National health insurance cannot be established on an economically and fiscally viable basis without the imposition of stringent medical cost-containment measures. Hospital and nursing-home rates, physician fees, and drug prices would have to be reduced. Administrative waste and inefficiency within the private health insurance industry, if not the industry itself, would have to be eliminated. Patient access to medical technology would have to be stringently rationed. National health insurance would impose financial losses upon every segment of the medical system—doctors, hospitals, and the private health insurance, pharmaceutical, and nursing-home industries. As a result, the health care industry has waged a pitched battle against national health insurance since 1920, when the American Medical Association (AMA) first announced its opposition to the program.[2]

The capacity of the health care industry to prevent the establishment of national health insurance has been enhanced by the growing importance of money in American politics. Since the mid-1970s, members of Congress have become increasingly dependent upon campaign contributions from interest groups to win reelection. Few, if any, interest groups have been more generous in providing campaign contributions to members of Congress than the health care industry, as we will see in Chapter 3.

During the early 1990s, the health care industry successfully used its substantial financial influence on Capitol Hill to blunt the significant political momentum toward medical reform unleashed by Democrat Harris Wofford's election to the Senate. Wofford made his support for national health insurance the centerpiece of his campaign, successfully using the issue to win a stunning upset victory in the 1991 United States Senate election in Pennsylvania. By successfully waging his legendary come-from-behind Senate victory on the issue of health care reform, Wofford provided dramatic and irrefutable evidence of the existence of strong public support for national health insurance. Further evidence of public support for national health insurance came in 1992, when Clinton was elected to the presidency campaigning on a pledge to achieve comprehensive health care reform. In the wake of Wofford's and Clinton's elections, congressional Democratic leaders, led by Senate Majority Leader George Mitchell of Maine, and joined by Clinton following his inauguration as President, stepped up their efforts to secure passage of a national health insurance bill. However, the health care industry responded by substantially raising its campaign contributions to members of Congress, preventing the Democratic majority on Capitol Hill from passing a national health insurance bill.[3]

National health insurance is unlikely to be established as long as members of Congress of both parties are heavily dependent upon campaign contributions from the health care industry to win reelection. The industry will oppose the establishment of national health insurance, since it is certain to include the imposition of stringent health care cost-containment measures, which would reduce the incomes of every segment of the medical system. The industry will use its substantial financial resources to target for defeat any member of Congress who supports the program. As a result, only a minority of members of Congress have been willing to defy the wishes of the industry and openly back the program.

Clinton was badly misfocused in pursuing his health care reform initiative. During the first nine months of his presidency, Clinton concentrated his time and energy on carefully developing a reasonable, balanced, and modest national health insurance plan which could gain support from all segments of American society with an interest in the health care system—Congress, the medical industry, business, the elderly, and the public as a whole. Clinton assumed that a national health insurance plan which embodied enough compromises and concessions to win the support of the major stakeholders in the health care system could be established.

However, Clinton failed to appreciate the substantial political obstacles which have prevented the establishment of national health insurance in the past and continue to do so. Those obstacles remain based upon the substantial financial ties existing between the health care industry and Congress. Clinton failed to understand that the enormous political clout the industry exerts on Capitol Hill makes passage of a national health insurance bill unlikely, regardless of how reasonable, balanced, and modest the plan is.

Clinton wanted the benefits of identifying himself with the politically popular cause of national health insurance, without having to undertake the politically difficult and arduous task of securing its establishment. An overwhelming majority of the public supports the establishment of a national health insurance program. By launching a campaign to establish such a politically popular program as national health insurance, Clinton won public support from a large segment of the population who have become alarmed at the rapid deterioration of the health care system and desire, if not demand, presidential leadership in addressing the issue of medical reform. By appearing to offer such leadership, Clinton succeeded in bolstering his sagging public approval ratings.

Indeed, polling data show that Clinton derived substantial political benefits from his campaign to establish national health insurance. During September 6–7, 1994, *USA Today*, CNN, and Gallup conducted a poll of 1,022 adults. The poll asked its respondents to rate Clinton's handling of four key issues, including health care policy. Sixty percent of the respondents approved of Clinton's handling of health care policy, and 36 percent disapproved. Popular approval of Clinton's handling of health care policy was higher than for any of the three other issues in which the public was asked to rate his performance.[4] Public approval of Clinton's handling of health care policy is consistent with popular support for national health insurance, a program which the president was committed to establishing. As a result, a substantial share of public support for Clinton's performance as president was derived from his commitment to health care reform.

Additional evidence of public support for Clinton's health care policy comes from a poll of 1,015 adults conducted by *USA Today*, CNN, and Gallup during March 27–29, 1995. The poll asked its respondents whether Clinton or the Republican congressional leaders were doing a better job in their handling of six key issues, including health care policy. Forty-seven percent of the respondents believed that Clinton was doing a better job handling health care policy, and 40 percent favored Republican congressional leaders. Health care was the only one of the six issues contained in the *USA Today*/CNN/Gallup poll in which the public preferred Clinton over Republican congressional leaders.[5]

Further evidence of public support for Clinton's health care policy comes from a poll of 1,039 adults conducted by *USA Today*, CNN, and Gallup during January 12–15, 1996. The poll asked its respondents whether they approved of Clinton and the early front-runner for the 1996 Republican presidential nomination, Senate Majority Leader Bob Dole of Kansas, in their handling of nine key issues, including health care. Forty-four percent of those polled said they approved of Clinton's handling of health care policy, compared to 35 percent for Dole.

Health care tied in fourth place, along with the economy and crime, among the nine issues in which the public was asked to rate Clinton's performance, behind education, foreign affairs, and Medicare. By contrast, health care tied next to last, along with education and crime, among the nine issues in which the public was asked to rate Dole's performance, ahead of only Medicare. Overall, health care tied in third place, along with crime, among the nine issues in which Clinton held his greatest advantage over Dole, behind education and Medicare.[6]

As we will see, the debate on health care reform resulted in sharp partisan divisions in Washington, with Clinton strongly favoring national health insurance, and congressional Republicans, led by Dole, adamantly opposed to the program. That health care ranked first among the four issues in which the public was asked to rate Clinton's performance in the 1994 *USA Today*/CNN/Gallup poll; and was virtually the only issue among the six contained in the 1995 *USA Today*/CNN/Gallup poll in which the public preferred Clinton over Republican congressional leaders indicates that an overwhelming share of the population support national health insurance, and that much of the popular backing for the President was derived from his commitment to establish the program. Further evidence of this fact is contained in the 1996 *USA Today*/CNN/Gallup poll, which shows Clinton maintaining an overwhelming advantage over Dole on the issue of health care.

Indeed, in a *Los Angeles Times* poll of 1,515 adults conducted during July 23–26, 1994, 45 percent of those polled approved of Clinton's performance as President. The *Los Angeles Times* poll asked Clinton supporters to state the major reason why they backed the President. Sixteen percent of the Clinton supporters said they backed the President because they "liked his health care proposals." Those expressing support for Clinton's health care policy represented the second largest group backing the president, behind only those who said that "he's trying" to do a good job but "needs more time."

Most importantly, health care policy represented the only issue attracting substantial public support for Clinton—a clear indication that much of the public support for the president was derived from his commitment to medical reform. Indeed, fully 7 percent of those polled cited Clinton's health care policy as the major reason why they backed the president. As a result, Clinton's commitment to health care reform gave him a major boost in his sagging public approval ratings, allowing him to command the support of a respectable, though hardly overwhelming, share of the population.

While Clinton's health care reform initiative generated substantial public support for the president, it also provoked significant popular opposition to him. The *Los Angeles Times* poll found that 47 percent of those surveyed disapproved of Clinton's performance as president. The *Los Angeles Times* poll asked those who disapproved of Clinton to state the major reason why they did so. Ten percent of those who disapproved of Clinton said that they did so because they "don't like his health care proposals." Those expressing opposition to Clinton's health care policy represented the third largest group who disapproved of the president. Health care was the only issue attracting substantial public disapproval of Clinton.[7]

On the surface, it would seem that Clinton did not gain politically from his health care reform initiative, since almost as many individuals opposed the president because of his commitment to national health insurance as supported him. However, those expressing opposition to Clinton due to his health care reform initiative were most probably conservative Republicans who would have opposed the president regardless of his stand on national health insurance. By contrast, those expressing support for Clinton due to his health care initiative were most likely liberal Democrats.

Those on the Left would have expected Clinton to pursue the liberal Democratic agenda, including health care reform. Clinton's failure to do so would have resulted in disillusionment within the liberal wing of the Democratic Party, costing him vital support from the Left. By pursuing his commitment to health care reform, Clinton succeeded in energizing and activating his liberal base within the Democratic Party, generating vital support for the president from the Left. While Clinton's health care reform initiative did alienate and anger the conservative wing of the Republican Party, the Right intensely opposed the president and, but for national health insurance, would have found another major issue on which to oppose him. Clinton gained politically from his health care reform initiative. His commitment to health care reform generated vital support for him among his natural allies on the Left, while alienating his traditional enemies on the Right, who could be expected to oppose him on almost every issue, even had the president joined conservative Republicans in opposing national health insurance.

Public approval of Clinton's health care policy was consistent with the fact that the president fully agrees with an overwhelming majority of the population that the medical system is in a state of disrepair, if not collapse, and is in dire need of reform. However, Clinton was unwilling to pursue the politically complicated and risky task of securing the establishment of national health insurance. If he had wished to obtain the adoption of national health insurance, then he would have had to create political conditions which would make its institution possible. To develop such conditions, Clinton would have had to act to loosen the solid financial links existing between Congress and the health care industry. He would have had to attempt to mobilize popular opposition to the overwhelming majority of members of Congress who are intent on sacrificing the health care needs of the public in order to continue their financial relationship with the industry. He would have had to impose substantial political costs on members of Congress who are insistent on pursuing their financial ties with the industry, and provide incentives for lawmakers to terminate their links with medical interest groups.

However, Clinton did virtually nothing to loosen the financial ties existing between Congress and the health care industry. Clinton failed even to call public attention to the financial links existing between the Congress and the industry, let alone take action to disrupt their relationship. Clinton's failure to challenge the financial bonds existing between Congress and the industry was due to partisan reasons. Practically all campaign contributions from the health care industry go to incumbent members of Congress, most of whom were Democrats until Republicans gained control of the legislative branch following the 1994 elections. As a result, Democratic members of Congress were far more dependent upon industry contributions than their Republican counterparts during the era in which Democrats controlled the legislative branch.

Accordingly, any attempt by Clinton to disrupt the financial ties existing between Congress and the health care industry would have provoked a confrontation between the president and the Democratic majority on Capitol Hill, who were heavily dependent upon the medical system for financial support. Clinton would have antagonized the Democratic majority in the 103rd Congress, had he attempted to publicly humiliate and embarrass them by exposing and publicizing their financial relationship with the industry. The public would have been angered, if not outraged, had they come to the conclusion that by being so dependent upon the health care industry as a source of financial support, the Democratic congressional majority had rendered themselves incapable of establishing national health insurance. Such a conclusion would have jeopardized the

Democratic congressional majority's claim to represent the middle class, many of whom are uninsured and have either little or no access to health care.

Clinton had the capacity to do substantial political damage to the Democratic majority in the 103rd Congress by publicly exposing the financial ties existing between them and the health care industry. However, he decided to avoid imposing such damage, since it would poison his relationship with the Democratic congressional majority. He opted instead to maintain a cordial, if not friendly, working relationship with the Democratic congressional majority. He refrained from even mentioning in public the close financial ties existing between the Democratic congressional majority and the health care industry. As a result, the overwhelming majority of Democratic, as well as Republican, members of Congress will continue to serve the financial interests of the industry, at the expense of the health care needs of the public, without having to pay any political price for doing so.

Members of Congress found any number of excuses to ignore Clinton's pleas for swift passage of a national health insurance bill. They complained that establishment of national health insurance would result in a substantial tax increase; drive small firms which do not currently provide their working families group coverage out of business, creating high unemployment; and require the stringent rationing of health care resources, depriving the insured population of access to vital life-saving and -enhancing medical technology. All those excuses collectively served as a convenient smoke screen for the single, central, overriding reason why the overwhelming majority of members of Congress cannot accept national health insurance: because it is opposed by the health care industry, which represents a major source of financial support for incumbent lawmakers. By failing to challenge, let alone disrupt, the financial ties linking the industry to Congress, Clinton practically assured the failure of his health care reform initiative. In the end, Clinton failed to demonstrate that he was up to the politically difficult and arduous task of reforming the health care system.

THE UNCERTAINTY OF PUBLIC OPINION ON NATIONAL HEALTH INSURANCE

A major factor which elevated national health insurance to a prominent place on the political agenda during the 1990s was the existence of strong public support for the program. The extent of public support for national health insurance was revealed in a poll of 600 adults conducted by Yankelovich Partners for *Time* and CNN during July 20–21, 1994. The poll asked its respondents the following question: "Should the federal government guarantee health care for all Americans?" Sixty-one percent of those polled said that "the federal government should guarantee health care for all Americans"; 33 percent believed that it should not.[8]

The *Time*/CNN poll shows the existence of overwhelming public support for making health care a right of American citizenship, with the federal government guaranteeing all individuals access to medical services. Given the fact that health care is currently a privilege of employment and income, not a right of American citizenship, the public believes that the medical system is in need of reform. During September 25–28, 1993, the *Los Angeles Times* conducted a poll of 1,491 adults, who were asked to "rate the nation's health care system." Fifty percent of the respondents said that the system "needs fundamental over-hauling"; 20 percent believed that it "needs many improvements"; 22 percent thought that it "needs some improvement"; 5 percent felt that it was "essentially good"; and 3 percent had no opinion. The *Los Angeles Times* poll found that 70 percent of the public believed that the health care system should be fundamentally reformed, if not completely overhauled—a clear indicator of popular dissatisfaction with the current arrangements for delivering and financing medical services.

The public is not so dissatisfied with the current health care system because they are unhappy with their own personal medical services or health insurance. Indeed, the 1993 *Los Angeles Times* poll just cited found that 76 percent of those asked expressed satisfaction with their own personal health care services.[9] The 1994 *Los Angeles Times* poll cited earlier asked its respondents whether they believed their insurance coverage was sound. Seventy-three percent of the respondents believed that their coverage was sound; only 23 percent thought it was unsound.[10] The *Los Angeles Times* polls show three-quarters of the public satisfied with their own personal health care services and insurance, which illustrates the fact that the health care system is doing a good job guaranteeing the insured population access to high-quality medical services.

The source of public dissatisfaction with the current health care system lies, not in public dissatisfaction with their own personal health care services or health insurance, but in the absence of any security in their insurance coverage. During the postwar period, the United States experienced the development of a voluntary, employment-based health insurance system in which business and the government assumed responsibility for providing the overwhelming majority of working families coverage. However, during the 1990s, the voluntary, employment-based insurance system underwent substantial deterioration, as large corporations, beset by competitive pressures, shrinking markets, and rising administrative costs, acted to downsize their operations by laying off millions of workers. In the meantime, the development of a severe recession from 1990 to 1991, combined with the weakest economic recovery in postwar history, which began in March 1991 and continues five years later, resulted in high unemployment, which shrunk the tax base, resulting in massive budget deficits at all levels of government. As a result, federal, state, county, and municipal governments laid off tens of thousands of public sector workers. Virtually all workers laid off by large corporations and government employers had group insurance, and lost their health care benefits when they lost their jobs. Many, if not most, of them became uninsured. Accordingly, the uninsured population swelled during the 1990s.

A majority of the public are working families covered by employment-based health insurance which is linked to their jobs. As a result, working families usually lose their insurance when they lose their jobs; and may experience difficulty finding a new employer willing to provide them coverage. Given the increasing job insecurity which the United States has experienced during the 1990s, practically all working families face a serious risk that they will lose their jobs and the insurance which comes with their employment in the not-too-distant future.

As the number of uninsured individuals has swelled due to the deterioration of America's voluntary, employment-based health insurance system, workers fortunate enough to keep their jobs, as well as their group coverage, saw their health care benefits shrink during the 1980s and 1990s. Soaring health care costs forced large corporations to reduce the medical benefits they provide their employed households in order to cut their business expenses. In addition, plagued with massive budget deficits, the federal government moved to reduce soaring Medicare costs by slashing coverage provided to beneficiaries under the program. Faced with shrinking health care benefits, working families and Medicare recipients were forced to shoulder an increasing financial burden for their medical expenses. As a result, practically all segments of society felt the combined pinch of soaring health care costs and shrinking medical benefits—working families, and elderly and disabled Medicare recipients.

Faced with the prospect of becoming uninsured, if they are not already, and with their group coverage shrinking, the public supported, and in some instances demanded, the establishment of a national health insurance program which would guarantee universal access to affordable health care during the early 1990s.[11] The rising public clamor for health care reform is the major factor which triggered intense efforts by Clinton and Democratic leaders in the 103rd Congress to establish national health insurance during 1993 to 1994. In pursuing their campaign to establish national health insurance, Clinton and congressional Democratic backers of the program were responding to the needs and demands of a substantial share of the public who had a strong and passionate commitment to health care reform.

However, public support for national health insurance, though strong, is also volatile. While an overwhelming majority of the public support national health insurance, they are reluctant to back any specific plan. The uncertainty of public support for any specific national health insurance program can be seen in popular skepticism toward Clinton's health care reform plan. Public support for the Clinton plan declined and finally collapsed during the ten months following its introduction by the president in his address before a joint session of Congress on September 22, 1993. The decline in public support for Clinton's national health insurance plan came after congressional Republican opponents of the program joined the private insurance industry in mounting an intense public relations campaign against the president's program. They argued that the Clinton plan would deprive the public of their choice of doctors, result in stringent and austere health care rationing, which would deny individuals access to life-saving and -enhancing medical technology, and raise health care costs, while reducing the quality of medical care. A substantial segment of the public found the case against the Clinton plan convincing and turned against it. With popular opposition to the Clinton plan now on the rise, and congressional leaders having failed to advance a credible alternative to the president's program, lawmakers saw no immediate and overriding public need to pass a national health insurance bill; the 103rd Congress adjourned in October 1994 without taking any action on health care reform.

BUSINESS OPPOSES CLINTON'S NATIONAL HEALTH INSURANCE PLAN

The health care industry's capacity to use its substantial political resources to prevent the establishment of national health insurance cannot alone explain the failure of medical reform during 1993–1994. Business, not the health care industry, had the potential to become the key player in determining the success of Clinton's campaign to establish national health insurance. The pivotal role business could play in the politics of national health insurance upon one single, central, overriding fact: The overwhelming majority of the public are working families covered by group health insurance financed by employers, most of whom are in the private sector.

As a result, a substantial minority of the population receive their health insurance through business. This gave business enormous influence in shaping the debate on health care reform during 1993–1994. Business could provoke a collapse of the health care system by merely terminating the group insurance that firms provide their working families. Many, if not most, working families cannot afford to purchase their own private insurance, are too young and healthy to qualify for Medicare, and are too "rich" to be eligible for Medicaid.

As a result, working families are dependent upon their employers for health insurance. Many, if not most, of them would become uninsured should their employers choose to terminate their group insurance. Accordingly, the termination of group insurance by business would add tens of millions of individuals to the ranks of the uninsured. In the absence of any coverage, the tens of millions of newly uninsured would be unable to finance the cost of their health care. They would have no alternative but to receive uncompensated care from charitable hospitals when they fell ill. This would force the health care system to contribute tens of billions of dollars in uncompensated care to the tens of millions of newly uninsured. A substantial segment of the health care system would go bankrupt providing such uncompensated care.

The financial solvency of the health care system is dependent upon the willingness of firms to continue financing group health insurance for their working families. Should business refuse to continue assuming this responsibility, then the government would have to do so, in order to avert the collapse of the health care system which would result from the termination of group insurance. As a result, through the simple elimination of group insurance, business could force the government to establish a national health insurance program, in which the state assumes from the private sector responsibility for providing coverage to working families.

Business had the capacity to use the substantial influence it wields over the health care system to shape the debate on national health insurance during 1993–1994. Business used its influence to oppose Clinton's national health insurance plan. True, business was by no means unanimous in its opposition to national health insurance. Large corporations were divided over this issue, with most big companies opposing national health insurance, while others supported it. In the meantime, small business was practically united in its opposition to the program.

The deep division within the business community over national health insurance deprived corporate supporters of the program of the ability to exert influence over the debate on health care reform. As we have seen, large corporations could have forced Congress to establish the program by terminating the group coverage they provide their working families. This would have raised the uninsured population by tens of millions, increased the amount of uncompensated care the health care system would have to provide the newly uninsured by tens of billions of dollars, bankrupted large segments of the medical industry, and forced Congress to reform the health care system in order to avert its collapse.

However, large corporations could not take any action to force Congress to establish a national health insurance program, since most big businesses were committed to preserving the current health care system. They wanted to continue to assume responsibility for providing their working families group insurance in order to avert the imposition of a federal mandate which would require them to finance any additional health care benefits for employed households beyond those which they were already offering. By requiring business to provide their working families a more generous package of health care benefits than is currently the case, such a federal mandate would have raised corporate medical costs. Business opposition to national health insurance was consistent with the need of large corporations to avert the imposition of such a costly federal mandate.

The willingness of most large corporations to continue providing their working families group health insurance guaranteed that the overwhelming majority of the public would remain insured and the health care system would continue to be adequately financed. As a result, Congress saw no clear and compelling public need to establish a national health insurance program. Large corporations which supported national health insurance could have attempted to force Congress to establish the program by terminating the group coverage they provide their working families. However, this would not have raised the number of uninsured substantially, since the overwhelming majority of large corporations opposing national health insurance would have continued to provide their working families group coverage. The willingness of most large corporations to continue assuming the responsibility for providing their working families group insurance deprived big businesses supporting national health insurance of the power to provoke a collapse of the health care system by terminating the coverage they provide their working families. And in the absence of such power, Congress could ignore the demands of some large corporations for action on health care reform.

While big business remained deeply divided over national health insurance, small business united to oppose the program. As a result, to the extent there was a coherent voice within the business community on national health insurance, it came from small firms, which opposed the program. Large corporations supporting national health insurance were unable to overcome the deep divisions within the big business community over the program in order to organize in backing it. Small business was able to use its unity against national health insurance in order to join the health care industry in organizing an effective campaign against the program. Unwilling to alienate the politically powerful small business lobby, in addition to the health care industry, Congress had no rational interest in establishing the program.

THE DIVISION WITHIN THE DEMOCRATIC PARTY OVER NATIONAL HEALTH INSURANCE

The business community was not the only group with a stake in health care reform which was divided over the issue. The same was true of the Democratic Party. Congressional Republicans are practically united in their opposition to national health insurance. Almost all the support for the program comes from within the Democratic Party. As a result, the program cannot be established without solid Democratic support.

Many congressional Democrats joined Clinton in supporting national health insurance. However, the Democratic Party was deeply divided over what kind of national health insurance program should be established. Most congressional Democrats supporting national health insurance backed a single-payer plan, in which the government would replace private insurance in financing most of the cost of health care. Democratic support for single-payer insurance was based upon the fact that private plans are wasteful and inefficient, generating tens of billions of dollars in excessive administrative costs annually. By eliminating the wasteful and inefficient private insurance industry, a single-payer plan represents perhaps the most economically feasible means to achieve universal coverage.

However, while the establishment of single-payer health insurance makes good economic sense, it is politically unfeasible. The private insurance industry represents one of the most well-organized and politically powerful interest groups in Washington. The industry opposes single-payer insurance, since it would result in the elimination of private plans and their replacement with a government program to provide universal coverage. Since single-payer insurance represents a threat to its very survival, the industry stands ready to defeat any single-payer insurance plan Congress might consider.

To avoid a politically bruising battle with the private health insurance industry, Clinton refused to even consider recommending the establishment of a single-payer plan. Instead, Clinton decided to achieve universal coverage through the imposition of a federal mandate requiring firms to provide their working families private insurance. As a result, the Clinton plan would have preserved the private insurance industry, in contrast to a single-payer plan, which would have eliminated and replaced voluntary plans with a government program to guarantee universal coverage. By preserving voluntary plans, Clinton hoped that his health care reform program would win the support of the private insurance industry.

However, by deciding to recommend the imposition of a federal mandate requiring employers to provide their working families group insurance, Clinton alienated congressional Democratic supporters of a single-payer program. They insisted that the employment-based insurance system be scrapped and replaced by a government program to achieve universal coverage. As a result, the Democratic Party was deeply divided over what kind of national health insurance plan should be established: between congressional Democratic supporters of single-payer insurance, and Clinton, who backed mandatory, employment-based insurance. This split within the party prevented the Clinton and Democratic congressional supporters of national health insurance from forging a consensus behind a single plan both sides could support, which derailed efforts to achieve health care reform during 1993–1994.

THE PLAN OF THIS BOOK

The remainder of this book analyzes in greater detail the political obstacles to health care reform outlined in this chapter.

Chapter 2 analyzes Clinton's national health insurance plan. No single individual, let along group, did more to shape the debate on health care reform during 1993 to 1994 than Clinton. He focused the public's and media's attention on health care reform; shaped, to some extent, popular opinion on the issue; determined the alternatives and options to be considered by Congress in any action its members might take on the issue; and developed a national health insurance plan, which defined the debate on health care reform. National health insurance dominated the political agenda during 1993–1994 as a result of Clinton's strong, sustained, and determined support for the program. Clinton's national health insurance plan became the focal point in determining how supporters and opponents of the program staked out their positions on health care reform.

Chapter 3 focuses on the financial relationship between Congress and the health care industry. It analyzes how the industry has effectively used its financial power to gain enormous influence over the making of health care policy on Capitol Hill.

Chapters 4 and 5 concentrate on the health care industry and Republican Party, respectively. They examine how both groups were able to mount public relations campaigns of their own which effectively undermined popular support for Clinton's national health insurance plan.

Chapter 6 turns to business opposition to national health insurance. It assesses how this opposition deprived Clinton of the support of an important constituency vital to the establishment of his national health insurance plan.

Chapter 7 deals with the severe split within the Democratic Party over national health insurance. It examines how this split prevented Clinton from building a Democratic majority in the 103rd Congress behind any single national health insurance plan, derailing his health care reform initiative.

Chapters 8 and 9 conclude with an assessment of the major reasons for the failure of Clinton's health care reform initiative.

This book concludes that Clinton's health care reform initiative was doomed to failure because the public was not ready for the kind of sweeping changes in the medical system the president's national health insurance plan promised to make. By imposing a radical overhaul of the health care system, Clinton's national health insurance plan provoked opposition from at least half the public, who were well insured and perceived the president's program as a threat to their continued access to health care. The existence of mounting public opposition to the Clinton plan destroyed any prospects for the establishment of national health insurance during the President's first, and possibly only, term.

Given the existence of widespread public satisfaction with the current health care system and popular opposition to any radical overhaul in the current arrangements for financing medical services, it is difficult to conceive how Clinton or any other president could have succeeded in securing the establishment of a national health insurance program during 1993–1994. As a result, it would be unfair to criticize Clinton for the failure of his health care reform initiative. However, Clinton can be fairly criticized for the naiveté he displayed in failing to appreciate the powerful political obstacles preventing the establishment of national health insurance. Indeed, Clinton aggressively pursued his health care reform initiative with little, if any, appreciation of those obstacles, which were sure to doom his efforts. This resulted in a false sense of complacency within the White House, since Clinton was certain, incorrectly as it turned out, that he would succeed in his campaign to establish national health insurance, despite the failure of similar efforts by previous presidents.

Neither Clinton nor other supporters of national health insurance in Congress, the media, and the academic community fully understood the political minefields which were sure to destroy the president's health care reform initiative. Clinton's health care reform initiative was the most serious and sustained presidential campaign to establish national health insurance in American history; and the failure of his efforts tells us much about the insurmountable political roadblocks which stand in the way of comprehensive health care reform. This book analyzes Clinton's health care reform initiative in order to facilitate a better understanding of precisely why the establishment of national health insurance has proven to be such a difficult, arduous, and seemingly impossible task.

Chapter 2

Clinton's National Health Insurance Plan: Addressing the Health Care Crisis

> Although America can still proudly boast the world's finest health professionals and astounding medical advances, our health care system is broken. If we go on without change, the consequences will be devastating for millions of Americans and disastrous for the nation in human and economic terms.[1]
>
> First Lady Hillary Clinton, Chair, President's Task Force on National Health Reform.

Perhaps Clinton's top priority when he entered the White House was to secure the establishment of a national health insurance plan which would guarantee universal access to affordable health care. Every individual would be guaranteed cradle-to-grave coverage. Consumers would be organized into health alliances to contain health care costs, and their efforts would be supported by the federal government, which would control medical expenses. The goal of Clinton's national health insurance plan was, in the president's words, to provide "every American health security; health care that can never be taken away; health care that is always there."[2]

To achieve his goal of guaranteeing "every American health care security," Clinton needed to convince the public that the medical system was in a state of disrepair, if not collapse; and that only through a fundamental overhaul of the arrangements for financing and delivering health care could the public desire for universal access to affordable medical services be achieved. Clinton attempted to do just that when he declared in his address to a joint session of Congress on September 22, 1993, that "this health care system of our is badly broken and it is time to fix it."[3] Clinton did not have to do much to support his argument that the health care system "is badly broken." He assumed the presidency as the United States was experiencing a health care crisis of unprecedented magnitude.

For nearly half a century—from the end of World War II in 1945 to the end of the Cold War in 1989—the labor force enjoyed access to permanent, full-time employment provided by both large corporations and federal, state, and local government. Practically all large corporations and government employers offer their working families group health insurance. However, as the United States entered the 1990s, both the public and private sectors undertook a painful restructuring of their operations, which resulted in massive job layoffs. Laid-off workers not only lost their jobs, but lost the group insurance which came with their employment, resulting in a substantial rise in the number of uninsured individuals.

In the meantime, soaring health care costs posed a threat to working families and the elderly, who were forced to pay a rising share of their incomes on medical services. Soaring health care costs also wreaked fiscal havoc on the federal government and states, which were forced to reduce spending on needed domestic programs to finance the skyrocketing cost of Medicare and Medicaid.

By the time Clinton entered the White House a rising uninsured population, combined with the soaring health care costs, was threatening the very foundations of the medical system. Those twin problems demanded urgent federal action on health care reform. As Clinton put it in his first presidential address to a joint session of Congress on February 17, 1993, "Our families will never be secure, our businesses will never be strong, and our government will never again be fully solvent until we tackle the health care crisis. We must do it this year."[4]

THE DECLINE OF THE VOLUNTARY, EMPLOYMENT-BASED HEALTH INSURANCE SYSTEM

During the first four decades of the postwar period, the United States enjoyed a voluntary, employment-based health insurance system, which was both politically acceptable and economically viable. Employers—mostly large corporations and federal, state, and local governments—offered virtually all their working families group insurance. Corporate and government workers enjoyed lifetime employment. As a result, they could expect to keep their group insurance for life, which guaranteed them and their families access to health care. Given the fact that working families could depend upon their employers to finance the cost of their health care, no strong public support existed for national health insurance during the 1940s and 1970s, when major campaigns were launched to establish the program. Rather, a substantial share of the public supported preserving the existing employment-based insurance system.[5]

However, the voluntary, employment-based health insurance system began to deteriorate during the 1990s. Thrust into an increasingly competitive market, large corporations were unable to continue operating without substantially reducing their costs. To do so, they had to downsize their operations by shrinking the size of their bureaucracies, which resulted in massive layoffs.

With large corporations laying off increasing numbers of workers, unemployment rose, and the tax base shrunk, depriving state and local governments of the revenues needed to finance their operations. This resulted in massive cuts in state and local government spending, and substantial layoffs of public sector workers. Virtually all laid-off corporate and government workers were covered by group health insurance, and lost their coverage when they lost their jobs. Many, if not most, of them and their families became uninsured.

Large corporations increasingly turned to hiring temporary and part-time workers to replace the permanent, full-time employees who had been laid off due to company downsizing. Temporary and part-time workers have become part of a contingency labor force. Contingency workers receive smaller salaries than permanent, full-time workers. While practically all permanent, full-time workers employed by large corporations receive pensions and group health insurance, few contingency workers do so. By paying lower salaries and not providing any pension or health care benefits, large corporations save substantial sums in replacing permanent, full-time employees with contingency workers.

Under increasing pressures to reduce costs in order to remain competitive in their industries, large corporations began to replace their permanent, full-time employees with contingency workers during the 1990s. This resulted in an expansion of the contingency labor force and a corresponding shrinkage in the number of permanent, full-time workers. Since most permanent, full-time workers have group health insurance, while most temporary and part-time workers do not, the growth of a contingency labor force coupled with the shrinkage in the permanent, full-time labor force resulted in a reduction in the number of working families receiving employment-based health care benefits. The share of the public covered by group insurance fell from 58.4 percent in 1988 to 52.6 percent in 1994.[6]

Consistent with the increasing instability of the voluntary, employment-based health insurance system, a substantial share of the public is seriously concerned about the prospect of losing their coverage and becoming uninsured. The 1994 *Los Angeles Times* poll cited in the previous chapter asked its respondents the following question: "How concerned are you that in the next few years you will lose the health care coverage you currently have?" Thirty-six percent of those polled said that they were "very concerned" about the prospect of losing their insurance; 24 percent were "somewhat concerned"; 30 percent were either "not too concerned" or "not concerned at all"; and 10 percent were uninsured.[7] The *Los Angeles Times* poll shows that 70 percent of the public were seriously concerned about the prospect of losing their coverage and becoming uninsured, if they are not already—a clear indicator that people feel insecure about their long-term access to health care, which has fueled the popular demand for medical reform.

The public has every reason to fear the loss of their health insurance. In the United States public access to insurance is linked to employment, mostly with large corporations and the government, which remain the primary sources of health care benefits for working families. As large corporations and the government have continued to downsize their operations during the 1990s, laying off an increasing number of their workers, the likelihood of employed households losing their insurance has increased, resulting in the heightened public anxiety concerning the security of their health care benefits, which the *Los Angeles Times* poll revealed.

Economic restructuring and corporate and government downsizing expanded the ranks of the uninsured during the 1990s, as many, if not most, laid-off corporate and government workers lost their group health insurance, along with their jobs, and were unable to find employers willing to provide them coverage, assuming they could find any jobs at all. Newly-laid-off and uninsured corporate and government workers joined a large number of workers who were already uninsured because their employers, mostly small businesses, do not provide them any group coverage. In the meantime, insured workers fortunate enough to keep their jobs saw their coverage shrink as employers feverishly slashed the health care benefits they provide their employed households in order to reduce their costs. With both uninsured population expanding and the amount of group insurance available to working families shrinking, a substantial minority of the public found themselves increasingly cut off from access to health care.

Even as the ranks of the uninsured swelled due to mass layoffs of insured workers, the economy enjoyed a modest, though sustained, economic recovery following the recession which gripped the United States during 1990 to 1991. With the economy enjoying a moderate expansion beginning in 1991, a large segment of the labor force felt more secure in their jobs, and the group health insurance which comes with their employment, than they did during the recession-plagued early 1990s. The economic recovery relieved many workers of the anxieties which they felt during the early 1990s concerning the possibility that they might lose their jobs, along with their group insurance. Feeling more secure in their jobs, those workers had less reason to fear that they might lose their jobs, along with their group insurance.

Corporate and government downsizing, combined with the modest economic expansion during the 1990s, has created a paradoxical situation in which a substantial segment of the public are losing their access to health care, at the same time that another significant part of the population are feeling more secure in their coverage. Laid-off corporate and government workers are losing their group health insurance along with their jobs, with many, if not most of them, becoming uninsured, with little, if any, access to health care. In the meantime, a large segment of the labor force are enjoying greater job security, assuring that they will continue to keep the coverage which comes with their employment.

The paradox of one segment of the public losing their access to health care, with another portion of the population feeling more secure in their coverage, is revealed in a poll of 800 adults conducted during January 17–18, 1996 by Yankelovich Partners for *Time* and CNN. The poll asked its respondents "compared to three years ago, are you and your family better or worse off'' relating to six socioeconomic conditions, including ''your ability to get good health care.'' Thirty-eight percent of those polled said that they and their families were worse off in terms of their ''ability to get good health care,'' 35 percent stated that they were better off, and 27 percent reported that they were the same. Those saying that they and their families were worse off in 1996 than they were three years earlier ranked access to health care fourth on their list of the six socio-economic conditions which they believed had deteriorated, behind crime, local public schools, and the availability of leisure time. On the other hand, those saying that they and their families were better off than they were three years earlier listed access to health care third on their list of the six socioeconomic conditions they believed had improved, behind the quality of products on the market and their standard of living.[8] The *Time*/CNN poll shows that corporate and government downsizing and layoffs of insured workers, the failure of many, if not most, small businesses to provide their working families group health insurance, together with cutbacks in employee health care benefits, have resulted in a third of the public increasingly cut off from access to health care, while the modestly improved state of the economy during the mid-1990s has led to another third of the population seeing themselves more secure in their coverage, with the remaining third showing no change in their health security.

During the early 1990s, the public had deep anxieties about their ability to maintain their access to health care, given the high unemployment rate the United States suffered during and following the recession of 1990–1991. Those without jobs are likely to be uninsured, since they lack access to employment-based health insurance, and are unlikely to have the financial means to purchase their own coverage. However, as the United States began to experience a modest economic expansion during the mid-1990s, public concerns over their access to health care eased, as the unemployment rate declined dramatically. With the modest economic expansion bringing greater job security to some, though not all, workers, increasing numbers of working families were assured that they could keep their employment-based insurance.

The decline in public concern over health care can be seen in two polls conducted by Yankelovich Partners for *Time* and CNN in September 1993 and August 1994, respectively. The polls asked a representative of the public the following question: ''What is the main problem facing the country today?'' The share of the public citing health care as America's most important problem declined from 13 percent in September 1993 to 7 percent in August 1994. In September 1993 health care ranked third on the public's list of the most important problems facing the United States, behind crime and unemployment. By August 1994, health care had slipped to fourth place on that list, behind crime, politicians and government, and the lack of morals.[9] The *Time*/CNN polls show a substantial decline in public concern over health care, as the modest economic expansion the United States enjoyed during the mid-1990s reduced the unemployment rate, strengthened job security, and assured a substantial number of working families the ability to keep their employment-based insurance, and maintain their access to medical services.

While a substantial share of the public enjoys greater health security than was the case during and shortly following the recession of 1990–1991, an equally significant segment of the population is becoming increasingly cut off from their access to health care as a result of economic restructuring and corporate and government downsizing, as we have seen. With a shrinking share of the population covered by employment-based health insurance, the overall health security of the public continues to deteriorate, even as a minority of the population manages to hold onto to their jobs, and the coverage which comes with their employment.

Working families not covered by employment-based health insurance have few options available to them in securing health care benefits. They could purchase their own private plans. However, private insurance is very expensive. Few families can afford private insurance.

Moreover, to limit their financial liabilities, private health insurance plans exclude pre-existing medical conditions from the coverage they provide and refuse to extend health care benefits to individuals with chronic ailments. As a result, even if working families can afford private insurance, they may not be able to purchase it: because either they cannot secure coverage for the pre-existing medical condition they have, rendering their insurance practically worthless; or obtain any health care benefits at all due to the chronic ailments they suffer from, which make them uninsurable at any cost.

If they are unable to purchase their own private health insurance, working families might be eligible for either Medicare or Medicaid. However, both programs maintain stringent eligibility requirements. Relatively few working families qualify for coverage under either program.

Medicare provides coverage to three groups: the elderly, individuals who have received Social Security Disability Insurance benefits for at least two years, and persons undergoing kidney dialysis or who have had a kidney transplant.[10] Since practically all working families are nonelderly and able-bodied, few of them qualify for Medicare.

States are required to provide Medicaid to Aid to Families With Dependent Children (AFDC) and Supplemental Security Income (SSI) recipients. States may also provide coverage to the medically needy, who include all individuals falling within the categories covered by either AFDC or SSI, and whose incomes after medical expenses do not exceed a third of the maximum AFDC payment.[11] Due to the existence of highly restrictive Medicaid eligibility requirements, only the very poor who fall within one of the categories covered by welfare qualify for the program. In 1994 only 58 percent of the poor were covered by Medicaid.[12]

Table 2.1
The Employment and Income Status of the Uninsured During 1993–1994

Employment Status	Percent of the Uninsured
Full-time, full-year	55
Part-time or part-year	29
Unemployed	16
Annual Income	
Under $10,000	24
$10,000 to $19,999	28
$20,000 to $29,999	19
$30,000 to $49,999	17
$50,000 or Over	12
Income as a Percentage of the Poverty Line	
Below the Poverty Line	28
100 Percent to 200 Percent	32
200 Percent to 400 Percent	27
400 Percent or Above	13

Sources: The Henry J. Kaiser Family Foundation, *Uninsured in America: Straight Facts on Health Reform*, April 1994; The Henry J. Kaiser Foundation, the League of Women Voters Education Fund, and the Robert Wood Johnson Foundation, *Critical Choices in Health Reform*, p. 3; Diane Rowland, *Directions for Health Reform: Testimony Before the Committee on Labor and Human Resources, United States Senate*, March 15, 1995.

A RISING NUMBER OF UNINSURED INDIVIDUALS

An increasing number of working families have no group health insurance, are too poor to purchase their own private plans, too "rich" to qualify for Medicaid, and too young and healthy to be eligible for Medicare. They have no alternative but to become uninsured. In 1993 37.8 percent of workers not covered by group insurance had no coverage.[13] Middle-class working families—too poor to afford private insurance, and too "rich" to qualify for public insurance—represent the overwhelming majority of the uninsured. As Table 2.1 shows, most of the uninsured were members of middle-class working families. Eighty-four percent of the uninsured were members of working families, and 59 percent middle class, earning annual incomes of from 100 percent to less than 400 percent of the poverty line.

The fact that the uninsured are without coverage because employer-provided health insurance is becoming increasingly unavailable, while private coverage is all but unaffordable, is borne out by a 1993 poll jointly conducted by the Henry J. Kaiser Family Foundation, Commonwealth Fund, and Louis Harris.

The poll asked a representative sample of uninsured individuals why they were without coverage. Fifty-nine percent of those polled said they were uninsured because they could not afford private coverage, 22 percent said they were either unemployed or worked for employers who did not provide them with health care benefits, 7 percent said they were uninsured by choice, and 3 percent said they were uninsurable because they suffered from preexisting medical conditions which prevented them from finding any insurance company willing to cover them. The Kaiser/Commonwealth/Harris poll shows that the overwhelming majority of the uninsured have no coverage, not by choice, but because they cannot find employers willing to provide them insurance, and lack the financial means to purchase their own health benefits, with many of them uninsurable at any cost due to chronic illness.[14]

By the early 1990s, the health insurance system was beginning to unravel. As corporations continued to downsize their operations by laying off massive numbers of workers, millions of individuals lost their group insurance when they lost their jobs. As health care costs soared, employers began terminating the group coverage they provided their working families because they could no longer afford to pay for their private insurance. Other self-insured individuals dropped their coverage because they too could no longer afford to pay for it. As a result of widespread job layoffs combined with the increasing unaffordability of private insurance, massive numbers of individuals were losing their coverage during the 1990s. On September 15, 1993, Families USA issued a report which found that 2.2 million individuals were losing their insurance every month.[15]

As increasing numbers of individuals lost their health insurance during the 1990s, the number of uninsured persons rose substantially. The number of individuals who were uninsured during any given day increased from 33.7 million in 1988 to 40.9 million in 1993.[16] The share of the public who were uninsured during any given day grew from 13 percent to 15.3 percent during the same period.[17]

While 40.9 million individuals were uninsured during any given day in 1993, the number of persons without coverage during that year was even greater. In 1993 51.3 million individuals, representing 19.9 percent of the public, were uninsured during either all or part of the year. Many of the uninsured go without coverage for long periods. In 1993 22 percent of the uninsured went without coverage for less than four months; 24 percent did so from four months to less than eight months; 19 percent did so from eight months to less than a year; and 35 percent did so for a year or longer.[18]

Many workers who have been laid off and lost the group health insurance which came with their employment during the 1990s have sought and qualified for Medicaid coverage, despite the program's restrictive eligibility requirements. With an increasing number of working families losing their group insurance and seeking Medicaid coverage as an alternative, Medicaid enrollments have risen substantially. The share of the public covered by Medicaid rose from 7.8 percent in 1988 to 11.4 percent in 1994.[19] Nevertheless, many workers who have been laid off and lost the group insurance which came with their employment are still unable to meet Medicaid's stringent eligibility standards and have had no alternative but to go uninsured. As a result, the expansion of Medicaid enrollments has served to ameliorate, but not reverse, the increase in the number of uninsured which has continued throughout the 1990s.

The uninsured must pay the entire cost of their health care, except for those medical services which they can secure from charitable hospitals. As a result, the uninsured face powerful financial barriers impeding their access to health care. By contrast, the insured pay a substantially smaller share of their health care expenses out of pocket, since much, if not most, of the cost of each insured family's medical services is financed by third-party payers—either the government or private health insurance. In 1991 third-party payers financed 76 percent of the cost of health care, with another 5 percent funded by charitable institutions, leaving patients paying only 19 percent of their medical expenses out of pocket.[20] Accordingly, the insured face few, if any, financial barriers impeding their access to health care.

With third-party payers financing most of the cost of their health care, insured individuals tend to seek immediate treatment for illnesses, and rarely postpone visits to the doctor, when necessary. By contrast, because they must pay the entire cost of their health care, except those medical services which they might secure from charitable hospitals, the uninsured tend to postpone treatment for illnesses, until they develop severe, or even life-threatening complications, which demand immediate medical attention, if not forego needed health care altogether. In 1993, 71 percent of uninsured adults postponed receiving needed health care, compared to only 21 percent of their privately-insured counterparts. Thirty-four percent of uninsured adults went without needed health care altogether, compared to only 7 percent of their privately-insured counterparts.

Because they tend to postpone treatment for illnesses, if not forego medical treatment altogether, many, if not most, uninsured individuals pay no visits to the doctor during any given year. By contrast, because they tend to seek immediate medical attention for illnesses, the insured usually pay regular visits to the doctor. In 1987 50 percent of uninsured individuals under the age of sixty-five paid no visits to the doctor, compared with only 26 percent of their privately-insured counterparts.

By failing to seek immediate medical attention, when needed, the uninsured tend to develop illnesses, which result in severe, or even life-threatening complications. By contrast, the insured usually seek immediate medical attention, which allows their doctors to treat their illnesses early, before complications develop, if not prevent ailments altogether. Because the insured have better access to health care than the uninsured, those without coverage tend to be sicker than those with it. In 1987 the uninsured were hospitalized 2.8 times more than the privately-insured for diabetes, 2.4 times more for hypertension, twice more for immunizable conditions, 1.4 times more for asthma, 1.2 times more for congestive heart failure, and 1.1 times more for a ruptured appendix.

Health care providers are compensated for most of the medical services they provide their insured patients, who tend to have the financial means to pay for whatever services are not covered by their insurance. As a result, health care providers extend all the medical services their insured patients need. By contrast, health care providers are unlikely to be compensated for treating the uninsured, since they lack insurance and, often, the financial means to pay for their health care. Accordingly, health care providers usually extend only the minimal health care required to treat their uninsured patients, and often withhold needed medical services from them. The uninsured are 80 percent less likely to receive an angiography than the privately insured, 45 percent less likely to receive a total hip replacement, 40 percent less likely to receive coronary artery bypass grafting, 29 percent less likely to undergo coronary artery bypass surgery, and 28 percent less likely to receive an angioplasty.

Because the uninsured tend both to be sicker than the insured and receive to less health care than the insured, those without coverage suffer substantially higher mortality rates than those with it. Adjusted risk of death is 25 percent higher for the uninsured than the privately insured; and the uninsured are up to three times more likely to die in the hospital than the privately insured.[21]

The health, and very lives, of the 40.9 million individuals who are uninsured remains at severe risk, since the data just presented clearly shows those with no coverage are at grave risk of suffering catastrophic and life-threatening illnesses, and even death. The uninsured fully recognize this, since practically all uninsured individuals are without coverage, not by choice, but because employment-based insurance is increasingly unavailable, and private insurance is all but unaffordable, as we have seen. The uninsured must go without coverage because of economic circumstances beyond their control, not by choice.

SOARING HEALTH CARE COSTS

Even before voluntary, employment-based health insurance began to crumble during the 1990s, the United States had been plagued by soaring health care costs which began with the establishment of Medicare and Medicaid in 1965. Nineteen sixty-five marks the year in which development of the insurance system was finally completed. The system is based upon three programs: group insurance for working families, Medicare for the elderly and disabled, and Medicaid for the poor. As a result of those three programs, the overwhelming majority of the public has remained insured since 1965. In 1993 84.7 percent of the public was insured.[22]

As a result of the existence of a health insurance system which provides coverage to the overwhelming majority of the public, most of the cost of health care is financed by third-party payers—either the government or private insurance, as we have seen. This has served to insulate the insured public from the high cost of health care, allowing them to utilize more medical services than would otherwise be the case if they had to pay the full cost of their health care out of pocket. This is especially true among the elderly, 99.7 percent of whom are insured, either through Medicare or Medicaid, and have virtually unlimited access to health care.[23] The elderly tend to be less healthy and utilize substantially more health care than their nonelderly counterparts.[24]

Third-party payers finance a greater share of the cost of hospital care than any other single health care service. In 1992 third-party payers financed 95 percent of the cost of hospital care.[25] The fact that practically the entire cost of hospital care is financed by third-party payers provides the insured public access to costly, hospital-based medical technology. The proliferation of costly medical technology represents perhaps the major source of soaring health care costs.[26]

The high utilization of health care has driven up its cost. The cost of health care rose from 5.9 percent of the GDP in 1965 to 14.3 percent in 1993.[27] Per capita health care spending, measured in 1990 dollars, increased from $1,136 in 1970 to $2,604 in 1990.[28] From 1980 to 1993 health care costs rose 199 percent, compared to 71 percent for the consumer price index (CPI).[29] The United States spends substantially more on health care than any other nation, despite the fact that this country is the only advanced industrial democracy with a significant share of its popularion which is uninsured.[30] In 1989 the United States spent 28.5 percent more on health care on a per capita basis than the next highest medical spender—Canada.[31]

Soaring health care costs represent a threat to the standard of living of working families. Employers have responded to rising costs by reducing the group health insurance coverage they provide their working families, forcing them to bear a greater financial burden for their medical expenses. The Labor Department found that from 1982 to 1989 the average monthly employee contribution to group health insurance plans provided by large and medium-size companies covering 31 million workers rose 167 percent, far exceeding the 25 percent increase in their wages during the same period.[32]

As the cost of their health care continues to substantially outpace their wage increases, working families have had to spend a rising share of their income on medical services. In a report issued on November 22, 1993, Families USA found that the share of income families spent on health care rose from 9 percent in 1980 to 13.1 percent in 1993.[33] The average cost of health care for families rose from $1,749 to $7,739 during the same period.[34] In 1993 families paid an average of $5,190 for their health care, with their employers financing the remaining $2,549 of their medical bill.[35] Families USA estimated that the average cost of health care for families would rise to $14,517 by 2000, representing 18.4 percent of their income, in the absence of far-reaching medical reform.[36]

As health care costs have soared, so has the cost of private health insurance. The average cost of private insurance for a family rose from $1,740 in 1980 to $5,160 in 1994.[37] In 1994 the average cost of private insurance for a household represented 13.3 percent of the median family income of $38,782 that year.[38]

Addressing the Senate floor on August 9, 1994, Majority Leader George Mitchell of Maine warned that the average cost of private insurance for a family would rise to $10,800 by 2000, in the absence of comprehensive health care reform.[39]

Employers pay most of the cost of group health insurance for their working families. However, the share of the premiums employers pay for group insurance is income which would have otherwise gone into the paychecks of their workers. As a result, workers indirectly bear the cost of the portion of their group insurance benefits financed by their employees through lost wages. Accordingly, soaring health care costs have taken a bigger bite out of workers' paychecks.

On October 27, 1993, the White House Domestic Policy Council issued a report entitled *Health Security: The President's Report to the American People*, which summarized the Clinton Administration's case for health care reform. The report found that had the share of payroll employers spent on health care been held to its 1975 level, the average wage would have been $29,630 in 1992, compared to the actual wage, which was $28,494 that year—$1,136 less than it otherwise would have been, representing a 3.8 percent reduction in income. The report estimated that the average wage will be $29,280 in 2000, in the absence of comprehensive health care reform. By contrast, the report predicted that, if comprehensive health care reform is achieved, then the average wage will be $29,846 in 2000. As a result, failure to reform the health care system during the 1990s will cost workers $566 in lost wages, representing a 1.9 percent reduction in income, by the turn of the twenty-first century.[40]

As we have seen, soaring health care costs have resulted in shrinking group health insurance coverage, as employers have acted to reduce the health care benefits they provide their working families in order to cut their business expenses; and a reduction in the standard of living, as employed households have been forced to bear an ever-larger share of the financial burden for their own medical services. Polling data show that the public is concerned, if not alarmed, over the financial threat posed to the middle class by soaring health care costs. The 1994 *Los Angeles Times* poll cited earlier asked its respondents the following question: "Do you prefer a plan limiting the amount of medical or insurance bills, at the risk of limiting availability [of health care], or do you prefer a free market system even if it might mean higher costs for the average person?" Forty-seven percent of those polled believed that the federal government should limit health care costs; and 40 percent thought that medical expenses should be determined by market forces.[41]

Consistent with public support for the imposition of federal limits on health care expenses, a substantial segment of the population believes that medical cost containment should be a top priority on the national agenda. During January 4–6, 1996, Celinda Lake and Ed Goas conducted a poll of 1,000 registered voters for *U.S. News & World Report*. The poll asked its respondents to define what changes could the federal government make which "would help average families the most." Twenty percent of those polled said that the federal government could most "help average families" by controlling health care costs. Health care cost containment ranked third on the list of three federal actions the public believed could most "help average families," behind a middle-class tax cut and a balanced federal budget.[42]

The *Los Angeles Times* and *U.S. News & World Report* polls show that the public fully understands that soaring health care costs represent a threat to both the middle class's access to medical services and its standard of living, and desires, if not demands, federal action to contain skyrocketing health care expenses. However, containing health care costs requires that the federal government impose stringent limits on the patient utilization of costly medical technology, which would result in severe health care rationing. As we will see, an overwhelming majority of the public opposes health care rationing, making it virtually impossible for the federal government to take any action to contain medical costs.

True, the 1994 *Los Angeles Times* poll suggests that the public is willing to accept limits on their access to health care as the sacrifice they must make to contain medical expenses. However, as we will see in Chapter 8, further examination shows that only a minority of the public is willing to accept any specific restrictions on its access to a number of costly medical technologies. In the absence of such restrictions, it will be virtually impossible for the federal government to contain soaring health care costs. The public holds contradictory attitudes on health care cost containment, demanding federal action to limit medical expenses, while rejecting the health care rationing which would result from such a move. The public's contradictory attitudes on health care cost containment is a major reason why the federal government has been unable to act upon the rising public clamor for health care cost containment.

Soaring health care costs represent a threat not only to the standard of living of working families, but to the elderly as well. As a result of soaring health care costs, Medicare spending rose from $4.5 billion in 1967 to $178 billion in 1995.[43] Burdened by massive budget deficits, the federal government has acted to reduce Medicare spending by slashing coverage under the program, requiring its beneficiaries to shoulder an increasing share of the financial burden for their health care. From 1966 to 1995 the deductible for Part A of Medicare, Hospital Insurance, rose from $40 to $716; the deductible for Part B, Medical Insurance, increased from $50 to $100; and the monthly Part B premium grew from $3.00 to $46.10.[44]

A major health care expense for the elderly is nursing-home care. Medicare provides no coverage for custodial care in a nursing home.[45] True, Medicaid provides such coverage. However, to qualify for Medicaid, elderly nursing-home residents must spend down their assets, until they can meet the means test required to be eligible for the program. In 1995 the average annual cost of a stay in a nursing home was $35,000. As a result, the elderly usually quickly exhaust their assets when they enter a nursing home. Once impoverished, the elderly secure Medicaid coverage to finance the remainder of their stay in a nursing home.[46]

True, the elderly could purchase private health insurance coverage for nursing-home care. However, such coverage is very expensive. In 1991 the annual cost of such coverage for a fifty-year-old individual was $852.[47] As a result, only a small fraction of the elderly can afford private nursing-home insurance coverage. In 1993 only 4 percent of the elderly were covered by private nursing-home insurance.[48]

With their Medicare benefits shrinking and lacking adequate coverage for nursing-home care, the elderly have been forced to shoulder an increasing financial burden for their health care. On February 25, 1992, Families USA issued a report which found that the share of income spent on health care by the elderly rose from 10.6 percent in 1961 to 17.1 percent in 1991. Per capita spending on health care by the elderly increased from $347 to $3,305 during the same period.[49]

In addition to reducing the standard of living of working families and the elderly, escalating health care costs have wreaked fiscal havoc on the federal government. Soaring Medicare and Medicaid costs have deprived the federal government of the revenues required to finance needed domestic programs and have absorbed much of the cuts in federal spending imposed under Clinton's deficit-reduction plan Congress passed in 1993. As Clinton put it in an interview with *Rolling Stone*,

We should be spending more money on defense conversion, more money on new technologies, more money on education and training. What are we doing? We're spending 16 percent more on Medicaid and 11 percent more on Medicare next year. Everything else [in the federal budget] is flat or cut. . . . If I'd had the money we cut from defense to spend on rebuilding America, it would have been more than enough. The tragedy is all the money went to . . . rising health care costs. The money we cut from the military would have been more than sufficient to lower unemployment, to increase growth, to give us what we need in education and training, were it not for the enormous inflation in health care costs.[50]

Rising health care costs have also wreaked fiscal havoc on the states, which share the financial burden of Medicaid with Washington. In 1994 the states financed 43 percent of the cost of Medicaid.[51] As a result of soaring health care costs, Medicaid spending rose from $734 million in 1966 to $156.5 billion in 1995.[52]

By 1993, Medicaid had become a massive financial burden on the states. This was graphically illustrated on July 26, 1993, when the National Conference of State Legislatures issued a report which found that in fiscal 1993 the states spent more on Medicaid than on higher education for the first time in history.[53] In his speech to the National Governors' Association in Tulsa on August 16, 1993, Clinton addressed the financial burden Medicaid had imposed on the states: "We know that State governments are literally being bankrupt by the rising cost of Medicaid—money that used to go to education, money that used to go to economic development, money that could have gone to law enforcement [is] going every year . . . for . . . health care.''[54]

CLINTON DEVELOPS A NATIONAL HEALTH INSURANCE PLAN

With the health care system in a state of disrepair, if not collapse, Clinton was committed to develop a national health insurance plan when he entered the White House. Just five days following his inauguration as chief executive, Clinton established the President's Task Force on National Health Reform, composed of the most influential members of his administration.[55] To illustrate that health care reform represented perhaps his most important domestic policy priority, the president appointed his closest and most influential adviser, First Lady Hillary Clinton, as chair of the task force. The purpose of the task force was to recommend a national health insurance plan Clinton would propose to Congress.

Upon announcing the establishment of the President's Task Force on National Health Reform, Clinton promised to recommend a national health insurance plan within the first hundred days of his presidency.[56] However, during the spring and summer of 1993, Clinton and Congress became absorbed and preoccupied with consideration of the president's deficit-reduction plan.[57] In order to avoid diverting Congress's attention from his deficit-reduction plan, Clinton decided to delay introduction of his national health insurance plan until passage of his economic program, which came on August 6. With his deficit-reduction plan now in place, Clinton introduced his national health insurance plan in an address to a joint session of Congress on September 22.[58]

Following the delivery of Clinton's address to a joint session of Congress, the administration developed a 1,342-page national health insurance bill, the Health Security Act, which defined the legislative details of the president's health care reform plan.[59] On October 27 Clinton went to Capitol Hill to personally present the bill to congressional leaders.[60] The bill was designed to rectify the two major problems which underlie the health care crisis—a rising uninsured population and escalating medical costs—by guaranteeing universal coverage, containing health care expenses, and making group insurance affordable for small business.

Guaranteeing Universal Health Insurance Coverage

The Health Security Act would guarantee universal coverage by building upon the current employment-based health insurance system. The bill would require all employers to provide their working families group insurance. Employers would be required to finance 80 percent of the cost of group insurance for their working families, with the remaining share funded by employees.[61] All unemployed and self-employed individuals would be required to purchase their own private insurance.[62] All individuals would receive a guaranteed health care benefit package, which would contain one of three different kinds of patient cost-sharing arrangements: low cost-sharing, high cost-sharing, and combination plans.

Individuals choosing a low cost-sharing private health insurance plan would enroll in a health maintenance organization (HMO). They would receive comprehensive coverage, with no deductibles or coinsurance charges, and only a $10 copayment for each visit to the doctor's office.

Individuals opting for a high cost-sharing plan would be free to choose their own doctors. However, they would have to assume responsibility for a substantial share of their own health care costs. Families would have to pay an annual deductible of $400 and a 20 percent coinsurance charge.

Individuals choosing a combination plan would enroll in a preferred-provider organization (PPO). They would receive the same comprehensive coverage provided to HMO enrollees, as long as they used only PPO doctors and hospitals. However, if they received services outside their PPO they would have to assume the same cost-sharing responsibilities as those with high cost-sharing plans.

A stop-loss limiting the maximum annual amount families would pay in out-of-pocket health care expenses to $3,000 would be imposed. The stop-loss would apply to all individuals, regardless of which type of plan they choose.[63]

Each state would be required to establish one or more regional health alliances, which would contract with private health insurance plans to provide coverage to the public.[64] All individuals in firms employing 5,000 or fewer workers, persons employed by federal, state, and local government, and self-employed and unemployed individuals would be required to join a health alliance in the region where they resided. Firms employing over 5,000 workers would be free to either join a regional health alliance or form their own corporate health alliance.[65] Each regional and corporate health alliance would offer to its members a choice of all qualified private health insurance plans operating in their area.[66]

All Medicaid recipients would be required to enroll in a regional health alliance. The government would provide all regional health alliances capitation payments to finance their enrollment of Medicaid recipients. They would choose from among the private plans contracting with their regional health alliance.[67]

Medicare beneficiaries would only be allowed to enroll in a regional health alliance at the request of their state governments, and upon the approval of the secretary of health and human services (HHS). Medicare beneficiaries would not be allowed to enroll in a regional health alliance unless they were guaranteed private health insurance coverage at least as comprehensive as that provided by Medicare.[68]

All private health insurance plans would be required to provide the guaranteed health care benefit package to any member of a regional or corporate health alliance desiring enrollment. They would be prohibited from either denying coverage to any individual due to chronic ailments he or she may suffer from, or excluding preexisting medical conditions from the health care protection provided to subscribers. They would be required to charge community-rated premiums, reflecting the cost of providing health care to the entire community.[69] They would also be required to use single, standardized forms for processing medical claims and reimbursing health care providers.[70]

The federal government would provide subsidies to employers who were members of a regional health alliance to finance the purchase of group health insurance for their working families. The federal subsidies would be sufficient to limit employer contributions to group insurance to from 3.5 percent to 7.9 percent, depending upon the size and average wage of each firm. No employer would pay in excess of 7.9 percent of payroll for group insurance. Employers with seventy-five or fewer workers would be limited to paying from 3.5 percent to 7.9 percent of their payroll for group insurance, depending upon the average wage of each firm. Small businesses with an average wage of under $12,000 would pay no more than 3.5 percent of payroll for group insurance. As the average wage rose, so would the share of payroll each small business would be required to pay for group insurance. Small businesses with an average wage of $24,000 or more would pay no more than 7.9 percent of payroll for group insurance.[71]

The federal government would also provide subsidies for families with incomes up to 150 percent of the poverty line who are members of a regional health alliance. The federal subsidies would cover the cost of premiums, deductibles, and coinsurance charges low-income families would have to pay under their private health insurance plans. The amount of the federal subsidy provided to each low-income family for the purchase of private insurance would depend upon its income and the average premium available to that household within the health alliance to which it belongs; the lower the income and higher the average premium, the greater the subsidy each low-income family would receive.[72]

The Health Security Act would expand health insurance coverage for the elderly. Medicare would be expanded to include coverage for prescription drugs. Medicare beneficiaries would pay a $250 deductible and a 20 percent coinsurance charge for prescription drugs. A stop-loss limiting the maximum annual amount Medicare beneficiaries would pay for prescription drugs to $1,000 would be imposed.[73] A comprehensive package of home health care benefits would be provided to all elderly and disabled individuals.[74]

Containing Health Care Costs

In addition to guaranteeing universal health insurance coverage, the Health Security Act would impose stringent health care cost-containment measures. Strict limits would be imposed upon the rise in Medicare and Medicaid spending. The rate of growth in Medicare spending would decline from 11.6 percent in 1994 to 4.1 percent in 2000. The rate of growth in Medicaid spending would fall from 16.5 percent to 4.1 percent during the same period. During this period,

Medicare spending would be reduced by $124 billion and Medicaid spending by $114 billion.[75]

In addition to Medicare and Medicaid spending, stringent limits would be imposed upon the cost of private health insurance. Beginning in 1996, the rate of growth in private insurance premiums would be tied to the CPI. In 1996 the rate of growth in premiums could not rise more than 1.5 percent above the CPI. The rate of growth in premiums would decline further until 1999 and thereafter, when they could not exceed the increase in the CPI.[76]

To administer the health care cost-containment measures provided for under the Health Security Act, a seven-member National Health Board would be established.[77] The Board would determine a per capita private health insurance premium target for each regional and corporate health alliance, based upon total national health care spending, adjusted for regional variations in medical costs. If the average premium of any health alliance exceeded its premium target, then a tax would be imposed on all private plans charging excessive premiums and on all health care providers receiving reimbursements from those plans. The tax imposed on a private plan would be equal to 100 percent of the excess revenues the plan earned by charging premiums above the premium targets for each health alliance; and the tax imposed on a health care provider would be equal to 100 percent of the excess reimbursements the provider received from private plans charging such premiums. Revenues from the tax on private plans would be used to finance the subsidies the federal government would provide to employees to fund their purchase of group insurance for their working families.[78] No regional health alliance would be allowed to contract with any private plan which charged a premium 20 percent or more in excess of the average premium paid by members of the alliance.[79]

A major goal of the Health Security Act was to reduce soaring health care costs. In the absence of comprehensive health care reform, medical spending will rise from $940 billion in 1993 to $1,631 trillion in 2000. Health care costs will increase from 14.3 percent of the GDP to 18.9 percent during the same period. The annual rise in health care costs will grow from 5.4 percent to 8 percent.

On September 7, 1993, the White House Domestic Policy Council released a document entitled *The President's Health Security Plan*, which summarized the provisions of the Health Security Act. The document provided a detailed outline of the reductions in national and health care spending which would result from the imposition of stringent cost-containment measures under the bill. By 2000, the bill would reduce health care costs to $1,495 trillion, representing 17.3 percent of the GDP. The annual rise in health care costs would decline to 4 percent. Over the period 1993 to 2000, health care spending would be reduced by $701 billion.[80]

During the period 1994 to 2000, the Health Security Act would increase federal health care spending by $350 billion. This would result largely from the cost of federal subsidies to provide coverage to the uninsured, and expanded

Table 2.2
Percentage of Insured and Uninsured Workers by Firm Size in 1993

Number of Workers in Firms	Percent of Workers Covered By Health Insurance From Their Employers	Percent of Workers Covered By Other Health Insurance	Percent of Uninsured Workers
Under 10	23.6	44.5	31.9
10 to 24	39.4	35.6	25.0
25 to 99	51.9	27.2	20.9
100 to 499	62.0	23.9	13.1
500 to 999	67.1	22.9	10.0
1,000 or Over	70.9	19.8	9.3
TOTAL	57.8	15.9	26.3

Source: Robert Pear, "Health Advisers Plan Exemption for Big Business," *New York Times*, April 26, 1993, p. A10.

health care benefits for the elderly. However, the bill would generate $441 billion in savings in federal health care spending during 1994–2000. This would result mostly from reductions in Medicare and Medicaid spending, and revenues earned from the tax imposed upon private health insurance plans which charge excessive premiums. As a result, the bill would result in a net reduction in federal health care spending of $91 billion during 1994–2000.[81]

Making Group Health Insurance Affordable for Small Business

Perhaps the most important goal of the Health Security Act was to make private health insurance affordable for small business. As we have seen, 84 percent of the uninsured are members of working families. The reason why so many working families are uninsured is that many, if not most, small businesses do not provide their employed households group coverage. By contrast, all government entities and practically all large corporations offer their working families group insurance; and most of their employed households choose to accept and share the cost of such coverage. In 1991 only 32 percent of all firms employing under 25 workers offered their working families group insurance, compared to 81 percent of all businesses employing from 25 to 100 workers, 95 percent of all companies employing from 100 to 999 workers, and 98 percent of all corporations employing 1,000 workers or over.[82]

In 1993 38 percent of all workers in firms with less than 100 employees were not covered by group health insurance. As Table 2.2 shows, the provision of group insurance is dependent upon the size of firms. The larger the firm, the greater the share of workers covered by group insurance. By contrast, the smaller the firm, the lower the share of workers covered. As a result, most workers in

Table 2.3
Percentage of the Uninsured by Firm Size During 1992–1993

Number of Workers in Firms	Percent of Workers	Percent of the Uninsured
Self-employed	–	14
Under 25	20[a]	26
25 to 99	13	13
100 to 499	15	10
500 or Over	45	21
Unemployed	7	16

Source: Robert Pear, "Health Advisers Plan Exemption for Big Business," *New York Times*, April 26, 1993, p. A10; Diane Rowland, Barbara Lyons, Alina Salganicoff, and Peter Long, "A Profile of the Uninsured in America," *Health Affairs*, Spring 1994, p. 285.

[a]Includes the self-employed.

firms employing 25 or more individuals are covered by group insurance. On the other hand, most workers in firms employing less than 25 individuals are not covered.

Because they usually do not receive group health insurance, workers in small business represent a large share of the uninsured, as Table 2.3 shows. By the same token, because they usually obtain insurance from their employers, workers employed with either large corporations or the government constitute a small share of the uninsured. Self-employed individuals and workers in firms employing less than 25 individuals represent only 20 percent of the labor force, yet 40 percent of all uninsured workers. By contrast, workers in firms employing 500 individuals or more represent 45 percent of the labor force, but only 21 percent of all uninsured workers.

Why do practically all large corporations and federal, state, and local governments offer their working families group health insurance, while many small businesses do not? The answer lies in the fact that group insurance premiums are currently experience-rated; premiums reflect the cost of health care for each group. Experience-rating hurts small business because its health care costs are unpredictable and subject to unforeseen increases. By contrast, experience-rating does not adversely affect large corporations because their health care costs are predictable and stable. Large corporations fare well under experience-rated premiums, while small firms do not, due to the difference in the ability to pay for health care which exists between big and small business.

Because they have large numbers of contributing members, large groups have substantial financial resources to fund their health care costs, including catastrophic medical expenses. Given the availability of substantial financial resources, large groups experience modest and predictable increases in their health insurance premiums on an annual basis. As a result, insurance is affordable for large groups. Large corporations do not face overwhelming financial difficulty providing their working families group insurance.

By contrast, because they have small numbers of contributing members, small groups have limited financial resources to fund their health care costs. Private health insurance premiums must be raised substantially to cover the cost of treatment for any member of a small group who suffers a catastrophic illness or injury. As a result, small groups face massive and unpredictable rises in their premiums during any given year when any of their members suffers a catastrophic illness or injury. In 1992 33 percent of all small businesses suffered increases in their premiums of from 25 to 100 percent, and 51 percent experienced increases of less than 25 percent. By contrast, only 12 percent had no change in their premiums, with 4 percent enjoying decreases.[83] Because small firms face enormous and unanticipated increases in their premiums whenever a member of their working families suffers a catastrophic illness or injury, insurance is virtually unaffordable for small business. As we have seen, many small businesses are financially incapable of providing their working families group insurance.

The Health Security Act would make group health insurance affordable for small business by prohibiting private health insurance plans from charging experience-rated premiums. Rather, they would have to charge community-rated premiums, as we have seen. Under community-rating, insurance premiums would have to reflect the cost of health care for the entire community, comprising tens of thousands, hundreds of thousands, or millions of residents. During any given year, the overwhelming majority of residents in each community will incur only modest health care costs. Only a small fraction of the residents will require costly treatment for catastrophic illnesses.

Because the overwhelming majority of their residents will remain healthy during any given year, communities experience relatively modest and predictable increases in their health care costs on an annual basis. As a result, insurance premiums will rise at a moderate and controllable pace under community-rating. Accordingly, community-rating will make group insurance affordable for small business. Moreover, by providing federal subsidies to assure that premiums do not exceed 7.9 percent of payroll, the Health Security Act would make group insurance affordable even for the least profitable small businesses, which would have difficulty financing health care costs for their working families.

In addition to experience-rating, another major factor making group health insurance unaffordable for small business is administrative costs. Each large corporation and federal, state, and local government employs thousands, tens of thousands, or even hundreds of thousands of workers. Only a single bureaucracy is needed to process medical claims and reimburse health care providers for each corporation and government employer. As a result, large corporations and government employers can be insured efficiently, with only minimal bureaucracy and paperwork.

By contrast, private plans must maintain separate bureaucracies to process medical claims and reimburse health care providers for each insured small business. Hundreds of thousands of small businesses are insured. The need to maintain a separate bureaucracy to administer the group insurance of each small business results in massive duplication of administration and paperwork in the small group insurance market, in contrast to large corporations and government entities, which can be insured much more efficiently. Administrative costs consume 40 percent of the group health insurance premiums paid by small business, compared to only 5 percent for large corporations.[84] The bureaucratic inefficiency in the administration of group insurance for the small business market is a major reason why small firms pay an average of 35 percent higher insurance premiums for the same coverage offered to large corporations.[85]

The Health Security Act would reduce the administrative costs in the small group health insurance market. Employers with 5,000 workers or fewer would be required to secure their coverage through a health alliance in their area. All the small businesses in each area would be insured through a single health alliance. This would allow thousands of small businesses to enroll in any private plan contracting with a health alliance. A single bureaucracy would be able to process medical claims and reimburse health care providers for the thousands of small businesses which would be covered by each private plan. As a result, the Health Security Act would allow small businesses to be insured, with a minimum of bureaucracy and paperwork, reducing the administrative costs in the small group insurance market. Those reduced costs would be passed on to small firms through lower premiums, making group insurance affordable for small business.

THE ROLE OF HEALTH ALLIANCES

Perhaps the most innovative reform in the health care system the Health Security Act would impose is the establishment of health alliances. They would fundamentally change the way private health insurance is purchased and health care costs are determined.

Currently private health insurance is independently purchased by millions of firms, governments, families, and individuals. The Health Security Act would require consumers of private insurance to join health alliances, which would serve entire regions.[86] As a result, no more than several dozen regional health alliances would be in operation under the bill.

True, employers with over 5,000 workers could form their own corporate health alliances. However, employers which do so would not be entitled to any federal subsidies to assist them in purchasing group health insurance costing in excess of 7.9 percent of payroll.[87] Rather, they would have to pay the full cost of such group insurance. Few large employers would be willing to do this. As a result, most large employers would opt to join regional alliances, which would entitle them to federal subsidies to purchase costly group insurance.

Under the Health Security Act, no more than several dozen regional health alliances and another several dozen corporate health alliances would be in operation. Accordingly, the bill would result in a far-reaching reorganization and consolidation of the private health insurance marketplace, requiring the millions of firms, governments, families, and individuals who currently buy voluntary plans independently to join no more than several dozen health alliances, which would serve as insurance purchasing agents for the entire population.

The primary goal of health alliances would be to contain health care costs through two means: First, they would operate on the basis of a medical budget, which would be achieved through stringent, federally imposed limits on the amount of private health insurance premiums they would have to pay; and second, they would use their collective bargaining power to secure the most comprehensive coverage available at the lowest possible cost.

Containing Health Care Costs Through Federal Regulation

The reorganization and consolidation of the private health insurance marketplace would permit the National Health Board to impose a national health care budget. This would be achieved through the establishment of a per capita premium target for each health alliance. A stringent tax would be imposed upon private plans which charged premiums in excess of the premium target.

To avoid paying stiff taxes, private health insurance plans would have to restrain the growth of their premiums to assure that they did not exceed the National Health Board's premium targets. This would require private plans to contain health care costs. Physician and dental fees, hospital rates, and drug prices would have to be reduced. Public access to medical technology would have to be stringently rationed. Administrative waste and inefficiency within the private insurance industry would have to be reduced.

Health care providers and the pharmaceutical companies would oppose any reductions in their charges. They would also resist restrictions on public access to medical technology they provide their patients and customers. Such actions would reduce physician, dental, hospital, and pharmaceutical incomes, which are largely based upon the excessive charges health care providers and drug companies impose for their goods and services and physician and hospital over-utilization of medical technology in treating catastrophic illnesses.

Health care providers and the pharmaceutical industry would be reluctant to provide goods and services to health alliance members, since the National Health Board would impose stringent limits on the premiums private health insurance plans contracting with health alliances could charge. As we have seen, such limits would result in a reduction in physician, dental, hospital, and pharmaceutical incomes. However, all families in firms employing 5,000 or fewer workers and Medicaid recipients would be members of a health alliance under the Health Security Act. The same would be true of all Medicare beneficiaries, if each state, upon approval of the HHS secretary, chose to enroll them in a health alliance. Firms employing over 5,000 workers would be given the option of establishing their own corporate health alliances in lieu of joining a regional health alliance. However, those firms would only be entitled to federal subsidies to assist them in providing group insurance to their working families if they joined a regional health alliance. As a result, practically all large corporations would voluntarily join a regional health alliance.

Practically the entire population—working families, Medicaid recipients, and perhaps Medicare beneficiaries—would be enrolled in a health alliance under the Health Security Act. Those individuals would be prohibited from purchasing private health insurance outside of a health alliance. The only means by which those individuals would be able to secure their health care outside of a health alliance would be through the direct purchase of their medical services out of pocket, which only the wealthiest persons would have the financial capacity to do.

With practically the entire population enrolled in a health alliance, health care providers and pharmaceutical companies which refused to provide goods and services to health alliance members would be deprived of practically all their patients and customers. The only patients and customers they would have access to would be the relative handful of wealthy individuals who would opt to pay for their health care services out of pocket in lieu of joining a health alliance. As a result, health care providers and pharmaceutical companies which refused to provide services to health alliance members would have few, if any, patients and customers. They would go out of business. To survive financially, health care providers and the pharmaceutical companies would have to provide goods and services to health alliance members, regardless of how little reimbursement they would receive under the stringent limits on the private health insurance premiums the National Health Board would impose.

Private health insurance plans would also be reluctant to contract with health alliances, given the stringent limits on their premiums the National Health Board would impose. Such limits would reduce the income of private plans. True, private plans would not have to absorb all the financial losses which would result from the limits imposed on their premiums. As we have seen, health care providers and the pharmaceutical industry, not private insurance, would have to sustain the lion's share of the financial losses—through reductions in physician and dental fees, hospital rates, drug prices, and restrictions on public access to medical technology.

However, health care providers and pharmaceutical companies would refuse to contract with private health insurance plans which reduced their incomes excessively. Private plans unable to contract with a sufficient number of health care providers and pharmaceutical companies would be unable to extend their subscribers sufficient access to medical services. They would go out of business. To survive, private plans would have to contract with an adequate number of health care providers and pharmaceutical companies. To do so, they would have to reimburse health care providers and pharmaceutical companies reasonably well.

As a result, in order to meet the limits on their premiums the National Health Board would impose, private health insurance plans would have to go beyond reducing the cost of health care services and drugs; they would have to reduce their own costs. They would have to curtail their administrative waste and inefficiency. They would have to downsize their operations by streamlining their bloated bureaucracies. This would result in a substantial loss of jobs and income in the private insurance industry.

Private health insurance plans could avoid any limits on their premiums by refusing to contract with health alliances. The National Health Board would only have the authority to impose limits on premiums paid by health alliances. Private plans could charge whatever premiums they wished to individuals not belonging to a health alliance.

However, under the Health Security Act virtually all privately insured individuals would be members of a health alliance. As a result, private health insurance plans refusing to contract with health alliances would have no business. To survive, private plans would have to contract with health alliances, regardless of how low the premiums they would be allowed to charge.

Containing Health Care Costs Through Collective Bargaining

As we have seen, the National Health Board would contain health care costs by imposing limits on the premiums private health insurance plans could charge health alliances under the Health Security Act. However, the bill would not rely upon premium limits alone to contain health care costs. Rather, health alliances would also be expected to contain health care costs on their own through the collective bargaining power they would exert in the medical marketplace.

Private health insurance is currently purchased by millions of firms, families, and individuals. No one group of insurance purchasers, not even large corporations, represents more than a small fraction of the insurance market. As a result, no group has sufficient bargaining clout to limit the amount it pays for insurance. Rather, it must accept whatever premium a private plan charges for insurance. This gives the private insurance industry control of coverage and health care costs. The industry profits by providing consumers the least amount of insurance available at the highest possible premiums. To limit their financial liabilities and maximize their revenues, private plans provide consumers inadequate, costly insurance.

The Health Security Act would strengthen the collective bargaining power of health care consumers by organizing them into health alliances. To save their members money, health alliances would only contract with private health insurance plans which provided the most comprehensive coverage available at the lowest possible premiums. Health alliances would refuse to contract with private plans which provided them inadequate, costly insurance. As we have seen, practically all consumers would be organized into health alliances. As a result, private plans which failed to contract with health alliances would go out of business. They would have to provide comprehensive, low-cost insurance in order to attract business from health alliances.

Health alliances would transfer power within the health care marketplace from the private health insurance industry to consumers. To survive, the industry would have to both expand the coverage it offers consumers and reduce its costs. Accordingly, health alliances would result in a reduction in health care costs, in addition to the premium limits the National Health Board would impose. Such a reduction in health care costs would result in a further slash in the incomes of health care providers and the private insurance and pharmaceutical industries—adding to the financial losses the medical system would sustain from those premium limits.

CONCLUSION

The Health Security Act represented an ambitious attempt to achieve far-reaching health care reform. The foundation of the bill lay in the establishment of health alliances which would serve as the institutional framework for achieving universal health insurance coverage combined with health care cost containment. Practically all individuals would be required to join a health alliance. Each health alliance would operate on the basis of a stringent budget achieved through the strict ceilings on private health insurance premiums the National Health Board would impose. Under the bill, health care providers and the private insurance and pharmaceutical industries would be required to accept substantial reductions in their incomes through those limits on insurance premiums. Further reductions in their incomes would come from the ability of health alliances to exert their collective bargaining power to guarantee their members the most comprehensive insurance available at the lowest possible cost.

Given the threat the Health Security Act posed to the financial interests of the health care industry, practically every medical interest group united in opposition to the bill. The industry was well-positioned to prevent passage of the bill through the enormous political clout medical interest groups exert on Capitol Hill, as we will now see.

Chapter 3

The Financial Relationship Between Congress and the Health Care Industry

> Nearly every President since Harry Truman has tried to push major health care reform through Congress, but only Lyndon Johnson succeeded. The failure of so many attempts to enact reform . . . and the enduring protections for [health care industry] interests are tribute to a flood of private money and political action committee (PAC) contributors [from medical interest groups] who have acquired veto power in key congressional committees over any proposal that seriously threatens their narrow interests.[1]
>
> Joseph A. Califano, Jr., Secretary of Health, Education, and Welfare, 1977–1979.

The health care industry has historically opposed national health insurance because the program cannot be established on a fiscally and economically viable basis without the imposition of stringent cost-containment measures, which are certain to inflict substantial financial losses upon every segment of the medical system. Since the early 1990s, the basic resource the industry has used to prevent establishment of the program has been money. Through its massive campaign contributions to members of Congress, the industry has succeeded in wielding enormous influence on Capitol Hill. The industry has used its influence to prevent the establishment of national health insurance.

The health care industry has long represented a financial powerhouse on Capitol Hill as a result of the political activities of the AMA's American Medical Political Action Committee (AMPAC). Since 1968, AMPAC has been one of the top two contributors to congressional campaigns among all PACs, with the exception of 1980, when it briefly slipped to third place.[2]

Since the defeat of the Hospital Cost Containment Act, the health care industry's financial power on Capitol Hill has mushroomed. Over the period 1980 through 1990, the industry provided $100 million in campaign contributions to congressional candidates.[3] Incumbent senators were major beneficiaries of contributions from the industry. During 1979–1994, the industry provided $40.1 million in contributions to incumbent senators.[4]

The massive campaign contributions the health care industry provided to congressional candidates during the 1980s were due to the rise of medical interest group PACs. During the 1960s and 1970s, the AMA was the only health care interest group with a strong PAC. However, by the beginning of the 1980s, the AMA was joined by virtually every major health care interest group, each of which established at least one, and in some cases several, strong PACs of its own. Doctors, dentists, optometrists, chiropractors, podiatrists, nurses, hospitals, nursing homes, and drug and private health insurance companies all had their own PACs.

The proliferation of strong medical PACs during the 1980s allowed the medical industry to emerge as a major source of campaign contributions to congressional candidates. During 1980–1991, health care industry PACs contributed $62 million to congressional candidates.[5] Health care professionals contributed $28 million, the private health insurance industry $19 million, the pharmaceutical industry $9 million, and the hospital industry $6 million.[6]

Like all other PACs, practically all the campaign contributions from medical PACs go to incumbent members of Congress. The reason is simple. Interest groups seek to gain influence on Capitol Hill, rather than pursue a particular political or ideological agenda. Practically all incumbent members of Congress are reelected.[7] As a result, interest groups can only gain influence on Capitol Hill by allying themselves with incumbent members of Congress. By devoting practically all their campaign contributions to incumbent members of Congress, interest groups maintaining PACs, like the health care industry, have succeeded in wielding substantial political clout on Capitol Hill.

To assure the health care industry maximum influence on Capitol Hill, medical PACs have provided campaign contributions to practically every member of Congress, regardless of his or her partisan affiliation or ideology. Of the $62 million in contributions from health care industry PACs which went to congressional candidates during 1980–1991, $43.2 million was provided to 519 of the 534 lawmakers who were in office in 1991.[8]

THE CAMPAIGN TO ESTABLISH NATIONAL HEALTH INSURANCE OPENS IN THE 102ND CONGRESS

With virtually every major health care interest group maintaining at least one strong PAC, the medical industry was well positioned to use its financial influence on Capitol Hill to prevent the establishment of national health insurance during the 1990s. The first opportunity the industry had to demonstrate its newly developed financial clout on Capitol Hill came in the 102nd Congress. It opened in 1991 with Mitchell announcing that health care reform would be his top legislative priority.[9] Accordingly, on June 5, 1991, Mitchell introduced the

HealthAmerica Act, which would have guaranteed universal access to affordable health care.[10] In introducing the HealthAmerica Act, Mitchell vowed to pass a national health insurance bill in the 102nd Congress. "It is my hope, my expectation and my intention to enact meaningful health care reform in this Congress," Mitchell declared.[11]

On January 22, 1992, the Senate Labor and Human Resources Committee approved a slightly modified version of the HealthAmerica Act. Mitchell greeted the committee's action by reiterating his pledge to quickly pass a national health insurance bill. "It is my intention to make every effort to see that meaningful health care reform is passed in this Congress," Mitchell declared.[12]

THE EMERGENCE OF NATIONAL HEALTH INSURANCE AS A MAJOR CAMPAIGN ISSUE

Mitchell's efforts to pass a national health insurance bill came in the midst of a U.S. Senate election in Pennsylvania, which proved to be major watershed in the eighty-year history of America's debate on health care reform. The election pitted Democratic senator Harris Wofford against his Republican challenger, Richard Thornburgh. Wofford had been an obscure secretary of labor and industry in Pennsylvania, having never before been elected to public office when he was appointed to fill the unexpired Senate term of the late John Heinz in May 1991.[13] By contrast, Thornburgh was a prominent political figure in both Pennsylvania and Washington, having served as a two-term governor of the state before becoming attorney general in the Reagan and Bush administrations.[14]

Because he was less known than Thornburgh, Wofford began the Senate campaign as the underdog, given virtually no chance of winning the election. When the campaign opened in June 1991, Wofford trailed Thornburgh by the seemingly insurmountable margin of 67 percent to 20 percent. Miraculously, however, Wofford succeeded in scoring a stunning upset victory, defeating Thornburgh by an overwhelming margin of 55 percent to 45 percent.[15]

A major factor in Wofford's surprise victory was the issue of national health insurance. Wofford made his support for the program a centerpiece of his campaign. In his most effective campaign sound bite, Wofford declared, "If criminals have a right to a lawyer, I think working Americans have a right to a doctor."[16] Thornburgh responded to Wofford's support for national health insurance by denouncing it as a costly program, which would drive many small firms out of business, create higher unemployment, and require a substantial tax increase.[17]

Polling data show that national health insurance was the single most important issue which determined how Pennsylvanians voted in the Senate election. Additional polling data showed widespread concern among Pennsylvanians over both their access to and the cost of health care.[18] This suggests that like other Americans, Pennsylvanians recognize that massive job layoffs by large corporations and state and local government have resulted in the widespread loss of group coverage among previously insured working families. Meanwhile, large corporations and the federal government have acted to reduce soaring health care costs by cutting the coverage provided under group insurance and Medicare, respectively. Threatened by the prospect of losing their jobs and the group insurance which comes with them, and forced to shoulder an increasing share of the financial burden of their health care as a result of shrinking medical benefits, an overwhelming majority of Pennsylvanians, like Americans as a whole, support, and in some cases are demanding, health care reform. By supporting national health insurance, Wofford gained a substantial number of votes from Pennsylvanians concerned, if not alarmed, by the financial and physical danger the worsening health care crisis poses to all but the wealthiest individuals.

By successfully using his support for national health insurance to win his stunning upset victory, Wofford demonstrated the political appeal of national health insurance. He showed that, given the gravity of the health care crisis, voters want medical reform to be a top priority on the national agenda and are predisposed, if not certain, to vote for candidates supporting national health insurance. This was good news for the Democratic Party. National health insurance will require government intervention to restructure the health care system in order to guarantee universal access to affordable medical services. Accordingly, as the party supporting activist government, the Democrats are better suited politically to lead on the issue of health care reform than are the Republicans. In contrast to the more activist Democrats, Republicans tend to favor minimal government and are less likely to support increased government involvement in the health care system.

As a result, the public has greater confidence in the Democrats on the issue of health care reform than they do in the Republicans. During October 22–26, 1993, Peter Hart and Robert Teeter conducted a poll of 1,508 adults for the *Wall Street Journal* and NBC News. The poll asked its respondents the following question: "Which party, the Democratic Party or the Republican Party, would do a better job handling the following" eight issues, including health care. Forty-four percent of the respondents said that the Democrats "would do a better job handling" health care; only 16 percent believed the Republicans would do so. Eighteen percent trusted neither party on the issue of health care, while another 16 percent believed in both. Health care ranked first among the eight issues in which the public was asked to rate the Democrats. By contrast, health care ranked second to last among those same eight issues in which the public was asked to rate the Republicans, behind only race relations.[19] The *Wall Street Journal*/NBC News poll showed that the public was looking to the Democrats to provide leadership on health care reform, and had little trust in the Republicans on this issue.

With the public expecting the Democratic Party to assume responsibility for achieving health care reform, and with Wofford's stunning upset victory demonstrating the popular appeal of this issue, Clinton made his support for national health insurance a centerpiece of his 1992 presidential campaign. Clinton's Republican opponent, President George Bush, attacked his Democratic rival for supporting national health insurance. Bush warned that national health insurance would impose added costs on small business, which would have to assume the financial burden of providing working families group coverage under the program. Unable to shoulder this financial burden, many small firms would either go out of business or lay off workers to escape responsibility for having to provide them group insurance, resulting in rising unemployment. In addition, the federal government would have to substantially raise taxes to finance the subsidies which would be required to assist small businesses in providing their working families group insurance. As Bush saw it, national health insurance would be an unmitigated disaster for the economy, resulting in small business failures, higher unemployment, and higher taxes.[20]

Clinton dismissed Bush's attacks against national health insurance. In his speech to the Democratic National Convention in New York accepting the party's presidential nomination, Clinton attacked Bush for his failure to provide leadership on the issue of health care reform. In contrast to Bush, Clinton promised to provide such leadership, if elected to the presidency. "He won't take on the big insurance companies and the bureaucracies to control health care costs and give us affordable health care for all Americans," Clinton charged. "But I will."[21] Polling data show that Clinton's decisive election victory was based upon the substantial number of the votes he received from the significant share of the electorate who considered health care reform to be the most important issue in the 1992 presidential campaign.[22] Alienated, if not angered, by Bush's opposition to national health insurance, those voters easily turned to Clinton, given his pledge to take action on the issue of health care reform if elected.

During 1991–1992, substantial pressure began to build for health care reform. As we have seen, Wofford's stunning upset election victory, which was largely based upon his support for national health insurance, demonstrated the popular appeal of health care reform. Clinton's election, also based largely upon his support for national health insurance, assured that health care reform would be at the top of the president's agenda when he took office. Polling data show that the public was looking to the Democratic Party to provide leadership on the issue of health care reform. With the Democrats now in control of the White House and Congress, it seemed that the political system was finally ready to establish national health insurance in 1993, after having repeatedly failed to do so for the previous half century. In the aftermath of Clinton's decisive election victory, the prospects for health care reform never looked better.

THE HEALTH CARE INDUSTRY RAISES ITS CAMPAIGN CONTRIBUTIONS TO CONGRESSIONAL CANDIDATES

The improved prospects for health care reform represented a financial threat to the medical industry. National health insurance cannot be established on a fiscally and economically sound basis without the imposition of stringent controls on health care costs, which are certain to reduce the incomes of every part of the medical industry. As a result, the industry was determined to blunt the substantial momentum toward health care reform which developed during 1991–1992 by significantly raising its campaign contributions to congressional candidates.

During 1991–1992, the health care industry provided $41.4 million in campaign contributions to congressional candidates. From 1989–1990 to 1991–1992, industry contributions to congressional candidates rose by 31 percent. By contrast, contributions from all sources rose by 10 percent during the same period.[23] As Michael Podhorzer, a health care policy analyst for Citizen Action, a public interest group, put it, the increase in health care industry campaign contributions was "nothing short of an explosion."[24]

The substantial rise in campaign contributions from the health care industry was led by a significant increase in donations from medical PACs. Medical PAC contributions to congressional candidates doubled from $11.6 million during 1989–1990 to $23.2 million during 1991–1992.[25] By contrast, contributions from all PACs rose by 15 percent during the same period.[26] During 1989–1990 to 1991–1992, contributions from PACs representing the health professions rose from $7.1 million to $9.7 million; the private health insurance industry $900,000 to $9.4 million; the pharmaceutical industry $2.3 million to $3 million; and the hospital and nursing-home industries $1.3 million to $1.5 million.[27] The substantial increase in campaign contributions to congressional candidates by medical PACs was concentrated among three key interest groups: the AMA, the American Dental Association (ADA), and the American Chiropractic Association. During 1989–1990 to 1991–1992, the AMA raised its contributions by 23 percent to $2,936,086; the ADA increased its contributions by 70 percent to $1,420,958; and the American Chiropractic Association raised its contributions by 234 percent to $641,746.[28]

Like all PACs, practically all campaign contributions from health care industry PACs went to incumbent members of Congress. The reason for this is simple. Interest groups, like the health care industry, use campaign contributions to gain political influence on Capitol Hill. Since practically all members of Congress are reelected, interest groups can only secure such influence by establishing close relationships with incumbent lawmakers. To develop such relationships, interest groups act as a secure and reliable source of financial support for incumbent members of Congress.

As Table 3.1 shows, nearly two-thirds of the campaign contributions to congressional candidates from medical interest groups during 1991–1992 came from the twenty-four largest medical PACs. Nearly half of the contributions to congressional candidates from medical interest groups during 1989–1990 came from twelve of those twenty-four medical PACs. Representing every major segment of the health care system, the twenty-four medical PACs included interest groups representing doctors, dentists, optometrists, podiatrists, chiropractors, nurses, hospitals, nursing homes, and insurance companies. The fact that every

Table 3.1

Campaign Contributions to Congressional Candidates From the Twenty-four Largest Health Care Industry PACs During 1989–1990 and 1991–1992 in Dollars

Contributor	Contributions During 1989–1990	Contributions During 1991–1992
American Medical Association	2,127,348	2,936,086
American Dental Association	762,022	1,420,958
National Association of Life Underwriters	n.a.	1,372,600
American Academy of Ophthalmology	412,566	801,527
American Chiropractic Association	n.a.	641,746
Independent Insurance Agents of America	n.a.	590,798
American Council of Life Insurance	n.a.	577,430
American Hospital Association	451,689	505,888
American Family Life Assurance Company	n.a.	503,000
American Podiatry Association	n.a.	401,000
Prudential Insurance Company of America	188,970	400,835
American Optometric Association	292,750	398,366
American Health Care Association	180,505	382,019
American College of Emergency Physicians	n.a.	330,725
American Nurses Association	281,240	306,519
Massachusetts Mutual Life Insurance Company	n.a.	282,338
Association for the Advancement of Psychology	n.a.	273,743
Metropolitan Life Insurance Corporation	276,471	266,342
National Association of Independent Insurers	n.a.	240,725
Northwestern Mutual Life Insurance Company	n.a.	240,580
American Physical Therapy Association	n.a.	198,941
Eli Lilly & Company	150,700	195,530
Pfizer Inc.	125,750	188,100
Schering-Plough Corporation	115,525	186,050
TOTAL	5,365,536	13,641,846

Sources: Tim Brightbill, "Political Action Committees: How Much Influence Will $7.7 Million Buy?" in Vincente Navarro, *Why the United States Does Not Have a National Health Program* (Amityville, N.Y.: Baywood Publishing, 1992), pp. 124–25; Vincente Navarro, *Dangerous to Your Health: Capitalism in Health Care* (New York: Monthly Review Press, 1993), p. 34; "To Give and to Receive," *Wall Street Journal*, September 23, 1993, p. A6.

major segment of the health care industry makes substantial campaign contributions to members of Congress assures that lawmakers will be responsive to the concerns of all the major health care interest groups.

Most of the increase in campaign contributions from medical PACs came from a single source: the private health insurance industry. From 1989–1990 to 1991–1992, insurance PAC contributions rose an astounding 900 percent, nine times the overall increase in medical PAC contributions during the same period.[29] Why did the insurance industry raise its contributions by such a massive amount? The answer lies in the fact that no segment of the health care industry is more threatened by medical reform than insurance companies.

HEALTH CARE REFORM AND THE PRIVATE HEALTH INSURANCE INDUSTRY

The private health insurance industry is wasteful and inefficient, generating tens of billions of dollars in excessive administrative costs annually. There are 1,500 private plans operating in the United States.[30] Each plan maintains its own bureaucracy to process medical claims and reimburse health care providers, generating a duplication of administrative overhead and paperwork, which adds to medical costs. In addition, the private insurance industry is intensely competitive. Private plans must compete for business by spending substantial sums on marketing, advertising, and sales to solicit business, which adds more to health care costs.

Finally, private health insurance plans must limit their financial liabilities to remain in business. They do so by denying enrollment to individuals with chronic and costly ailments and exclude preexisting medical conditions from the coverage they provide their subscribers. This requires private plans to maintain large underwriting departments to examine the health history of each new applicant for coverage in order to deny health care benefits to those individuals who would represent a financial liability to the insurance company, which adds even more to health care costs.

Public health insurance represents a much more efficient alternative to private plans in financing the delivery of health care. This fact is illustrated by the case of Medicare, the federal insurance program for elderly and disabled Social Security beneficiaries.

The federal government contracts with only a small handful of private plans to process medical claims and reimburse health care providers under the program. In 1995 the federal government contracted with only thirty-two private plans to do so under Part B of the program, which covers physician services.[31] The existence of no more than a few dozen private plans to process medical claims and reimburse health care providers guarantees a minimum of administration and paperwork, which has served to restrain the growth of Medicare costs.

Unlike private health insurance, Medicare provides coverage to its beneficiaries on a compulsory basis. The federal government does not spend one dime soliciting business under the program. The cost of marketing, advertising, and sales under the program is practically nonexistent.

Every elderly and disabled Social Security recipient has the right to Medicare benefits. There are no underwriting departments to review applications for coverage to determine the health history of each new applicant for Medicare coverage in order to deny health care benefits to those elderly and disabled individuals who would represent a financial liability to the federal government.

The absence of underwriting departments substantially reduces administrative costs under the program.

The case of Medicare shows that public health insurance is efficient because the government uses no more than a handful of insurance companies to process medical claims and reimburse health care providers, keeping administrative overhead and paperwork to a minimum. Coverage is provided on a compulsory basis, eliminating the costs of marketing, advertising, sales, and underwriting. By contrast, private insurance is wasteful and inefficient because the existence of a multiplicity of voluntary plans competing for business results in excessive administrative overhead and paperwork, and generates additional costs for marketing, advertising, sales, and underwriting.

The fact that public health insurance is more efficient than private plans is supported by a comparison of administrative costs between public and private insurance. In 1988 Canada's single-payer insurance program spent only 3 percent of its revenues on administrative costs. America's federal insurance program for the elderly and disabled, Medicare, spent only 2.3 percent of its revenues on administrative costs that same year.[32] By contrast, in 1991 the private insurance industry spent 16 percent of its revenues on administrative costs.[33]

By generating excessive administrative overhead and paperwork, and spending substantial sums on marketing, advertising, sales, and underwriting, the private health insurance industry represents a major source of the waste and inefficiency within the health care system, squandering tens of billions of dollars which could be better used to provide coverage to the uninsured. As a result, the health care reform initiatives launched during the 1990s have concentrated on restricting the role of private insurance in financing medical services, or even eliminating voluntary plans altogether. The most important such initiative pursued in the 102nd Congress was the HealthAmerica Act. It would have established a play-or-pay insurance plan in which employers would have been required to either provide their working families group coverage or pay a payroll tax to finance a government program to extend health care benefits to the uninsured.[34] The bill was sponsored by a group of leading Senate Democratic health care policy makers, including Mitchell; Edward M. Kennedy of Massachusetts, chairman of the Labor and Human Resources Committee, which exercises partial jurisdiction over health care reform in the Senate; John D. Rockefeller IV of West Virginia, chairman of the U.S. Bipartisan Commission on Comprehensive Health Care; and Donald Riegle of Michigan, chairman of the Subcommittee on Health for Families and the Uninsured of the Senate Finance Committee.[35]

By providing employers the option of paying a payroll tax to provide their working families public health insurance, the HealthAmerica Act would have resulted in the elimination of a substantial part of the private insurance industry. Because the administrative costs of public insurance are low, employers would have to pay a relatively low payroll tax to finance a government program to provide their working families coverage. By contrast, because the administrative costs of private insurance are high, voluntary plans would charge employers substantially higher premiums than the payroll tax they would pay to provide their working families the same coverage under a government program.

If given a choice, most employers would opt to provide their working families public, rather than private, insurance. By providing employers such a choice, the HealthAmerica Act promised to result in a massive shift of working families from private to public insurance, driving many, if not most, insurance companies out of business.[36] Accordingly, insurance PACs raised their campaign contributions to congressional candidates by a whopping 900 percent from 1989–1990 to 1991–1992 to assure the defeat of the HealthAmerica Act or any other health care reform bill which posed a threat to the financial interests of insurance companies.

THE HEALTH CARE INDUSTRY'S CAMPAIGN CONTRIBUTIONS TO MEMBERS OF IMPORTANT CONGRESSIONAL COMMITTEES

Perhaps the most distinguishing feature of the financial relationship between Congress and the health care industry is that much of the campaign contributions from medical interest groups go to members of four committees exercising jurisdiction over health care reform: the House Energy and Commerce and Ways and Means Committees; and the Senate Finance and Labor and Human Resources Committees. During 1980 to 1991, members of those four committees received $18 million in campaign contributions from medical PACs, representing 29 percent of all donations medical interest groups made to congressional candidates during this period.[37] During 1983 to 1993, medical PACs provided $6 million in campaign contributions to members of the House Ways and Means Committee; $5.5 million to members of the House Energy and Commerce and Senate Finance Committees, respectively; and $3 million to members of the Senate Labor and Human Resources Committee.[38] During 1980 to 1991, twelve of the twenty-one Senators who received over $200,000 from medical PACs were members of the Finance Committee; and all the top twenty-five House recipients of contributions from medical PACs served either in the House leadership or on the Ways and Means or Energy and Commerce Committees.[39] During 1979 to 1994, each committee member received an average contribution of $600,000 from medical PACs.[40]

As we have seen, campaign contributions from health care industry PACs to congressional candidates rose substantially during 1989–1990 to 1991–1992 to blunt the increased political momentum towards medical reform which developed in this period. As Table 3.2 shows, much of the increase in campaign contributions from medical PACs during 1989–1990 to 1991–1992 went to members of the four congressional committees exercising jurisdiction over medical reform. Moreover, much, if not most, of the contributions to the House Ways and Means and Energy and Commerce Committees went to members of

Table 3.2
Campaign Contributions From Health Care Industry PACs to the Congressional Committees and Subcommittees Exercising Jurisdiction Over Health Care Reform During 1989–1990 and 1991–1992 in Dollars

Congressional Committee or Subcommittee	Amount of Contributions During 1989–1990	Amount of Contributions During 1991–1992	Percent Increase in Contributions From 1989–1990 to 1991–1992
House Energy and Commerce Committee	1,523,028	2,049,559	34.6
Energy and Commerce Health Subcommittee	935,609	1,232,963	31.8
House Ways and Means Committee	1,423,580	1,889,246	32.7
Ways and Means Health Subcommittee	526,859	775,691	47.2
Senate Finance Committee	1,018,417	1,330,938	30.7
Senate Labor and Human Resources Committee	839,566	878,745	4.7

Source: Alissa J. Rubin, "With Health Overhaul on Stage, PACs Want Front Row Seat," *Congressional Quarterly Weekly Report*, July 31, 1993, pp. 2052–54.

their health subcommittees. During 1991–1992, 60.2 percent and 41.1 percent of campaign contributions from medical PACs to members of the House Energy and Commerce and Ways and Means Committees, respectively, went to those sitting on their health subcommittees.[41]

From 1991–1992 to 1993–1994, medical PACs raised their campaign contributions to members of Congress to prevent the political drive toward health care reform, which Clinton's election to the presidency unleashed. Congressional committees exercising jurisdiction over health care reform received the lion's share of the increase in contributions from medical PACs. From 1991–1992 to 1993–1994, the average contribution from medical PACs to members of the House Ways and Means and Energy and Commerce Committees rose by $27,000. By contrast, the average contribution from the industry to House members not serving on either of the two committees increased by only $3,000.[42]

Why does so much of the campaign contributions to members of Congress from medical PACs go to the committees exercising jurisdiction over medical reform? The answer lies in the critical role those committees play in the legislative process on health care reform. Except in unusual circumstances, neither the House nor the Senate will consider legislation on any issue until it has been approved by the committees exercising jurisdiction over this issue. Consistent with this rule, the House and Senate will not consider any national health insurance bill unless it has been approved by the committees in each house of Congress exercising jurisdiction over health care reform. Moreover, the House Energy and Commerce and Ways and Means Committees are unlikely to consider any national health insurance bill until it has been approved by their health subcommittees.

By concentrating its campaign contributions to members of the congressional committees and subcommittees exercising jurisdiction over health care reform, the medical industry succeeded in exerting substantial influence over those legislative bodies. The industry used this influence to frustrate the ability of those committees to approve a national health insurance bill. True, four of the five committees exercising jurisdiction over national health insurance approved health care reform legislation in the 103rd Congress. However, those committees approved health care reform legislation during June and July 1994, late in the second session of the 103rd Congress.

The full 103rd Congress was unable to consider health care reform legislation until July 2, 1994, when Senate Finance became the final committee exercising jurisdiction over national health insurance to approve a bill to overhaul the medical system. The Finance Committee's action paved the way for Mitchell to bring a national health insurance bill to the Senate floor on August 2. However, this gave the Senate only two months to pass health care reform legislation before the adjournment of the 103rd Congress on October 8. There was no way Congress could pass legislation so sweeping, complex, and controversial as to overhaul the health care system in such a short period. Recognizing this, House Democratic leaders saw no point in bringing national health insurance legislation of their own to the House floor for a vote. By dragging their feet, and waiting until almost the last minute to approve health care reform legislation, the committees exercising jurisdiction over national health insurance effectively destroyed prospects for passage of a bill to overhaul the medical system in the 103rd Congress.

By preventing the congressional committees which exercise jurisdiction over national health insurance from approving health care reform legislation on a timely basis, the medical industry blocked both the House and Senate from having to vote on a bill to overhaul the health care system in the 103rd Congress. Such a vote would have placed members of Congress in a politically difficult position. The overwhelming majority of the public support national health insurance. Given the political popularity of health care reform, members of Congress would have risked defeat the next time they ran for reelection if they voted against any national health insurance bill which might have reached either the House or Senate floor. However, they would have been forced to vote against such a bill, since the health care industry opposes national health insurance. Financially beholden to the industry, members of Congress will take no major action which is opposed by medical interest groups.

Members of the 103rd Congress needed to be spared from taking the politically risky, if not suicidal, action of voting against national health insurance legislation. To do so, they needed to prevent a national health insurance bill from reaching either the House or Senate floor sufficiently early in the life of the 103rd Congress to permit Democratic congressional leaders to schedule a vote on health care reform legislation. Such a bill could only be prevented from reaching either floor that early if the congressional committees exercising jurisdiction over health care reform delayed action on national health insurance until it was too late to permit a vote on legislation to overhaul the medical system. To assure this, the health care industry poured millions of dollars into the campaign coffers of members of those committees. This gave the industry enormous influence over the committees, which health care interest groups used to keep national health insurance legislation bottled up in those legislative bodies until the summer of 1994, just months before the 103rd Congress adjourned. As a result, the committees served as legislative choke points to delay and frustrate efforts by Democratic congressional leaders to bring national health insurance legislation to the House and Senate floors. This insulated members of Congress from having to take the politically dangerous action of voting against such a bill.

The role that congressional committees play in making it difficult for national health insurance legislation to reach either the Senate or House floor was perhaps best expressed by Richard Wade, vice president of the American Hospital Association (AHA). In explaining why the AHA contributes so heavily to the congressional campaigns of members of the House Ways and Means Committee, Wade bluntly admitted that "that's our gatekeeper committee in terms of health stuff."[43]

Members of Congress could oppose national health insurance without having to pay any political price for doing so. Many, if not most, members of both parties of the 103rd Congress, ranging across the ideological spectrum from left to right, declared their support for health care reform, even going so far as to sponsor legislation to extend coverage to at least some of the uninsured. By supporting health care reform, members of Congress succeeded in bolstering their popularity among their constituents, perhaps gaining the backing of millions of voters who favor, and in some cases are demanding, national health insurance.

In the meantime, the congressional committees exercising jurisdiction over health care reform acted to prevent national health insurance legislation from reaching either the House or Senate floor until the waning months of the 103rd Congress, after it was too late to schedule a vote on a bill to overhaul the medical system. This spared members of Congress from taking the politically detrimental action of voting against national health insurance legislation, which they would have to do, given their financial relationship with the health care industry. In the end, members of the Congress had it both ways: They pleased their constituents by promising to support health care reform, allowing them to gain the backing of the millions of voters who favor national health insurance; while satisfying the medical industry by refusing to take any action on national health insurance, enabling them to maintain their access to the millions of dollars in campaign contributions the industry provides. This ideal state of affairs for Congress will continue as long as the committees exercising jurisdiction over health care reform continue to keep national health insurance legislation from reaching either the House or Senate floor on a timely basis.

AN ANALYSIS OF CAMPAIGN CONTRIBUTIONS FROM THE HEALTH CARE INDUSTRY TO MEMBERS OF IMPORTANT CONGRESSIONAL COMMITTEES

Most of the campaign contributions from medical PACs going to the Senate Finance and Labor and Human Resources Committees during 1989–1992 went only to those members who were reelected in either 1990 or 1992. During 1991–1992, 86.4 percent and 72.8 percent of contributions going to members of the Senate Finance and Labor and Human Resources Committees, respectively, went to those who were reelected in 1992.[44] Moreover, committee members running for reelection in either 1990 or 1992 received most of their contributions during the two years prior to their reelection, as Table 3.3 reveals. Ten of the eleven members of the Senate Finance Committee who were reelected in either 1990 or 1992 received contributions from medical PACs. All ten of those received over 70 percent of their contributions during the two years prior to their reelection. Six of the eight members of the Senate Labor and Human Resources Committee reelected in either 1990 or 1992 received over 75 percent of the contributions during the two years prior to their victories.

Because most of the campaign contributions from medical PACs going to the Finance and Labor and Human Resources Committees during 1989–1992 went only to members reelected in either 1990 or 1992, those senators received substantially more donations than their committee colleagues up for reelection in 1994. As Table 3.3 shows, five of the eleven members of the Finance Committee and three of the eight members of the Labor and Human Resources Committee reelected in either 1990 or 1992 received contributions of over $200,000. Another four members of the Finance and Labor and Human Resources Committees, respectively, received contributions of between $100,000 and $200,000. Only one member of either committee received contributions of less than $25,000.

By contrast, all seven members of the Senate Finance Committee and all six members of the Senate Labor and Human Resources Committee up for reelection in 1994 received contributions of less than $100,000. Six members of the Finance Committee and two members of the Labor and Human Resources Committee received contributions of less than $25,000. Another two members of the Labor and Human Resources Committee received no contributions.

By making PAC contributions to members of the Senate Finance and Labor and Human Resources Committees only during their reelection campaigns the

Table 3.3
Campaign Contributions From Health Care Industry PACs to Members of the Senate Finance and Labor and Human Resources Committees During 1989–1992 in Dollars

Senator	Committee Membership	Year Up for Reelection	Amount of Contributions Received During 1989–1992	Percent of Contributions Received During Two Years Prior to Reelection
Daniel Coats (R-IN)	Labor	1992	416,663	53.7
John D. Rockefeller IV (D-WV)	Finance	1990	319,672	96.1
Tom Daschle (D-SD)	Finance	1992	299,624	75.6
Tom Harkin (D-IA)	Labor	1990	265,553	77.3
Christopher J. Dodd (D-CT)	Labor	1992	258,915	84.5
Bob Packwood (R-OR)	Finance	1992	247,852	100.0
Bob Dole (R-KS)	Finance	1992	238,807	81.9
Charles Grassley (R-IA)	Finance	1992	235,834	95.3
Bill Bradley (D-NJ)	Finance	1990	200,000	100.0
Max Baucus (D-MT)	Finance	1990	195,150	100.0
John B. Breaux (D-LA)	Finance	1992	188,241	93.5
Paul Simon (D-IL)	Labor	1990	115,141	99.9
Strom Thurmond (R-SC)	Labor	1990	113,557	99.1
Kent Conrad (D-ND)	Finance	1992	112,200	71.7
Barbara Mikulski (D-MD)	Labor	1992	112,204	86.5
Judd Gregg (R-NH)	Labor	1992	100,509	100.0
David Durenberger (R-MN)	Finance	1994	88,009	
Orrin G. Hatch (R-UT)	Labor	1994	82,080	

David Pryor (D-AR)	Finance	1990	81,990	100.0
Harris Wofford (D-PA)	Labor	1994	51,625	
Nancy Kassebaum (R-KS)	Labor	1994	27,000	
Daniel Patrick Moynihan (D-NY)	Finance	1994	19,500	
John H. Chafee (R-RI)	Finance	1994	17,400	
Paul Wellstone (D-MN)	Labor	1990	12,755	52.9
William V. Roth (R-DE)	Finance	1994	11,000	
John C. Danforth (R-MO)	Finance	1994	6,000	
George Mitchell (D-ME)	Finance	1994	5,500	
Edward M. Kennedy (D-MA)	Labor	1994	2,000	
Malcolm Wallop (R-WY)	Finance	1994	250	
David L. Boren (D-OK)	Finance	1990	0	
Jeff Bingaman (D-NM)	Labor	1994	0	
James M. Jeffords (R-VT)	Labor	1994	0	

Source: Alissa J. Rubin, "With Health Overhaul on Stage, PACs Want Front Row Seat," *Congressional Quarterly Weekly Report,* July 31, 1993, p. 2054.

health care industry has enhanced its influence in the two committees, since medical interest groups serve as a source of financial support for committee members only during their reelection campaigns, when they are in most need of assistance. By providing financial support to members of the Senate Finance and Labor and Human Resources Committees when they are in most need of assistance, the health care industry can expect the two committees to favor medical interest groups on issues of concern to them.

As Table 3.4 shows, the Senate Finance and Labor and Human Resources and the House Energy and Commerce and Ways and Means Committees, like Congress as a whole, received campaign contributions from every major segment of the health care industry. As in the case of Congress, the fact that members of the committees receive contributions from a wide and diverse group of different health care interest groups assures that they will be responsive to the concerns of all organized constituencies within the medical system.

Table 3.4
Campaign Contributions From Major Medical Interest Groups to Members of the Senate Finance and Labor and Human Resources and House Energy and Commerce and Ways and Means Committees During 1989–1992 in Dollars

Contributor	Amount Received by House Energy and Commerce Committee	Amount Received by House Ways and Means Committee	Amount Received by Senate Finance Committee	Amount Received by Senate Labor and Human Resources Committee
American Medical Association	397,766	346,686	62,473	54,000
American Dental Association	242,350	173,600	59,000	52,000
American Academy of Ophthalmology	192,704	136,383	53,500	N.A.
American Hospital Association	114,241	106,693	71,000	61,269
Independent Insurance Agents of America	99,716	76,557	57,977	44,211
American Health Care Association	81,600	61,600	N.A.	N.A.
American College of Emergency Physicians	80,640	61,850	71,000	N.A.
American Optometric Association	77,800	55,650	N.A.	N.A.
American Podiatry Association	70,500	54,300	45,000	53,000
American Chiropractic Association	66,050	N.A.	63,997	71,998
American Family Life Assurance Company	59,500	60,500	N.A.	N.A.
TOTAL	1,482,869	1,133,819	484,047	382,278

Source: Alissa J. Rubin, "With Health Overhaul on Stage, PACs Want Front Row Seat," *Congressional Quarterly Weekly Report*, July 31, 1993, p. 2051.

THE HEALTH CARE INDUSTRY CONTINUES ITS CAMPAIGN CONTRIBUTIONS TO THE 103RD CONGRESS

Clinton's election to the presidency confronted the health care industry with a new challenge. During 1993 and 1994, Clinton pursued an intense and relentless campaign to secure the establishment of national health insurance. He

Table 3.5
The Seven Largest Campaign Contributors to Congressional Candidates Among Medical Interest Groups From January 1, 1993, to May 31, 1994, in Dollars

Interest Group	Contribution
American Medical Association	977,704
American Dental Association	630,553
National Association of Life Underwriters	612,301
American Hospital Association	551,266
American Nurses' Association	444,446
Independent Insurance Agents of America	371,260
American Family Life Assurance Company	345,850
TOTAL	3,933,380

Source: Katharine Q. Seelye, "Lobbyists Are the Loudest in the Health Care Debate," *New York Times*, August 16, 1994, p. A1.

succeeded in generating an unprecedented level of public interest in and initial support for national health insurance. As a result, the 103rd Congress came under intense pressure to pass a national health insurance bill. To blunt the substantial political momentum toward health care reform Clinton unleashed, the health care industry increased its campaign contributions to members of Congress.

From January 1, 1993, to July 31, 1994, the health care industry provided $38 million in campaign contributions to congressional candidates.[45] Much of those contributions came from medical PACs. From January 1, 1993, to May 31, 1994, medical PACs made $26.4 million in campaign contributions to congressional candidates.[46] Table 3.5 shows that seven interest groups served as the source of one-sixth of all the contributions made by medical PACs during this period. Campaign contributions to congressional candidates from the health care industry rose substantially during 1991–1992 to 1993–1994. During January 1, 1993 to March 31, 1994, contributions to congressional candidates from the industry increased 52 percent over the same period during the 1991–1992 congressional election cycle. Contributions from medical PACs grew 24 percent during the same period.

Much of the increase in campaign contributions to congressional candidates from the health care industry came from private health insurance companies. From January 1, 1993 to March 31, 1994, contributions to congressional candidates from the private insurance industry rose 42 percent over the same period during the 1991–1992 congressional election cycle.[47] The industry has the most to lose from national health insurance, since it threatens not just the financial interests but the very existence of insurance companies. By imposing stringent health care cost-containment measures, national health insurance would reduce the incomes of health care providers, while forcing private plans to slash their administrative costs, driving many, if not most of them, out of business. As a result, insurance companies have the greatest political incentive to prevent the establishment of national health insurance among all medical interest groups; and they acted to do so by increasing their financial influence on Capitol Hill during 1993–1994. Accordingly, insurance companies have far outpaced every other segment of the health care industry as a growing source of campaign contributions to members of Congress.

The health care industry feared that Clinton would succeed in securing the establishment of a national health insurance program, imposing stringent cost-containment measures, which would reduce the incomes of every segment of the medical system. As a result, the industry acted to increase its financial influence over Capitol Hill in order to prevent Clinton from obtaining the adoption of the program. As Podhorzer put it, "What's happening . . . is that a lot of people [in the health care industry] who will be affected [by medical reform] are saying to themselves, 'Oh, my gosh, my business is on the line.' These are, after all, people like doctors and insurance company executives who have a lot of discretionary income and are able to make those [congressional campaign] donations."[48] The health care industry made no secret of the fact that its massive campaign contributions to members of Congress were designed to blunt the substantial political momentum toward medical reform which occurred during the 1990s. As Tom Goodwin, public affairs director of the Federation of American Health Systems, representing the for-profit segment of the hospital industry, put it, "We spend our money on those members [of Congress] most interested in maintaining the current [health care] system."[49]

THE HEALTH CARE INDUSTRY LOBBIES AGAINST MEDICAL REFORM

In addition to campaign contributions, the health care industry undertook an intensive lobbying campaign to prevent the establishment of national health insurance. In fact, most of the money spent by the industry to block the institution of national health insurance was devoted, not to campaign contributions to congressional candidates, but to lobbying and other related activities. On November 3, 1994 Citizan Action issued a report which showed that the industry had spent $100 million to defeat efforts to establish national health insurance during 1993 to 1994, including $60 million for lobbying, advertising, public relations, and organizing; and $40 million in campaign contributions to congressional candidates.[50]

The health care industry spent more money to influence the outcome of the debate on medical reform than interest groups have on any other issue in American history. As the Center for Public Integrity puts it, "There is no issue of public policy in which the sheer strength of . . . special interests have so overwhelmed the [political] process as in the health care reform debate."[51] In pursuing its campaign to prevent the establishment of national health insurance, the health care industry focused its efforts on lobbying Congress. As Ellen Miller,

Executive Director of the Center for Responsive Politics puts it, "This is the biggest-scale lobbying effort that's ever been mounted on any single piece of legislation, both in terms of dollars spent and people engaged."[52]

The health care industry was well positioned to lobby against national health insurance. The number of medical interest groups which were represented by lobbyists in Washington soared from 117 in 1979 to 741 in 1992. By 1992, virtually every major medical interest group was represented by lobbyists in Washington.

In 1992 212 medical interest groups represented in Washington had their own PACs.[53] Medical interest groups with both financial and lobbying power on Capitol Hill were well positioned to exert influence over Congress. By providing campaign contributions to incumbent members of Congress, medical interest groups were assured that lawmakers would be especially susceptible to the influence which lobbyists representing the health care industry would attempt to exert on Capitol Hill. Members of Congress would be reluctant to reject the influence of lobbyists representing medical interest groups with their own PACs, given the dependence of lawmakers on the health care industry as a source of campaign contributions.

As Table 3.6 shows, an influential handful of lobbyists representing the health care industry had previously served in the federal government, and were well connected with either the executive or legislative branch. As a result, those health care industry lobbyists had good connections on Capitol Hill, and maintained strong relationships with members of Congress serving on the key committees exercising jurisdiction over medical reform. Lobbyists representing the health care industry maintained good access to those members of Congress who played a key role in the legislative process on medical reform. They used this access to press the health care industry's case against medical reform. When combined with the health care industry's massive campaign contributions to members of Congress, the ability of medical interest groups to retain highly influential Washington lobbyists allowed the industry to wield substantial political clout on Capitol Hill, which it used to prevent the establishment of national health insurance.

THE HEALTH CARE INDUSTRY PREVENTS MEDICAL REFORM IN CONGRESS

The massive increase in campaign contributions to members of Congress from the health care industry during 1991–1992 derailed Mitchell's efforts to pass a national health insurance bill in the 102nd Congress. Clinton's own campaign to establish national health insurance was sidetracked by another flood of contributions from the industry to members of Congress during 1993–1994. The industry's representation on Capitol Hill by a handful of highly influential and well-connected Washington lobbyists only added to the power of medical in-

Table 3.6
Influential Lobbyists Representing the Health Care Industry

Lobbyist	Former Position	Currently Lobbies For
Kenneth Bowler	Staff Director for the House Ways and Means Committee	Pfizer Inc.
Martin Gold	Counsel to Senate Majority Leader Howard Baker	Association for the Advancement of Psychology
Bill Gradison	Member of the House Ways and Means Committee	Health Insurance Association of America
John Jonas	Tax Counsel for the House Ways and Means Committee	Massachusetts Mutual Life Insurance Company, Metropolitan Life Insurance Corporation, and the National Association of Life Underwriters
Robert Leonard	Chief Counsel and Staff Director of the House Ways and Means Committee	Alliance for Managed Competition (Consisting of Aetna Life and Casualty Company, Cigna Corporation, Metropolitan Life Insurance Corporation, Prudential Insurance Company of America, and The Travelers Corporation)
Frank McLaughlin	Aide to Speaker of the House Tip O'Neill	The American Dental Association
Dawson Mathis	Representative in Congress	Massachusetts Mutual Life Insurance Company and Metropolitan Life Insurance Corporation
John Salmon	Aide to House Ways and Means Committee Chairman Daniel Rostenkowski	Federation of American Health Systems
Deborah Steelman	Member of the Office of Management and Budget in the Bush Administration	Aetna Life and Casualty Company and the Pharmaceutical Manufacturers' Association
Richard Verville	Assistant Secretary of Health, Education, and Welfare	Academy of Physical Medicine and Rehabilitation, Joint Council on Allergy and Immunology, and Medical Group Management

Gordon Wheeler	Member of the Congressional Liaison Office and the Office of Management and Budget in the Bush Administration	Health Insurance Association of America

Sources: Joseph A. Califano, Jr., *Radical Surgery: What's Next for America's Health Care* (New York: Times Books, 1994), pp. 266–67; Viki Kemper and Viveca Novak, "What's Blocking Health Care Reform?" in Nancy F. McKenzie, ed., *Beyond Crisis: Confronting Health Care in the United States* (New York: Meridian Books, 1994), p. 598.

terest groups to prevent the establishment of national health insurance during 1991–1994.

The Democratic majority in Congress could not act upon Mitchell's and Clinton's pleas for swift passage of national health insurance legislation without jeopardizing their access to campaign contributions from the industry. This is especially true since practically all contributions from health care industry PACs go to incumbent members of Congress, most of whom were Democrats until Republicans won control of both houses of the legislative branch for the first time in forty years following the 1994 elections. During 1991–1992, 61 percent of all contributions from health care industry PACs went to Democrats, and 39 percent to Republicans.[54]

Financially beholden to the health care industry, congressional Democrats are reluctant to take any action which might antagonize medical interest groups. The health care industry remains adamantly opposed to national health insurance, since it cannot be established on a fiscally and economically viable basis without imposing stringent cost-containment measures, which are certain to inflict substantial financial losses upon every segment of the medical system. Congressional Democrats had no choice but to ignore Mitchell's and Clinton's calls for quick action on health care reform. Had they passed a national health insurance bill, congressional Democrats would have risked loss of the substantial campaign contributions they receive from the health care industry, which would have used its financial resources to target for defeat those congressional Democrats supporting national health insurance. The Republican Party remains staunchly opposed to national health insurance. As a result, the health care industry can easily target a Democratic member of Congress supporting national health insurance for defeat by financing the campaign of his or her Republican challenger, who could be expected to oppose the program. To avoid antagonizing the health care industry, which could spell the end of their political careers, congressional Democrats ignored Mitchell's and Clinton's pleas for swift passage of a national health insurance bill, handing them a stinging political setback and undermining their credibility as party leaders.

CONCLUSION

During 1991–1994, Congress came under intense pressure to pass a national health insurance bill. The elections of Wofford and Clinton, which were achieved largely on the basis of their support for national health insurance, provided Congress irrefutable evidence that an overwhelming majority of the public backed health care reform. Mitchell's and Clinton's campaigns to establish national health insurance placed additional pressure upon Congress to pass a health care reform bill.

To blunt the political momentum for health care reform, the health care industry acted to strengthen its influence on Capitol Hill by making massive campaign contributions to members of Congress. Those contributions were concentrated among members of the congressional committees exercising jurisdiction over health care reform. This allowed the health care industry to exert enormous influence over those committees, preventing them from approving national health insurance legislation on a timely basis, and sending it to the House and Senate floors in time for a vote before the 103rd Congress adjourned. As a result, members of Congress were spared from taking the politically dangerous action of voting against national health insurance legislation, which they would have had to do given the fact that the health care industry opposes any such measure. Financially beholden to the industry, members of Congress cannot pass any national health insurance bill without jeopardizing their access to campaign contributions from medical interest groups, and risking defeat the next time they run for reelection.

Because the congressional committees exercising jurisdiction over health care reform served to prevent any national health insurance bill from reaching either the House or Senate floor until almost the last minute before the 103rd Congress adjourned, members of Congress were assured that they would not have to vote on legislation to overhaul the medical system. This allowed many, if not most, members of Congress to take the politically popular position of supporting health care reform, gaining the backing of voters who favor national health insurance. In the meantime, members of Congress would not have to take any action on national health insurance legislation, which would remain bottled up in the committees exercising jurisdiction over health care reform. By failing to take such action, members of Congress would be able to maintain their access to campaign contributions from the health care industry, which remains adamantly opposed to national health insurance. Members of Congress could stake out a position on health care reform that would assure them both votes from their constituents and money from the health care industry, providing lawmakers the political and financial resources to remain in office.

Chapter 4

The Health Care Industry Opposes Clinton's National Health Insurance Plan

It was only when it became clear that we weren't getting anywhere [with the Clinton Administration] on two or three central [health care reform] issues that I became convinced we had to carry our message [against Clinton's national health insurance plan] more broadly to the public.[1]

Bill Gradison, President, Health Insurance Association of America.

On September 22, 1993, the health care industry confronted perhaps the most serious challenge to its power when Clinton introduced his national health insurance plan in his address before a joint session of Congress. By delivering his address in prime time before a nationwide audience, Clinton succeeded in placing the issue of health care reform at the very top of the national agenda. This is the last thing the health care industry could have wanted. No national health insurance plan can be established on an economically and fiscally viable basis without the imposition of stringent cost-containment measures, which are certain to inflict substantial financial losses upon the medical industry.

As a result, any movement toward health care reform poses a financial threat to the medical industry, which needed to derail Clinton's campaign to establish national health insurance. True, Clinton's campaign had practically no chance of succeeding, given the close financial relationship existing between Congress and the health care industry. Financially beholden to the industry, members of Congress refused to seriously consider establishing a national health insurance program, given the fact that it is adamantly opposed by medical interest groups.

Nevertheless, the overwhelming majority of the public support national health insurance, as we saw in Chapter 1. A slight, though real, chance existed that Congress might defy the health care industry and pass a national health insurance bill, if lawmakers came under intense public pressure to do so. To prevent the establishment of national health insurance, the industry needed to go beyond providing massive campaign contributions to members of Congress, and raise public doubts about the wisdom and necessity of health care reform.

No single medical interest group was more committed to the fight against national health insurance than the private insurance industry. The reason for this is simple: no segment of the health care system was more threatened by the program than the private insurance industry.

National health insurance threatened only to reduce the incomes of health care providers. However, national health insurance represented a threat, not just to the financial position, but the very existence of the private insurance industry. A single-payer insurance plan, sponsored by dozens of congressional Democrats, would have scrapped and replaced private plans with a government program to provide coverage to the public. True, Clinton's national health insurance plan, the Health Security Act, would have preserved the private insurance industry. However, as we saw in Chapter 2, the bill would have imposed stringent limits on insurance premiums, which would have substantially reduced the revenues of private insurance companies, driving many, if not most, of them out of business. Moreover, the bill would have prohibited private insurance from excluding preexisting medical conditions from the coverage they provide their subscribers and from denying health care benefits to individuals with chronic illnesses. By requiring private insurance companies to provide coverage for costly illnesses, the bill would have raised the financial liabilities of insurance firms, shrinking their revenues, and driving still more of them out of business. With its very existence threatened by Clinton's national health insurance plan, the private health insurance industry mounted an all-out public relations campaign to turn popular opinion against the president's program.

Despite the financial threat it posed to the health care industry, Clinton's national health insurance plan promised to benefit one key segment of the medical system: primary-care doctors. By guaranteeing the public the option of joining HMOs, which heavily utilize the services of primary-care doctors, the Clinton plan promised to provide general practioners a financial windfall. As a result, the Clinton plan won the support of interest groups representing primary-care doctors.

However, the dominant voice representing the health care industry on Clinton's national health insurance came, not from interest groups representing primary-care doctors, but from the private insurance industry, which mounted an intense public relations campaign to mobilize popular opposition to the president's program. Primary-care doctors were completely drowned out in their support of the Clinton plan by the loud and shrill voice of opposition to the president's program mounted by the private insurance industry. Charging that the Clinton plan would result in health care rationing, the industry attempted to mobilize popular opposition to the President's program. When combined with the Republican Party's own public relations campaign against the Clinton plan, the industry succeeded in turning public opinion against the president's program, as we will see.

THE DIVISION WITHIN THE MEDICAL PROFESSION
OVER NATIONAL HEALTH INSURANCE

Traditionally, the medical profession has led the health care industry's fight against national health insurance every time it has assumed a prominent place on the political agenda. During the 1940s, the AMA single-handedly mounted a public relations campaign against Truman's drive to establish national health insurance, which prevented its adoption.[2] The AMA's fight against national health insurance was consistent with the fact that the overwhelming majority of doctors were opposed to the program during the 1940s.[3] Massive campaign contributions to members of Congress from AMPAC played a key role in the House's rejection of the Hospital Cost Containment Act, which President Carter had recommended. The bill would have imposed stringent hospital cost-containment measures. The defeat of the bill deprived Carter of the means to create an economically and fiscally viable basis for the establishment of national health insurance, derailing his campaign to institute the program.[4]

However, the medical profession did not lead the fight against Clinton's campaign to establish national health insurance. This was due to the fact that the previously strong physician opposition to national health insurance had largely dissipated in the half century since the AMA's campaign against the program during the 1940s. By 1993, the medical profession had become deeply divided over the issue of health care reform.

The division within the medical profession over the issue of health care reform surfaced in 1993, when physician interest groups took opposing sides on the Health Security Act. Opposing the bill was the AMA, the largest physician interest group, representing 290,000 doctors, or 43 percent of all physicians in the United States.[5] In a letter to Clinton released on December 16, 1993, AMA Executive Vice President James Todd charged that the bill would impose "excessive" government regulation of the medical profession, which would undermine "the physician's role in medical decision-making."[6]

Of special concern to the AMA were the stringent limits on private health insurance premiums the Health Security Act would impose. To comply with those limits, private plans would have to reduce physician fees and limit the number of services doctors could provide, which were sure to result in a substantial reduction in physician incomes. In his appearance before the President's Task Force on National Health Reform on March 29, 1993, Raymond Scalletar, chairman of the AMA's board of trustees, warned that the medical profession would not cooperate with any federal effort to contain health care costs, since such action would result in medical rationing:

True effective cost control has never been achieved in this or any other economy through arbitrary caps on spending or price controls. They did not work in the 1970s, only delaying natural price increases and impeding supply of necessary goods and services. They also will not work in health care.

Price controls, or global budgets, mean arbitrary decisions that will, without basis, limit our ability to deliver needed medical care to our patients.

Scalletar concluded that the AMA would oppose the imposition of any health care cost-containment measures because they would limit "patients' access to medical care."[7]

As we saw in Chapter 2, the Health Security Act would establish a National Health Board, which would impose stringent limits on private health insurance premiums. In order to comply with those limits, private plans would have to substantially reduce their health care costs, including physician reimbursements, resulting in a decline in physician incomes. Determined to prevent any such decline in physician incomes, Richard A. Deem, the AMA's chief Washington lobbyist, announced in a letter to other physician interest groups that his organization would demand the elimination of the "regulatory price control/global budget authority of the National Health Board."[8]

As we saw in the previous chapter, the AMA remains one of the most powerful interest groups on Capitol Hill, consistently ranking among the top two contributors among all organized constituencies in the amount of campaign donations provided to congressional candidates. Given its massive financial power, the AMA had the political influence to steer members of Congress to oppose the stringent limits on private health insurance premiums the Health Security Act would have imposed. National health insurance cannot be established on a fiscally and economically viable basis without the imposition of stringent health care cost-containment measures. As a result, the AMA's capacity to kill the health care cost-containment measures included in the Health Security Act gave the interest group the power to defeat national health insurance altogether.

However, despite its massive financial power on Capitol Hill, the AMA was plagued by severe weaknesses in pursuing its efforts to defeat Clinton's national health insurance plan. The AMA has traditionally represented the single most politically powerful medical interest group; its power was based upon its capacity to speak on behalf of the entire medical profession. Prior to the 1990s, the AMA represented the unchallenged voice of the medical profession on health care policy. This was especially true during the 1940s, when the AMA succeeded in leading the entire medical profession in defeating Truman's campaign to establish national health insurance.

However, the AMA's capacity to speak on behalf of the medical profession on health care policy had greatly diminished by the 1990s. This became evident in 1993, when ten physician interest groups broke ranks with the AMA in announcing their support for the Health Security Act. The ten groups represented 300,000 doctors, mostly primary-care physicians, constituting 45 percent of all physicians practicing in the United States.[9] The most important of the groups supporting the bill was the American College of Physicians, the second largest physician organization after the AMA, representing 77,000 internists.[10] Other physician groups supporting the bill included the American Academy of Pedi-

Table 4.1
The Average Net Income of Various Medical Specialty Groups in 1991 in Dollars

Medical Specialty Group	Income
Cardiovascular Surgeons	296,880
Neurosurgeons	289,750
Orthopedic Surgeons	248,220
All Surgeons	233,800
Thoracic Surgeons	231,530
Radiologists	229,800
Anesthesiologists	221,100
Plastic Surgeons	209,840
Urologists	202,990
Obstetricians-Gynecologists	198,380
Pathologists	198,000
Cardiologists	193,200
Ophthalmologists	180,280
All Doctors	170,600
General Surgeons	166,000
Internists	111,900
Pediatricians	111,370
Psychiatrists	104,170
Family Practitioners	101,160
General Practitioners	89,820

Sources: Melinda Beck, Mary Hager, Patrick Rogers, and Susan Miller, "Doctors Under the Knife," *Newsweek*, April 5, 1993, p. 32; James Flanigan, "One Casualty of Clinton's Health Plan: Freedom to Choose," *Los Angeles Times*, September 22, 1993, p. D2; Sara Fritz, "A Profession on the Edge: New Doctors Face New Day," *Los Angeles Times*, May 24, 1991, p. A12; Hilary Stout, "Doctors, Seeing Health-Care System Faults, Lie Low As Clinton Drafts Plan That Could Curb Incomes," *Wall Street Journal*, March 2, 1993, p. A20.

atrics, the American Society of Internal Medicine, and the National Medical Association, an organization representing African-American doctors.[11]

Why was the medical profession deeply divided over the Health Security Act? Why did the profession fail to unite in opposition to national health insurance during the 1990s, as had been the case in the past? The answer lies in the deep socioeconomic divisions existing within the profession between specialists and primary-care doctors.

As Table 4.1 shows, specialists earn substantially more income than primary-care doctors. As a result, specialists would suffer substantially more financial losses than primary-care doctors would under any national health insurance program which would impose health care cost-containment measures. Such measures would focus on reducing the exorbitant fees specialists charge and limiting their excessive utilization of costly medical technology in the treatment of catastrophic illnesses and injuries. This would have imposed substantial financial losses upon specialists, whose high incomes are derived from their inflated fees and their liberal use of medical technology in performing costly diagnostic, therapeutic, and surgical procedures. By contrast, primary-care doctors earn substantially lower fees than specialists and usually do not utilize costly medical technology in their practices. As a result, national health insurance poses little, if any, financial threat to primary-care doctors. In opposing the Health Security Act, the AMA was representing the interests of specialists, who stood to suffer substantial financial losses from the president's program. By contrast, interest groups representing primary-care doctors had no problem supporting the bill, since it posed no significant financial threat to general practitioners.

Moreover, interest groups representing primary-care doctors had every reason to support the Health Security Act, since it promised to financially benefit general practitioners by raising their numbers and fees. The share of doctors specializing in primary care has suffered a severe decline, falling from 50 percent in 1961 to 33 percent in 1993.[12] The United States has the lowest share of its doctors specializing in primary care among all the advanced industrial democracies. In 1992 74 percent of all doctors specialized in primary care in Britain, 54 percent in Germany, and 47 percent in Canada.[13]

Why do most doctors prefer to enter a medical specialty, rather than engage in primary care? The reason is that specialists earn substantially more income than primary-care doctors, as we have seen. Attracted by the lure of high incomes, only 13.7 percent of all American medical students entering their profession became primary-care doctors in 1989. By contrast, 52.9 of all Canadian medical students entering their profession did so during the same year.[14] Because so few medical students entering their profession are becoming primary-care doctors, the share of all physicians specializing in general practice will decline further to 28 percent by 2010.[15]

Clinton was committed to reverse the decline in the number of primary-care doctors as a means of containing health care costs. A major source of soaring health care costs results from the fact that the medical profession is heavily specialized. Specialists charge higher fees and tend to provide more costly services, largely through their greater utilization of expensive medical technology, than primary-care doctors, as we have seen. As a result, health care costs cannot be reduced unless the medical system utilizes more primary-care doctors and fewer specialists.

To achieve this goal, the Health Security Act would require medical schools to raise the number of residency positions devoted to primary care by 7 percent annually for five years. During the same period, the number of medical residency positions devoted to specialties in which an excess supply of doctors existed would have to be reduced by 10 percent annually. At the end of five years, half of all students entering the medical profession would have to specialize in primary care.[16] To provide financial incentives for students to choose a career in primary-care medicine, federal reimbursements for services provided by general practitioners to Medicare beneficiaries would be raised substantially.[17]

The Health Security Act promised to provide additional financial benefits to primary-care doctors by requiring the public to join regional health alliances, which would give their members a choice of all qualified private health insurance plans operating in each given area. Included in this choice would be HMOs, which heavily utilize the services of primary-care doctors.[18] HMOs require their members to choose a primary-care doctor, who is responsible for managing the health care of all HMO patients. Primary-care doctors provide all the health care they are capable of rendering for their HMO patients. HMO patients may suffer illnesses or injuries which require specialist care. In that case, primary-care doctors will refer their patients to specialists who have been contracted by HMOs to provide services to their members.

Doctors are usually reimbursed on a fee-for-service basis; the more services they provide, the greater income they receive. By contrast, HMOs reimburse doctors on a capitation basis; they receive the same income regardless of how many services they provide their HMO patients. If the cost of providing services to each HMO member is less than the capitation payment the doctor receives for treating the patient, then the physician pockets the difference. On the other hand, if the cost of providing services to each HMO member exceeds the capitation payment the doctor receives for treating the patient, then the physician absorbs the financial loss. As a result, the fewer services doctors provide their HMO patients, the more income they can keep; while the more services physicians provide their HMO patients, the more income they lose. While fee-for-service reimbursement provides doctors financial incentives to extend more services than would otherwise be the case, the opposite is true under the capitation payments physicians receive from HMOs.

In addition, patients may not see a specialist except on referral from their primary-care doctor, often subject to the approval of the HMO. As a result, HMOs utilize primary-care doctors as gatekeepers to prevent patients from seeing specialists except when absolutely necessary.[19] HMOs require primary-care doctors to serve the health care needs of their patients to the maximum extent possible, with the provision of specialist care kept to an absolute minimum.

As we have seen, primary-care doctors charge lower fees and utilize costly medical technology less frequently than specialists. As a result of their heavy utilization of primary care doctors, HMOs provide their members fewer services, allowing them to extend health care at lower cost than other types of private health insurance plans. Those other types of plans include PPOs, which contract with select groups of health care providers to extend services at discount rates; and traditional indemnity plans, which reimburse doctors and hospitals at their full costs.

In 1994 the Congressional Budget Office (CBO) released a comparative study of the amount of health care services provided between HMOs on the one hand and PPOs and indemnity plans on the other. The CBO study found that in 1989 HMOs provided an average of 4 percent fewer services than PPOs, and 7 percent fewer services than indemnity plans.[20] Because they provide fewer services, HMOs charge substantially lower premiums than other types of private plans.

In 1992 the average premium for a working family enrolled in an HMO was $3,313, compared to $4,080 for those in indemnity plans and $3,708 for PPOs.[21]

Employers providing their working families group health insurance are currently free to offer whichever private plans they wish. In 1993 39 percent of all employers providing their working families group insurance did not offer their working families the option of joining an HMO.[22] Only a small share of the public belong to an HMO. In 1995 only 21.5 percent of the public did so.[23]

The Health Security Act would require health alliances to offer the public the option of joining any one of the qualified HMOs operating in their area.[24] Since HMOs provide comparable coverage at lower premiums than other private plans, many additional individuals would opt to join an HMO, if given the opportunity to do so, as would be the case under the bill. Accordingly, the bill would result in an expansion in HMO enrollments. This would financially benefit primary-care doctors, whose services are heavily utilized by HMOs. This would also undermine the financial interests of specialists, since HMOs seek to reduce the utilization of the services of specialists by using primary-care doctors as gate-keepers to keep HMO patients away from specialists.

The Health Security Act promised to financially benefit primary-care doctors by raising their numbers and increasing patient utilization of their services through the expansion in HMO enrollments. Primary-care doctors must currently compete against specialists, who provide many, if not most, of the services performed by general practitioners. As a result, specialists have siphoned off many patients who would go to primary-care doctors, which is a major reason why general practitioners earn substantially less income than specialists.

By expanding the number of primary-care doctors and reducing the supply of specialists, while enlarging HMO enrollments, the Health Security Act would result in greater patient utilization of general practitioners and less use of specialists, leading to a rise in the incomes of primary-care physicians. Their incomes would further increase from the more generous Medicare reimbursements they would receive under the bill. With an increasing number of patients seeing primary-care doctors, specialists would suffer substantial financial losses under the bill.

The Health Security Act promised to financially benefit primary-care doctors at the expense of specialists. As a result, interest groups representing primary-care doctors lined up behind the Health Security Act, while the AMA, voicing the concerns of specialists, opposed the bill. The division within the medical profession over the bill is reflected in polling data. During October 1–18, 1993, *USA Today*, CNN, and Gallup asked 502 doctors whether they supported or opposed Clinton's national health insurance plan. Fifty-eight percent of the doctors opposed the Clinton plan, and 38 percent supported it.[25] The division of physician opinion over the Clinton plan revealed in the *USA Today*/CNN/Gallup poll roughly parallels the split within the medical profession: between the two-thirds of all doctors who are specialists, and would tend to oppose the Clinton plan; and the remaining third who are primary care physicians, and would generally support it.

With the medical profession deeply divided over Clinton's national health insurance plan, doctors were unable to play an important public role in shaping the debate over health care reform during the 1990s. True, the profession was hardly irrelevant to this debate. As we saw in the previous chapter, AMPAC has almost always remained among the top two contributors to congressional campaigns among all PACs. The AMA, in conjunction with other medical interest groups, used its enormous financial influence on Capitol Hill to prevent passage of a national health insurance bill during 1991 to 1994, when health care reform assumed a high priority on the political agenda.

However, the division within the medical profession over national health insurance limited the AMA's influence in the debate on health care reform. During the 1940s, the AMA succeeded in leading its successful campaign against Truman's drive to establish national health insurance because the profession was practically united in its opposition to the program. Yet, as we have seen, this was not the case during the 1990s. Clinton's national health insurance plan pitted primary-care doctors, who generally supported the President's program, against specialists, backed by the AMA, who tended to oppose it.

With the medical profession deeply divided over Clinton's national health insurance plan, the AMA was unable to go beyond engaging in muted opposition to the president's program. The AMA could not mount an intense public relations campaign against the Clinton plan, since such action would have antagonized primary-care doctors, who stood to gain from the President's program, as we have seen. Constituting 43 percent of all doctors, the AMA is the largest and most inclusive physician interest group, representing the needs and concerns of all segments of the medical profession. Any active effort by the AMA to derail the Clinton plan could have provoked a flood of resignations from the interest group by primary-care doctors. The lack of primary-care physician members would have damaged the AMA's credibility, which is based upon its claim to represent the entire medical profession. The AMA could not actively oppose the Clinton plan without damaging itself. As a result, the AMA was largely a bystander in the debate on health care reform during 1993 to 1994, with the interest group too weakened by deep divisions within the medical profession to lead the health care industry in its fight against the Clinton plan.

THE HIAA LAUNCHES ITS PUBLIC RELATIONS CAMPAIGN AGAINST CLINTON'S NATIONAL HEALTH INSURANCE PLAN

With the AMA hamstrung in its ability to fight Clinton's national health insurance plan, the primary responsibility for leading the health care industry's campaign against the president's program fell on the shoulders of private insurance companies. Unlike the medical profession, which was deeply divided over the issue of health care reform, the private insurance industry was united in its opposition to national health insurance. While national health insurance promised to reduce the incomes of specialists, while financially benefiting primary-care physicians, the program threatened the very existence of the private insurance industry, as we have seen. As a result, private insurance companies had no problem in joining together in mounting an all-out offensive against the program.

Leading the campaign against Clinton's national health insurance plan was the largest interest group representing the private insurance industry: the Health Insurance Association of America (HIAA), an organization composed of 271 companies, which collectively control 35 percent of the private health insurance market.[26] On September 8, 1993, the HIAA launched a television advertising campaign designed to mobilize public opposition to the Clinton plan.[27] The campaign featured two advertisements, starring a couple named Harry and Louise. Adam Clymer has perhaps best summed up the messages conveyed in the two advertisements:

In the first of the [HIAA's] two advertisements, a couple seated at a kitchen table reminisces fondly about an old health insurance plan and worries whether a new one [required under the Clinton plan] would cover them as well. An announcer says, "The Government may force us to pick from a few health plans designed by government bureaucrats." And the woman says, "Having choices we don't like is no choice at all."

In a second advertisement, the same couple is shown agreeing that something needs to be done about health care but they complain about the details of the Clinton plan. The woman says, "The Government caps how much the country can spend on health care and says, 'That's it!' "

The man asks, "So what if our health plan runs out of money?" The woman shrugs and says, "There has got to be a better way."[28]

The HIAA's two television advertisements against Clinton's national health insurance saturated the airwaves during the months following the president's introduction of his program in his address before a joint session of Congress on September 22, 1993. By May 1994, the HIAA had spent a whopping $14 million on its advertising campaign.[29] With the HIAA's advertisements appearing daily on virtually all the nation's television networks, few, if any, individuals were able to escape exposure to the interest group's commercials. By displaying its message against the Clinton plan before virtually the entire nation, the HIAA's advertising campaign had a powerful effect in shaping the debate on health care reform during 1993–1994.

The HIAA coupled its television advertising campaign against Clinton's national health insurance plan by organizing and financing the establishment of the Coalition for Health Insurance Choices (CHIC). The purpose of CHIC was to mobilize grassroots opposition to the Clinton plan. By December 1993, the CHIC had enrolled 20,000 members, mostly representing business and the private insurance industry. The HIAA's television advertisements against the Clinton plan included an 800 telephone number for the CHIC. The public was invited to call the 800 number for information on the organization's activities. Each individual who called received a letter from Bob Myers, a member of the CHIC's board of advisers and former chief actuary of the Social Security Administration. On the front of the envelope carrying Myers's letter stood the following message typed in bold capital red letters, which summarized his theme: "DON'T LET GOVERNMENT TAKE CONTROL OF YOUR HEALTH CARE."

In his letter, Myers asked the public to join the CHIC in its fight against Clinton's national health insurance plan. Myers repeated the case against the Clinton plan made by the HIAA in its television advertising campaign. He warned that the federal government would deprive consumers of their right to choose their own private insurance under the Clinton plan:

The Clinton Administration says it wants to preserve access and choice [in health care]. However, it would be access within the confines of government-created "mandatory health alliances." These new government monopolies would put government at the controls of America's health care system . . . making important decisions that should only be made in a free and competitive market.

In addition, Myers charged that Clinton's national health insurance plan would impose stringent cost-containment measures and result in severe health care rationing:

Not only does the Administration want to force most Americans into mandatory health alliances, it wants to limit the amount Americans can spend on each alliance through arbitrary spending limits on health care. We agree costs must be controlled, but arbitrary spending caps raise serious concerns. What happens if your health alliance reaches its limit? Will it mean rationing of care, long lines and limits on covered procedures? Will it reduce quality of care?[30]

THE HIAA'S CAMPAIGN OF DECEPTION AGAINST CLINTON'S NATIONAL HEALTH INSURANCE PLAN

The HIAA's public relations campaign against Clinton's national health insurance plan infuriated the administration's chief spokesperson on health care reform: the first lady. In a speech to 2,000 members of the American Academy of Pediatrics in Washington on November 1, 1993, Hillary Clinton denounced the HIAA's public relations campaign, charging that it had told "great lies" about the president's program.[31] She could not have been more correct. The two major arguments the HIAA made in its public relations campaign against the Clinton plan—that it would restrict the ability of consumers to choose their own private plans and would result in severe health care rationing—were false and misleading.

The HIAA's charge that Clinton's national health insurance program would limit the ability of consumers to choose their own private plans is false; the opposite is in fact true. The Clinton plan would actually expand the range of choices consumers would have in selecting their own private insurance. Practically all privately insured individuals are currently covered through their employers. In 1994, 88.8 percent of all privately insured individuals were.[32] Every employer restricts the number of private plans their working families may choose to enroll in. Virtually no employer provides his or her working families the option of choosing to enroll in any one of all the private plans operating in a given area. Employers in fact often provide their working families only one private plan.

As we have seen in Chapter 2, Clinton would require most individuals to join regional health alliances. These would offer their members a choice to enroll in any one of all the qualified private health insurance plans operating in their area. As a result, Clinton's national health insurance program would provide the public the widest possible range of choices in selecting a private plan. The HIAA's charge that the Clinton plan would restrict the ability of consumers to choose their own private insurance could not be further from the truth. As Hillary Clinton put it in her address, "One of the great lies that is currently afoot in the country is that the President's plan will limit [consumer] choice [of private plans]. To the contrary, the President's plan enhances choice."[33]

The HIAA's claim that the health alliances to be established under Clinton's national health insurance plan would serve as "government monopolies" which would "put government at the controls of America's health care system" is also false. The purpose of health alliances would be to provide the public affordable access to health care. They would not interfere in the delivery of health care, which would remain under the control of medical providers.

The HIAA's warning that Clinton's plan to limit increases in private health insurance premiums would result in stringent health care rationing represents a cynical exercise in fear mongering. The federal government needs to take action to contain soaring health care costs. Business will not be able to afford continuing to provide their working families with health insurance if health care costs are allowed to continue to skyrocket unchecked. Firms will have no alternative but to terminate the insurance they provide their working families. Unable to afford their own private insurance and ineligible for either Medicare or Medicaid, those working families will go without coverage, resulting in additional tens of millions of uninsured individuals. The health care system will have to provide tens of billions of dollars in uncompensated care to those newly uninsured individuals, resulting in a financial collapse of a large part of the medical industry, which will leave hundreds, perhaps thousands, of communities without access to health care.

The United States can no longer maintain a rational and sustainable health care system in the absence of medical cost-containment measures, a fact that HIAA chose to ignore. As a result, Clinton's plan to contain health care costs through limits on private health insurance premiums is entirely justifiable. The HIAA's claim that such limits would result in stringent health care rationing is misleading. The health care rationing which would exist under the Clinton plan would be the same as that existing in every other advanced industrial democracy, all of which have national health insurance programs. Costly medical technology of only limited value in treating catastrophic illnesses and injuries would be severely rationed. However, relatively inexpensive primary care which has proven highly effective in treating illnesses at their early stages, before complications develop, would be freely provided. The Clinton plan would create a more cost-effective health care system in which medical procedures whose benefits greatly exceed their costs would be freely provided, while medical treatments whose costs greatly exceed their benefits would be stringently rationed.

A health care system cannot function in a rational and effective manner unless it provides the public access to the primary care which allows doctors to treat illnesses at their early stages, when it can be done with minimum pain and expense, if not to prevent ailments altogether. The health care system currently imposes financial barriers on patient access to primary care by requiring individuals to shoulder a substantial share of the financial burden for their medical services. This is especially true in the case of the uninsured, who must pay the entire cost of their health care, except for those medical services they receive from charitable hospitals. While restricting patient access to primary care, especially among the uninsured, the health care system imposes no limits on patient utilization of medical technology, which, as we saw in Chapter 2, represents the primary source of rising health care costs. Even uninsured individuals receive free access to costly medical technology from charitable hospitals when they suffer catastrophic illnesses and injuries. By rationing patient utilization of costly medical technology, which is often of only marginal value in treating catastrophic illnesses and injuries, health care cost-containment measures could free up the financial resources a medical system needs to concentrate on the provision of primary care. By guaranteeing universal health insurance coverage, limiting patient cost-sharing requirements, and imposing limits on insurance premiums to provide private plans financial incentives to avoid wasting their resources on the excessive utilization of costly medical technology, the Clinton plan would assure the public greater access to primary care than they currently have.

Every advanced industrial democracy except the United States imposes limits on its health care costs.[34] Such limits have not impeded the ability of any individual to receive access to primary care. The same would be true under Clinton's national health insurance plan. While the HIAA's charge that the Clinton plan would result in severe health care rationing is technically true, the interest group fails to point out that restrictions on public access to health care would be limited to costly medical technology of only limited value, and that the savings resulting from such rationing would be used to provide the public greater access to primary care than they currently have. The HIAA attacked health care rationing, but the interest group failed to advance any alternative which would reduce the soaring medical costs which threaten the very survival of the health care system.

The HIAA's attacks against Clinton's national health insurance plan served as a thinly disguised cover for the real reason why the interest group opposed the president's program—that it would undermine the financial interests of the private insurance industry. The Clinton plan would provide consumers the organizational clout to bargain with the private insurance industry through the establishment of health alliances, representing tens of thousands, hundreds of thousands, or even millions of individuals. Health alliances would refuse to contract with private plans which failed to provide the most comprehensive coverage available at the lowest possible premium. Since practically the entire public would belong to a health alliance, private plans which failed to contract with a health alliance would go out of business. To survive, private plans would have to provide efficient, low-cost health care to health alliance members. To do so, private plans would have to substantially reduce their administrative costs, which would result in a significant decline in their revenues, driving many, if not most, of them out of business. Further declines in revenues and insurance company bankruptcies would come through the limits on private insurance premiums the Clinton plan would impose. Finally, the Clinton plan would prohibit private plans from denying individuals with costly chronic illnesses health care protection and from excluding preexisting medical conditions from the coverage they provide their subscribers. This would result in a substantial increase in the financial liabilities of private plans, which would further cut into their revenues, and drive still other insurance companies out of business.

CONCLUSION

In launching its campaign against Clinton's national health insurance plan, the HIAA represented itself as a defender of the public interest—fighting against the president's program because it would limit the right of consumers to choose their own private plan and deprive them of access to health care. However, those false charges served as a smoke screen to hide the fact that the HIAA was motivated purely by self-interest in pursuing its public relations campaign against the Clinton plan. The HIAA opposed the Clinton plan for one central, overriding reason: that it would give the federal government and consumers the power to reduce health care costs, which would have forced insurance companies to streamline their operations, slashing their revenues, driving many, if not most, of them out of business.

The HIAA fully recognized that it could not successfully mobilize public opposition to the Clinton plan on the basis of its threat to the financial interests of the private insurance industry. Only a small fraction of the public has a financial stake in the industry. The public could not care less about the financial welfare of the industry. As a result, the HIAA sought to mobilize popular opposition to the Clinton plan on the basis of claims the public would be sympathetic with: that the president's program would limit consumer choice in and patient access to health care. By cynically concocting those false charges to unfairly discredit the Clinton plan, the HIAA showed that it was willing to go to any lengths to defend the financial interests of the private insurance industry.

Chapter 5

The Republican Party Launches Its Campaign to Defeat Clinton's National Health Insurance Plan

> There will be a positive Republican alternative [to Clinton's national health insurance plan]. If the [Clinton] plan is as bad as we've heard, our alternative won't be swept under the rug.[1]
>
> Haley Barbour, Chairman, Republican National Committee.

In pursuing its public relations campaign against Clinton's national health insurance plan, the HIAA received valuable support from the Republican Party, which launched an offensive of its own to politically discredit the president's program. Republicans had two reasons for opposing national health insurance.

First, Republican congressional leaders, like their Democratic counterparts, are recipients of massive campaign contributions from the health care industry. Operating under the financial influence of the industry, Republican congressional leaders cannot seriously consider supporting national health insurance because it is stridently opposed by medical interest groups.

Second, the Republican Party is dominated by an affluent membership, which has the financial capability to gain access to health care, without any government assistance. As a result, there is little support for national health insurance among the Republican rank and file. Moreover, national health insurance might have resulted in a tax increase to finance expanded access to health care, especially among the poor and uninsured. Such a tax increase would have had a negative financial impact upon the Republican Party's relatively affluent membership base. In addition, by reducing financial barriers impeding public access to health care, national health insurance threatened to raise patient utilization of medical services, driving up their cost. To contain health care costs, the government would have to stringently ration health care, especially costly medical technology. This threatened access to health care among affluent Republicans, who have the insurance coverage and financial means to secure all the medical services they need, and whose utilization of health care would be sharply curtailed under government mandated health care rationing.

With its congressional leaders financially beholden to the health care industry and its affluent members certain to be hurt by national health insurance, the Republican Party joined the private insurance industry in mounting an all-out public relations campaign against Clinton's national health insurance plan. This campaign succeeded in turning public opinion against the Clinton plan during the ten months following its introduction by the president in his address before a joint session of Congress on September 22, 1993. With public opinion shifting against the Clinton plan, Congress saw no clear and compelling need to establish national health insurance. As a result, all hopes for adopting national health insurance ended by July 1994, with polls showing a plurality of the public opposed to the president's plan.

THE REPUBLICAN PARTY LAUNCHES ITS PUBLIC RELATIONS CAMPAIGN AGAINST CLINTON'S NATIONAL HEALTH INSURANCE PLAN

The Republican Party's decision to oppose Clinton's national health insurance plan was based upon the fact that Republicans are less supportive of national health insurance than the public as a whole. Moreover, a plurality of Republicans opposed Clinton's national health insurance plan, unlike Democrats, an overwhelming majority of whom initially supported the president's program.

As we saw in Chapter 1, a *Time*/CNN poll conducted in July 1994 found that 61 percent of those surveyed said that ''the federal government should guarantee health care for all Americans''; 33 percent stated that it should not. However, support among Republicans for national health insurance was substantially weaker than that of the public as a whole. During March 28–30, 1994, *USA Today*, CNN, and Gallup asked 468 Republicans whether they either supported or opposed ''guaranteed health coverage.'' Forty-seven percent of Republicans supported ''guaranteed health coverage''; 33 percent opposed it; and 18 percent said that the issue did not matter to them.[2]

In addition to their weak support for national health insurance, an overwhelming majority of Republicans opposed Clinton's health care reform plan. During September 25–28, 1993, the *Los Angeles Times* asked 1,491 adults the following question: ''Do you approve or disapprove of the health care reform proposals Clinton has proposed to Congress?'' Fifty-four percent of the respondents approved of Clinton's national health insurance plan; 24 percent disapproved of it; and 22 percent did not know. However, the *Los Angeles Times* poll found a wide partisan divergence in public opinion on the Clinton plan. Sixty-four percent of Democrats and 55 percent of independents supported the Clinton plan, compared to only 38 percent of Republicans. Forty-five percent of Republicans opposed the Clinton plan, compared to only 21 percent of independents and 12 percent of Democrats.[3]

As we saw, Republicans tend to oppose national health insurance, unlike the public as a whole, who generally support the program, for one simple reason: Republicans are generally more affluent than the public as a whole. As a result, Republicans usually have the insurance coverage and financial means to maintain their access to health care, unlike a large share of the public, who do not. Moreover, national health insurance could result in higher taxes and rationing of health care, both of which would hurt Republicans. Because they are generally wealthier than the public as a whole, Republicans would have to bear the brunt of higher taxes to finance national health insurance. In addition, since they tend to already have access to health care, Republicans would have to face restrictions on their utilization of medical services under any government rationing of health care which would result from the establishment of the program. Republican opposition to Clinton's national health insurance plan was based largely upon the party's desire to protect the interests of its members.

Bob Dole and the Politics of Health Care Reform

Spearheading the Republican fight against Clinton's national health insurance plan was Senate Republican Leader Bob Dole of Kansas. In leading the Republican fight against the Clinton plan, Dole was motivated more by self-interest than by the interests of his party. Dole was perhaps the health care industry's strongest ally in Congress. Dole's close relationship with the industry was based upon financial considerations.

Among the 100 members of the Senate, Dole ranked thirteenth in campaign contributions received from the health care industry from 1979 to 1994, amassing a total of $707,794 in donations during this period.[4] Among the 535 members of the 102nd Congress, Dole ranked eleventh in the amount of campaign contributions received from health care industry PACs during 1991–1992, garnering $262,552. Among the 100 members of the Senate, Dole ranked tenth in health care industry contributions during this period.

Dole's principal campaign contributions came from private insurance companies, which, as we have seen, had the most to lose from national health insurance, and represented the strongest source of opposition to the program within the health care industry.[5] Given the threat national health insurance poses to the financial interests of private insurance companies, which served as a major source of contributions to Dole, the Senate Republican leader became among the most vociferous congressional opponents of national health insurance.

The health care industry had good reason to provide Dole massive campaign contributions. As Senate Republican leader since 1985, Dole had substantial influence in determining the Republican congressional agenda on critical issues, like health care reform. Dole also served as a member of the Finance Committee, which shares jurisdiction over health care reform with the Labor and Human Resources Committee in the Senate. As we saw in Chapter 3, committee members receive substantial campaign contributions from health care industry PACs.

The industry uses its financial influence over the committee to keep health care reform legislation from coming to the Senate floor. With the exception of 1994, the committee has remained faithful to the interests of the industry, preventing any health care reform legislation from reaching the Senate floor. By helping to keep, for the most part, health care reform legislation bottled up in committee, Dole became an important ally of the medical industry, and a major beneficiary of its financial largess.

Finally, Dole was the early front-runner for the 1996 Republican presidential nomination, having gained widespread national attention as Senate Republican leader. No president has done more to generate public interest in and support for health care reform than Clinton. As a result, Clinton's defeat in the 1996 presidential election is sure to become a top political priority of the health care industry. The massive campaign contributions the industry made to Dole served to allow the Senate Republican leader to raise his political profile as the primary Republican challenger to Clinton in 1996. Given the political damage done to the health care industry by Clinton's relentless and tireless efforts to secure the establishment of national health insurance and by the first lady's stinging attacks against the private insurance industry, medical interest goups need a friend in the White House. As the industry's most powerful congressional ally, no Republican presidential candidate can be counted upon to serve the financial interests of the medical system better than Dole. Accordingly, the industry had a financial stake in Dole's presidential campaign.

Dole was committed to defend the financial interests of the health care industry as a result of the massive campaign contributions he received from medical interest groups. He quickly became perhaps the industry's chief ally on Capitol Hill once health care reform emerged as a major issue on the national agenda in 1991. On June 5, 1991, Mitchell and other Senate Democrats introduced the HealthAmerica Act. As we saw in Chapter 3, the bill would have established a play-or-pay insurance plan. Employers would have been required to either provide their working families group insurance or pay a payroll tax to finance a government program for the uninsured.

As we will see in Chapter 6, many, if not most, small businesses do not provide their working families group health insurance. The HealthAmerica Act was primarily aimed at requiring small business to do so. As a result, Dole denounced the bill, charging that its requirement that employers provide their working families insurance would impose an excessive and onerous financial burden upon small business. "Now that the federal government is running in the red and state governments are faced with budget deficits that rise each year, the Democrats are looking for a new pocket to pick, and small business will fill that role," Dole charged.[6]

On February 6, 1992, Bush countered the HealthAmerica Act with a health care reform plan of his own. The Bush plan would have provided lower- and middle-class individuals tax credits to purchase their own private insurance.

However, the Bush plan neither guaranteed universal health insurance coverage nor contained health care costs.[7]

Nevertheless, Dole endorsed Bush's health care reform plan, despite its inadequacies. Addressing the Senate floor the day Bush introduced his health care reform plan, Dole repeated his charge that by requiring firms to provide their working families group health insurance, the Democratic Party's play-or-pay plan would impose a massive and unsustainable financial burden upon business, which would drive many companies into bankruptcy, resulting in massive job losses. "We can help low- and middle-income Americans buy insurance on the free market, as the President has proposed, or we can bury our businesses under a mountain of new mandates," Dole declared. "Americans want affordable health care, but they shouldn't have to pay for it with their jobs." Dole praised the Bush plan as a sensible alternative to play-or-pay insurance. "By helping individuals purchase health insurance with tax credits . . . President Bush has gone a long way toward addressing our health system's major problems."[8]

Dole Leads the Republican Campaign Against Clinton's National Health Insurance Plan

Clinton's election to the presidency allowed Dole to emerge as the chief Republican critic of national health insurance. With a Democratic president committed to health care reform now in office, Dole assumed leadership over the Republican Party's fight against national health insurance, taking every opportunity to thwart Clinton in his efforts to mobilize public support for the program. Dole undertook his campaign to derail Clinton's national health insurance plan as soon as the president became actively involved in winning public support for his program shortly after he entered the White House.

Clinton's first major effort to mobilize political support for his national health insurance plan came on August 16, 1993, when he went to Tulsa to rally the backing of the governors behind his health care reform program. Addressing a meeting of the National Governors' Association, Clinton denied Republican charges that his plan to require employers to provide their working families group insurance would impose a punitive and unbearable financial burden upon business, driving many firms into bankruptcy, and resulting in massive job losses. As Clinton put it,

If you reform the insurance system and all these . . . employers that are paying way too much now . . . wind up with reductions or no increases in [their insurance premiums] in the years ahead, that is more money that they're going to have to invest in creating new jobs in the private sector. If you reform the insurance system . . . and you limit the amount of payroll that someone can be required to put out in an insurance premium . . . you're increasing [jobs] dramatically.[9]

Clinton was correct in his argument that his national health insurance plan would not drive any firms out of business, resulting in job losses. The Clinton plan would allow employers to join health alliances, which would give firms the collective bargaining power to negotiate with the private insurance industry. Health alliances would contract only with those private plans which agreed to provide their members the most comprehensive coverage available at the lowest possible premium. As a result, health alliances would serve to reduce business health care costs. Further reductions in business health care costs would come through federal limits on private insurance premiums and the share of payroll firms would have to pay for group insurance; requiring all insurance premiums to be community-rated; and providing subsidies for employers to purchase group plans, all of which would allow them to extend their working families health care benefits on an affordable basis. Whether business would take advantage of its lower health care costs to create more jobs, as Clinton claimed, is questionable. Nevertheless, by reducing business health care costs, the Clinton plan would, at the very least, not result in either any corporate bankruptcies or job losses.

True, firms not providing their working families group health insurance would have to do so under the Clinton plan, which would require them to assume financial responsibility for the health care costs of their employed households, which they currently do not bear. Addressing the National Governors' Association the day following Clinton's appearance before the organization, Dole charged that a federal mandate for employers to provide their working families group insurance would drive many firms out of business, resulting in massive job losses. "Employer mandates would damage the economy and hurt those who need help the most—new hires, small businesses, and low-income workers," Dole claimed.[10]

Opponents of national health insurance, like Dole, argue that a federal mandate requiring businesses to provide their working families group coverage would result in massive job losses in one of two ways. To escape the financial burden of providing their working families group insurance, firms not currently offering health care benefits could lay off some employees. Alternatively, such firms could adhere to the federal mandate requiring them to provide their working families group insurance and pass on the cost of their health care benefits to consumers in the form of higher prices, which would render them uncompetitive in their industries, driving them out of business. A federal mandate requiring firms to provide their working families group insurance would result in massive job losses, either by making it unaffordable for business to maintain their workers, or by driving companies into bankruptcy.

However, Dole's charge that the imposition of a federal mandate requiring firms to provide their working families group health insurance would result in massive job losses is false, at least insofar as the Clinton plan is concerned. Dole ignored the fact that the Clinton plan would require firms to join health alliances, which would give businesses the collective bargaining power to reduce their health care costs. The federal government would further reduce business health care costs through the imposition of limits on private insurance premiums and the share of payroll firms would have to pay for group insurance. The federal government would provide subsidies to assure that no firm spent more than 7.9 percent of its payroll on group insurance. Finally, the Clinton plan would require that all insurance premiums be community-rated, assuring that no firm would experience a sudden and unpredictable increase in its health care costs as a result of catastrophic illnesses or injuries suffered by any of its working families. The combined effect of health alliances, federal regulation of business health care costs, subsidies to finance the cost of group insurance, and community-rated insurance premiums would assure that no firm would have to assume a substantial financial burden for the health care costs of its working families.

As a result, firms which currently do not provide their working families group health insurance would not suffer any undue financial hardship, let alone be driven out of business, by a federal mandate requiring them to assume responsibility for the health care costs of their employed households under the Clinton plan. Since the Clinton plan would make group insurance affordable for all firms, the imposition of such a mandate would probably not cost any jobs. Quite the contrary; by curbing the growth of health care costs, the Clinton plan could very well result in an increase in the number of jobs by allowing firms to use their medical savings to hire new workers, as the president claimed. Indeed, in 1993 the Employment Benefit Research Institute released a study which found that the Clinton plan would have essentially a neutral effect on the labor market, ranging from 666,000 jobs created to 168,000 jobs lost.[11]

On September 22, 1993, Clinton made his most ambitious attempt thus far to mobilize public and congressional support for his national health insurance plan when he delivered a prime-time television address before a joint session of lawmakers. In his address, Clinton assured the business community that his national health insurance plan would reduce their health care costs by providing firms the bargaining clout to secure coverage at lower premiums and limiting the share of payroll companies would have to spend on medical services for their working families. Accordingly, Clinton reiterated his claim that his national health insurance plan would neither drive any firms into bankruptcy nor cost any jobs:

If you're a small business owner who wants to provide health insurance to your family and your employees, but you can't afford it because the system is stacked against you, this plan will give you a discount that will make insurance affordable. If you're already providing insurance, your rates may well drop because we'll help you as a business person join thousands of others to get the same benefits big corporations get at the same price they get those benefits. . . .

If you're a large employer, your health care costs won't go up as fast, so that you will have more money to put into higher wages and new jobs and put into the work of being competitive in this tough global economy.[12]

Dole remained unpersuaded by Clinton's claim that his national health insurance plan would not cause business failures and job losses. Following Clinton's address, Dole once again repeated his charge that the president's program would impose "job-killing employer mandates."[13]

In January 1994 Dole intensified the Republican campaign against Clinton's national health insurance plan, taking his party's case against the president's program directly to the public. On January 1, 1994, Clinton delivered a radio address in which he refuted the HIAA's claim that his national health insurance plan would result in government control of the health care system. "Our health care reform plan is a guaranteed system of private insurance," Clinton reminded his listeners. "We'll maintain the health care system in private hands, improve the quality of health care, increase the choices you have as a consumer, and protect the doctor-patient relationship."[14]

Clinton's rejection of the HIAA's charge that his national health insurance plan would result in government control of the health care system was entirely correct. Since Clinton would leave the entire health care system, including most of the health insurance system, in private hands, no one could seriously argue that the president's program would result in any government control of medical care. The HIAA's charge that such a result would occur represented nothing more than a scare tactic designed to frighten the public into opposing the Clinton plan on the false grounds that it would result in an unwarranted government intrusion into the health care system.

However, Dole saw the HIAA's charge that Clinton's national health insurance plan would result in government control of the health care system as an effective argument for the Republican Party to use in mobilizing public opposition to the president's program. Following Clinton's radio address, Dole quickly took to the airwaves himself to deliver the Republican rebuttal to Clinton's speech, blasting the president's program for including "price controls, employer mandates, mandatory health alliances, and massive overdoses of government control" of the health care system.[15]

THE DEBATE OVER THE EXISTENCE OF A HEALTH CARE CRISIS

In January 1994 a new controversy arose which transformed the debate on health care reform. In 1993 national health insurance had emerged as a dominant issue on the political agenda because of the public perception that a health care crisis existed, which even opponents of medical reform did not question. Given the existence of a health care crisis, an overwhelming majority of the public supported, and in some cases was demanding, sweeping federal action to overhaul the medical system.

However, appearing on *Meet the Press* on January 9, 1994, Senator Daniel Patrick Moynihan of New York became the first major political figure to publicly question the existence of a health care crisis, emphatically declaring that "we do not have a health care crisis in America."[16] Moynihan's comments would not have received much attention had they been made by an inconsequential Republican congressional opponent of Clinton. However, Moynihan was a prominent Democratic congressional supporter of Clinton. As chairman of the Finance Committee, which shares jurisdiction over health care reform with the Labor and Human Resources Committee in the Senate, Moynihan was expected to play a prominent role in shepherding Clinton's national health insurance plan through Congress. Moynihan's comments unleashed a debate over the existence of a health care crisis which dominated the politics of national health insurance in January 1994.

In denying the existence of a health care crisis, Moynihan placed himself in direct opposition to Clinton. The president based his campaign to establish national health insurance on the existence of a health care crisis. To address this crisis, Clinton demanded urgent congressional action to adopt the program. The health care crisis resulted from the fact that a substantial share of the public remained uninsured, while medical costs continued to soar. As Clinton put it in an open letter to the public on October 27, 1993, which coincided with his introduction of the Health Security Act, "Next year we will spend over one trillion dollars on health care—and still leave 37 million Americans without health insurance."[17]

Moynihan's denial of the existence of a health care crisis made no sense. A rapidly growing uninsured population combined with soaring medical costs makes the existence of a health care crisis an undeniable reality. As Robert Kuttner put it, "Intellectually, Moynihan is a deft provocateur, but his airy dismissal of the health crisis is pure mischief. The ills of the health system are multiple."[18]

Moynihan's claim that no health care crisis existed was due to the close financial relationship the Senate Finance Committee chairman had established with the medical industry. During 1993–1994, the industry made a concerted effort to influence Moynihan to take action in order to prevent the Senate Finance Committee from approving national health insurance legislation. To secure such influence, the industry substantially increased its financial support for Moynihan, who was up for reelection in 1994. Campaign contributions from medical PACs to Moynihan skyrocketed from $19,500 during 1989–1992 to $259,685 from January 1, 1993, to March 31, 1994.[19]

The massive increase in campaign contributions to Moynihan from the health care industry is consistent with the fact that those serving on the two committees exercising jurisdiction over health care reform in the Senate—Finance and Labor and Human Resources—usually receive most of their financial support from medical interest groups during the two years prior to their reelection. By demonstrating financial support for members of the two committees when they need it most—during their reelection campaigns—the industry has succeeded in exerting enormous political influence over the committees and each of its members. Financially beholden to the health care industry as a result of the massive contributions he received from medical interest groups during 1993–1994, Moynihan could not support national health insurance, since it was opposed by practically all segments of the health care system. As a result, Moynihan needed to find some convenient justification for rationalizing his own inaction on health care reform. His argument that no health care crisis existed served as such a justification.

In addition to benefiting himself, Moynihan's claim that no health care crisis existed was designed to provide a convenient justification for the Senate Finance Committee's inaction on health care reform. As we saw in Chapter 3, committee members receive massive campaign contributions from medical PACs. The industry has used its financial influence over the committee to prevent its approval of a national health insurance bill. In the absence of the committee's approval, no national health insurance bill can reach the Senate floor. As a result, the committee has served as a useful tool for the health care industry to prevent a Senate vote on national health insurance legislation, sparing senators from having to take the politically risky action of voting against such a measure, given their close financial relationship with medical interest groups.

As we saw in Chapter 3, the Senate Labor and Human Resources Committee approved a national health insurance bill in the 102nd Congress, and did do so again in the 103rd Congress. The Finance Committee's refusal to follow the lead of the Labor and Human Resources Committee and approve a national health insurance bill had prevented a health care reform measure from coming to the Senate floor in the 102nd Congress. To prevent a national health insurance bill from coming to the Senate floor in the 103rd Congress, the Finance Committee needed to remain steadfast in its refusal to consider health care reform legislation. However, this became increasingly difficult to do, since the committee came under mounting public and presidential pressure to approve a national health insurance bill as a result of Clinton's intense and relentless campaign to establish the program, which had widespread popular support, as we have seen. To relieve the committee of this pressure, Moynihan had no alternative but to deny the existence of the health care crisis.

True, on July 2, 1994, the Senate Finance Committee followed the lead of the Labor and Human Resources Committee and approved a health care reform bill. However, as we will see in Chapter 8, Senate Finance was the only one of the four committees approving health care reform legislation in the 103rd Congress that failed to guarantee universal health insurance coverage. The Finance Committee's action prevented a bill guaranteeing universal coverage from going to the Senate floor. As a result, the Senate Finance Committee continued to serve as a stumbling block to passage of a national health insurance bill in the 103rd Congress.

Moynihan's denial of the existence of a health care crisis dealt a severe setback to Clinton's health care reform initiative. Following Moynihan's lead, congressional opponents of national health insurance could now argue that no urgent and compelling public need existed for the establishment of the program, since the health care system was not in a state of crisis, contrary to Clinton's claims. This served to defuse public and congressional pressure for the establishment of national health insurance, dealing a fatal blow to Clinton's health care reform initiative.

Clinton recognized that if Moynihan's claim that no health care crisis existed gained widespread public and congressional acceptance, then lawmakers would see no immediate and overriding need to establish national health insurance. Accordingly, Clinton set out to refute Moynihan's claim in his 1994 State of the Union address. Delivered to a joint session of Congress and broadcast in prime time, the address gave Clinton an opportunity to communicate directly with both the public and lawmakers, allowing him to make his case for the existence of a health care crisis before a national audience.

In his State of the Union address, Clinton took issue with the notion made by some members of Congress that no health care crisis existed:

I know there are people here who say there's no health care crisis. . . . Tell it to the 58 million Americans who have no coverage at all for some time of the year. Tell it to the 81 million Americans with those preexisting conditions. Those folks are paying more, or they can't get insurance at all. Or they can't even change jobs because they or someone in their family has one of those preexisting conditions. Tell it to the small businesses burdened by the skyrocketing cost of insurance. Most small businesses cover their employees, and they pay on average 35 percent more in premiums than big business or Government. Or tell it to the 76 percent of insured Americans, three out of four, whose policies have lifetime limits. And that means they can find themselves without any coverage at all just when they need it most. So if all of you believe there's no [health care] crisis, tell it to those people because I can't.[20]

THE POLITICS OF NATIONAL HEALTH INSURANCE: CLINTON VERSUS DOLE

On January 25, 1994, Clinton and Dole appeared on prime-time television to take their opposing positions on health care reform directly to the public. Clinton did so in his State of the Union address, which was immediately followed by the Republican rebuttal to the president's speech, delivered by Dole. In addition to refuting the notion that no health care crisis existed, Clinton devoted his State of the Union address to repeating the fact that his national health insurance plan would leave the medical system in private hands. "Our approach protects the quality of care and people's choices," Clinton noted. "It builds upon what works in the private sector, to expand employer-based coverage, to guarantee private insurance for every American."[21]

In the Republican rebuttal to Clinton's State of the Union address, Dole repeated the familiar charge that no health care crisis existed. "Our country has health care problems, but not a health care crisis," Dole declared. Dole reiterated his claim that Clinton's national health insurance plan would result in government control of the health care system. "We will have a [health care] crisis if we take the President's medicine—a massive overdose of government control'' of the medical system, Dole warned.

Dole produced a chart which purported to show that Clinton's national health insurance plan would result in the establishment of a vast network of new federal bureaucracies to govern the health care system. "The President's idea is to put a mountain of bureaucrats between you and your doctor," Dole warned. "The President is asking you to trust the government more than you trust your doctors and yourselves with your lives and the lives of your loved ones. More cost, less choice, more taxes, less quality, more government control and less control for you and your family—that's what the President's government-run [national health insurance] plan is likely to give you.''[22]

Clinton and Dole squared off again over the issue of health care reform in separate speeches they delivered to a meeting of the National Governors' Association in Boston on July 19, 1994. In his speech, Clinton urged the Republicans to abandon the inflammatory rhetoric they had used to unfairly discredit his national health insurance plan, and work with him to produce a practical solution to the health care crisis. "All I ask in the closing weeks of this debate [on health care reform] is that we take the political air out of the balloon and ask ourselves what will work for ordinary Americans," Clinton implored.[23]

However, Dole rejected Clinton's plea for Republicans to abandon the false characterizations they had used to unfairly malign the president's national health insurance plan. In his speech to the National Governors' Association, Dole repeated his charge that Clinton's national health insurance plan would result in government control of the health care system. "The health care system may not be perfect, but it is the best in the world," Dole told the governors. "It needs repair, but I'm not certain it needs a complete and total overhaul, and certainly not a complete and total takeover by the federal government.''[24]

During August 9–19, 1994, the Senate conducted a debate on health care reform, focusing its attention on a scaled-down version of Clinton's national health insurance plan, which Mitchell had introduced. As we will see in Chapter 8, Mitchell's health care reform bill would have provided federal subsidies designed to guarantee 95 percent of the public health insurance coverage by 2000.

In his speech on the Senate floor introducing his health care reform bill, Mitchell pleaded for bipartisan cooperation to assure passage of legislation to overhaul the medical system. "It is my goal that the Senate pass the best possible health care reform bill, not a bill with a Democratic label, or a Republican label . . . but simply the best possible bill that will reach the goal that we all should share, guaranteed private health insurance to provide high-quality health care for every American family," Mitchell declared. "I urge my colleagues, Democrats and Republicans alike, to join the debate, to offer constructive suggestions to improve my bill.''[25]

However, Dole flatly rejected Mitchell's pleas for bipartisan cooperation to pass health care reform legislation. "America has the best health care delivery system in the world," Dole flatly declared, arguing that the high quality of

American medicine was due to "the American commitment to the freedom of individuals, the freedom of markets, not the government." Echoing his previous attacks against Clinton's national health insurance plan, Dole claimed that Mitchell's health care reform bill would result in "more government control" over the health care system. "Will we trade in a health care system based on individual freedom, for one based on Government control?" Dole asked, in urging the Senate to reject the Mitchell bill.[26] Noting that the United States spent 14 percent of its GDP on health care in 1994, Dole urged the Senate to refrain from taking any action which would increase government involvement in the medical industry. "Let's not turn one-seventh of our national economy over to the Government and say, 'OK, you run the health care system,' " Dole pleaded.[27]

Dole's denial of the existence of a health care crisis represents perhaps the most irresponsible claim made by the Senate Republican leader in his campaign to malign and discredit Clinton's health care reform initiative. By rejecting the notion that a health care crisis existed, Dole displayed contempt for the welfare of the 40.9 million uninsured individuals who run the risk of being financially wiped out by an illness, or denied health care altogether when they need it, because they have no coverage. Dole also showed insensitivity toward the tens of millions of individuals who are only one job away from losing their group insurance, and should this occur, only one illness away from suffering either the physical or financial catastrophe which the uninsured must experience.

The overwhelming majority of the public found Dole's argument that the United States has health care problems, but no health care crisis, unpersuasive. During January 28–30, 1994, *USA Today*, CNN, and Gallup conducted a poll of 1,013 adults, who were asked whether they believed that the United States faced a health care crisis, or just health care problems. Fifty-seven percent of the respondents said that the United States faced a health care crisis; 42 percent stated that the nation had health care problems, but no health care crisis.[28]

In addition to being unpersuaded by Dole's claim that no health care crisis existed, the public initially doubted the Senate Republican leader's charge that Clinton's national health insurance plan would result in government control of the health care system. As we saw, the 1993 *Los Angeles Times* poll cited at the beginning of this chapter found that 24 percent of those surveyed disapproved of the Clinton plan. Asked why they disapproved, 22 percent said that the plan would result in the establishment of a new government bureaucracy and 12 percent considered it to be "socialized medicine."[29] That is, only 34 percent of those opposing the Clinton plan, representing 8 percent of the public, opposed the president's program because they feared that it would result in a government takeover of the health care system.

However, public concern that Clinton's national health insurance plan would result in a government takeover of the health care system rose substantially during the ten months following the president's introduction of his health care reform program in his address to a joint session of Congress on September 22,

1993. During August 8–9, 1994, *USA Today*, CNN, and Gallup conducted a poll of 1,016 adults, who were asked which prospect did they fear more: that health care reform will result in "too much government control" of the medical system, or that it would not lead to universal coverage. Fifty-three percent of those polled feared that health care reform would result in "too much government control" of the medical system, and 40 percent that it would not lead to universal coverage.[30]

Why did the public fear that Clinton's national health insurance plan would result in a government takeover of the health care system rise substantially during 1993–1994? The answer remains the massive public relations campaign against the Clinton plan mounted by the Republican Party and the private insurance industry. As we have seen, a key argument used by the Republicans and the insurance industry in their campaign to politically discredit the Clinton plan was that it would result in a government takeover of the health care system. The public doubted that Clinton's national health insurance plan would result in government control of the health care system when the president introduced his health care reform program in his address to a joint session of Congress on September 22, 1993. However, during the ten months following this address, the Republicans and insurance industry hammered away at the Clinton plan, repeatedly warning in public forums and in paid television advertisements that the president's program would result in a government takeover of the health care system. The *USA Today*/CNN/Gallup poll shows that the public found this argument convincing. Public fear that the Clinton plan would result in excessive government intervention in the health care system was a major factor in the success of the Republicans and the insurance industry in mobilizing popular opposition to the president's program.

By August 1994, Clinton had come to realize belatedly that the Republican–insurance industry argument that his national health insurance plan would result in a government takeover of the health care system was having an effect in undermining public support for his health care reform program. In his news conference on August 3, 1994, endorsing the health care reform plan Mitchell had introduced in the Senate the previous day, Clinton launched a counterattack against the Republicans and insurance industry, denying that he supported government control of the health care system:

We want to guarantee private, not government, insurance for every American. . . . The [Mitchell] proposals before Congress are less bureaucratic. They're more flexible. They provide more protection and support for small business. They contain a reasonable phase-in time over a period of years, to make sure we get it right. No bureaucrat will pick your doctor. You can keep your own [health insurance] plan or pick another. This approach controls government [health care] spending but relies on competitive forces in the free market to restrain the growth of private health insurance premiums.[31]

However, Clinton's claims that his health care reform initiative would not result in a government takeover of the medical system fell on deaf ears. A majority of the public rejected Clinton's argument, believing instead that the president's efforts would result in government control of the health care system. The public belief that Clinton's health care initiative would result in excessive government intervention in the medical system dealt a fatal blow to the president's campaign to establish national health insurance. With health care reform becoming synonymous in the public mind with big government, Clinton's health care reform lost political credibility and collapsed.

Consistent with their fear that Clinton's national health insurance plan would result in "too much government control" of the health care system, a majority of the public believed that the president's program would add to the bureaucracy and paperwork governing the management of medical care, much as Dole had argued. In his address before a joint session of Congress on September 22, 1993, Clinton attempted to reassure the public that his national health insurance plan would reduce the bureaucracy and paperwork within the health care system:

Our health care system must be simpler for patients and simpler for those who actually deliver health care—our doctors, our nurses, our other medical professionals. Today we have more than 1,500 insurers, with hundreds and hundreds of different forms. . . . These forms are time-consuming for health care providers, they're expensive for health care consumers, they're exasperating for anyone who's ever tried to sit down around a table and wade through them and figure them out.

The medical industry is drowning in paperwork. . . .

Under our proposal, there will be one standard insurance form, not hundreds of them. . . . Doctors, nurses, and consumers shouldn't have to worry about the fine print. If we have this one simple form, there won't be any fine print. People should know what it means.[32]

Clinton was correct in his argument that his national health insurance plan would reduce bureaucracy and paperwork in the health care system. As he mentioned, there are currently 1,500 private plans, each with its own bureaucracy to process medical claims and reimburse health care providers, generating a duplication of administrative overhead and paperwork. This proliferation of bureaucracy and paperwork is a major source of soaring health care costs.

As we have seen, Clinton's national health insurance plan would allow the public to join health alliances, which would provide consumers the bargaining clout to purchase the most comprehensive coverage available at the lowest possible premium. In addition, the federal government would impose limits on insurance premiums under the Clinton plan. Faced with shrinking premiums, insurance companies would be forced to reduce their administrative costs, which would result in a shrinkage in bureaucracy and paperwork. Other insurance companies would go out of business as a result of the revenue losses they would suffer from reductions in their premiums. With fewer insurance companies in business, and with those still in operation having to reduce their administrative costs, the overall amount of bureaucracy and paperwork in the insurance system would shrink under the Clinton plan.

Despite the fact that Clinton's national health insurance plan would result in a reduction in bureaucracy and paperwork within the health care system, a majority of the public refused to believe this. During September 23–24, 1993, Princeton Survey Research Associates conducted a poll of 751 adults for *Newsweek*. The respondents were asked the following question: "Will President Clinton's proposed health-care plan mean either more bureaucracy and paperwork or more simplicity for doctors and patients?" Forty-five percent of the respondents said that the Clinton plan would result in "more bureaucracy and paperwork"; 42 percent stated that it would lead to "more simplicity for doctors and patients." [33]

Given his close financial relationship with the health care industry, Dole needed to defuse the pressure building on Capitol Hill to establish national health insurance as a result of Clinton's health care reform initiative. National health insurance threatened the financial interests of the industry, and some means was needed to blunt the political momentum toward medical reform which developed during 1993 and 1994. Accordingly, Dole set out to derail Clinton's health care reform initiative by charging that the president's national national health insurance plan would result in government control of the health care system. Dole's charge was designed to exploit the unfounded fear held by a substantial share of the public that the Clinton plan would indeed result in government control of the health care system and add more bureaucracy and paperwork in the delivery of medical care. It represented a cynical exercise in political deception, a misleading attempt at fear mongering designed to scare the public into opposing the president's program, by playing upon people's suspicion of big government. Given the fact that roughly half the public feared that the Clinton plan would result in "too much government control" of the health care system and add more bureaucracy and paperwork to the financing and administration of medical services, Dole's charge was certain to strike a responsive chord among a large segment of the population. If this charge gained widespread public acceptance, then popular pressure for congressional action on health care reform would dissipate, relieving the medical industry of the devastating financial consequences which would result from the establishment of national health insurance. In leading the Republican campaign against the Clinton plan, Dole was serving the financial interests of the industry, which represented an important source of campaign contributions for the Senator.

GRAMM JOINS DOLE IN LEADING THE REPUBLICAN CAMPAIGN AGAINST CLINTON'S NATIONAL HEALTH INSURANCE PLAN

In leading his party's campaign against Clinton's national health insurance plan, Dole received valuable support from Senator Phil Gramm of Texas, an unsuccessful candidate for the 1996 Republican presidential nomination. Like Dole, Gramm's opposition to national health insurance was motivated more by self-interest, than the interests of his party. Like Dole, Gramm was the recipient of massive campaign contributions from the health care industry. Among the 100 members of the Senate, Gramm was the single largest recipient of contributions from the industry during 1979 to 1994, amassing a total of $1,235,520 in donations during his first nine years in the Senate from 1985 to 1994.[34] Among the 535 members of the 102nd Congress, Gramm ranked thirty-fourth in the amount of campaign contributions received from health care industry PACs during 1991 to 1992, garnering a total of $106,550, and among the 100 members of the Senate, ranked sixteenth in health care industry contributions during this period.

Gramm's principal contributions came from the medical profession, whose dominant interest group was the AMA.[35] As we have seen, the AMA opposed Clinton's national health insurance plan because it would impose stringent health care cost-containment measures, which would require the profession to suffer substantial financial losses. Gramm was committed to defending the AMA's interests in Congress, joining the interest group in opposing any health care cost-containment measures as a result of the massive campaign contributions the senator received from the profession.

With the possible exception of Dole, no member of Congress assumed a stronger leadership role in the Republican campaign against Clinton's national health insurance plan during 1993–1994 than Gramm. As the largest single recipient of campaign contributions from the health care industry in the Senate during the 1980s and 1990s, Gramm had a political obligation to preserve the financial interests of medical interest groups. Given the threat the Clinton plan posed to the financial interests of the industry, Gramm had no choice but to mount an aggressive attack against the president's program. Failure to do so would have jeopardized Gramm's close financial relationship with the industry.

In addition to his relationship with the health care industry, Gramm had political reasons to lead the Republican campaign against Clinton's national health insurance. He needed to establish himself as Dole's chief rival for the 1996 Republican presidential nomination. Gramm saw his campaign against the Clinton plan as a means of establishing his credentials as Dole's primary Republican opponent. As he opened his campaign for the Republican presidential nomination in February 1995, Gramm pointed to the pivotal role he had played in the defeat of the Clinton plan as a major reason why members of his party should rally around his candidacy. Addressing a meeting of the Conservative Political Action Conference in Washington on February 11, 1995, Gramm noted that he had been an early and vociferous opponent of the Clinton plan:

What I am proudest of is, at the darkest moment of the health care debate, when all Republican pollsters were saying to us: "It is political suicide to take on the health care bill straight on" . . . I stood up and said the Clinton health care bill is going to pass over my cold, dead political body. My political body is still alive. And the Clinton health care plan is deader than Elvis. [Elvis] may be back, but the Clinton health care bill is not coming back.[36]

As we have seen, Republicans generally opposed Clinton's national health insurance plan, unlike Democrats and independents, who tended to support the president's program. Opposition to the Clinton plan was especially intense among conservative Republican activists, who tend to play a dominant role in selecting their party's presidential nominee. Given the existence of strong Republican opposition to the Clinton plan among conservative party activists, Gramm hoped to win the support of right-wing Republicans by leading the fight against the president's program. With the solid support of conservative Republican activists, Gramm was almost certain to win his party's presidential nomination. The contribution which his leadership role in the Republican campaign against Clinton's national health insurance plan played in furthering the senator's 1996 presidential campaign was perhaps best expressed by James A. Barnes:

Gramm fought the Clinton proposal by raising . . . philosophical points that were consistent with Republican ideology, such as free markets and freedom of choice for patients. . . . Gramm's call to arms not only helped defeat the Clinton plan but also won converts to his presidential campaign. "It was during the health care debate that it became pretty obvious to me that Gramm was the instrument of change that I think is so important for the country," said Senator Paul Coverdell [of Georgia] who has endorsed the Texan's White House bid.[37]

Gramm joined the Republican campaign against Clinton's national health insurance plan following the president's introduction of his health care reform program in his address before a joint session of Congress on September 22, 1993. Gramm responded to Clinton's address by warning that "this is basically a health care plan that could bankrupt the government."[38] Gramm stepped up his attacks on the Clinton plan following the president's introduction of his national health insurance bill on October 27. Gramm responded to the introduction of the bill by continuing his denunciation of the Clinton plan. "The President is a good salesman. The First Lady is a good salesman," Gramm declared. "But the bottom line is, they're trying to sell you socialized medicine, and that is bad product."[39]

Gramm presented his argument against Clinton's national health insurance plan in an article published in the *Washington Times* and reprinted in the spring/summer 1994 issue of *Health Care News*, a publication of the Seniors Coalition, an interest group representing elderly individuals opposed to the president's program. In his article, Gramm repeated the familiar Republican charges that the Clinton plan would result in a substantial tax increase, health care rationing, massive job losses, and government control over all medical decision making.

Gramm charged that the Clinton national health insurance plan would drive up federal spending on health care, resulting in a substantial tax increase and health care rationing. "By any responsible measure, the Clinton plan is over-promised and underfunded," Gramm warned. "If it becomes law, taxes will have to be raised further or health care will have to be rationed—or both."

Gramm charged that Clinton's national health insurance plan would impose an onerous financial burden upon small businesses, which would force them to lay off workers. "Business costs, especially for small businesses, will rise sharply when government mandates that employers provide universal cover-age," Gramm warned. "As a result, jobs will be lost."[40] Gramm quoted studies which estimated that the Clinton plan would cost 3.1 million jobs, while placing another 9.1 million jobs at risk of being lost.[41]

Gramm charged that Clinton's national health insurance plan would result in government control of all medical decision making by requiring the public to secure access to health care through "government-run, regional health care col-lectives." Only individuals employed in firms with over 5,000 workers would be exempt from the requirement to join a health alliance under the Clinton plan. All other individuals would be prohibited from purchasing private insurance outside a health alliance.

As a result, unless they were employed by a large corporation or the govern-ment, the only other way that individuals could avoid having to secure their health care through a health alliance was to pay for their medical services out of pocket. Accordingly, Gramm warned that individuals not employed by a large corporation or the government or sufficiently wealthy to pay for their own health care out of pocket would be forced into "the Clinton health care system, where a National Health Czar will have the power to determine what doctors and hospitals can do, which doctors you can see, how much they can charge, what medications can they dispense, what new drugs and procedures will be devel-oped and how much you will pay."[42]

Gramm concluded that Clinton's national health insurance plan was nothing less than "socialized medicine":

Under the Clinton health plan, the federal government will decide what health plans are offered, what services are provided, what treatments are appropriate and paid for, how much money can be spent, what doctors will earn, what new "reasonably priced" drugs will be covered, [and] what specialties young interns can pursue. . . . If that's not so-cialized medicine, what is?[43]

In an article published in the February 8, 1994, edition of the *Wall Street Journal*, and reprinted in a 1996 Gramm presidential campaign newsletter, the senator repeated his charge that Clinton's national health insurance plan would result in "socialized medicine," and accurately predicted that public support for the president's program would collapse, resulting in its defeat. "The President says he wants to fix what's broken in American health care," Gramm declared. "The truth is, he wants to use what's broken as a justification for throwing out the whole system and adopting socialized medicine. When Americans discover this simple fact about the Clinton plan, his credibility will once again be lost and his plan will die.''[44]

Gramm's charge that Clinton's national health insurance plan would result in massive job losses was a familiar Republican argument against the president's program often repeated by Dole, as we have seen. We showed that this charge was false. Equally false are Gramm's charges that the Clinton plan would result in a substantial tax increase and government control of all medical decision making.

Gramm's charge that Clinton's national health insurance plan would result in a substantial tax increase is groundless, since the Clinton plan would impose stringent cost-containment measures, which would result in a reduction in health care costs—both public and private, as we saw in Chapter 2. Accordingly, the Clinton plan would not result in any tax increase.

Gramm conceded that Clinton's national health insurance plan would impose health care cost-containment measures by organizing consumers into health alliances, which would use their collective bargaining power to reduce health care costs, combined with the imposition of federal limits on private insurance premiums. However, in an article published in the April 11, 1993, edition of the *Los Angeles Times*, Gramm rejected the imposition of any such measures. Gramm was particularly strident in his rejection of any federal limits on health care costs. ''We know quite a bit about price controls and rationing,'' Gramm explained. ''From Hammurabi to Nixon, they have been employed in all times, in many places, and never, ever, have they worked.''[45] However, Gramm neglected to note that virtually every advanced industrial democracy except the United States imposes some form of health care cost-containment measures, which have succeeded in holding medical spending in Western Europe, Canada, and Japan substantially below that of this nation.[46] While ''price controls'' may not work in the rest of the economy, they have succeeded in containing health care costs, as international comparative analysis between the United States and the other advanced industrial democracies shows.

Gramm's rejection of any federal limits on health care costs might be understandable, given the fact that the senator is a conservative Republican who opposes government regulation of the marketplace. However, what is less understandable is Gramm's opposition to the establishment of health alliances. Unlike federal limits on health care costs, health alliances would contain health care costs through market, rather than regulatory, means. Health alliances would provide consumers the organizational clout they currently lack to bargain effectively with the private insurance industry to reduce health care costs. This should have satisfied Gramm. Conservative Republicans, like Gramm, have traditionally favored a free enterprise system in which consumers exercise their market sovereignty in compelling producers to provide the highest-quality product at the lowest possible cost. Health alliances would have done just that in the health care marketplace, allowing consumers to use their organizational clout to compel the private insurance industry to provide the most comprehensive coverage available at the lowest possible premium.

As a result, Gramm should have supported the health alliances; instead, he denounced them. "If consumer cooperatives the size of states can be efficient, why don't we see them operating in any other market?" Gramm asked in his *Los Angeles Times* article.[47] The answer to Gramm's question is simple: Health alliances have not been established at either the national or state level because they would serve to reduce health care costs, and slash the incomes of every segment of the medical industry. Since Congress, and perhaps even the state legislatures, are financially beholden to the health care industry, neither federal nor state lawmakers are willing to take action, such as the establishment of health alliances, which would undermine the interests of organized medical groups. In rejecting health alliances, Gramm contradicted his own conservative philosophy of free markets and consumer empowerment, insofar as health care was concerned; he had no other choice but to do so, given his dependence upon campaign contributions from the medical industry.

Gramm's charge that Clinton's national health insurance plan would result in government control of all medical decision making is perhaps the least persuasive of all the arguments against the president's program made by its opponents. Doctors and hospitals would be free to provide whatever services their patients need under the Clinton plan. Gramm's charge that the Clinton plan would establish a "National Health Czar," who would be responsible for determining what services patients would receive, is nonsense; it represents a convenient scare tactic concocted by the senator to frighten the public into opposing the Clinton plan, based upon the groundless fear that their access to medical services would be controlled by the government, not their doctors.

A critical part of Gramm's use of scare tactics to falsely discredit Clinton's national health insurance plan was his denunciation of the president's program as "socialized medicine." The term "socialized medicine" has long been used by opponents of national health insurance as a means to mobilize public opposition to the program.[48] The term implies that the program would give the government control of the health care system, and politicians and bureaucrats the right to decide when each individual may have access to health care and the conditions under which medical services are to be delivered. As a result, the term has been traditionally used by opponents of national health insurance, like Gramm, as part of a scare tactic designed to frighten the public into opposing the program based upon the false assumption that it would result in government control of all medical decision making.

In 1994 Gramm actively pursued the Republican campaign against Clinton's national health insurance plan, openly ridiculing the program in speeches before party and conservative groups. Addressing a meeting of the Conservative Political Action Conference in Washington on February 12, Gramm predicted that the public would reject the Clinton plan. "When the American people understand what Clinton's plan entails, in cost, jobs, and freedom, it is going to get a reception that is going to make the weather outside seem warm and wonderful,'' Gramm quipped, in a humorous reference to the severe winter weather which gripped the Northeast in 1994.[49]

Addressing a meeting of the Southern Republican Leadership Conference in Atlanta on April 30, Gramm accurately predicted that there was no chance that Congress would pass the Clinton plan. "There is a big difference between Elvis and the President's health care plan . . . Elvis may be out there alive somewhere,'' Gramm quipped, in a humorous reference to the frequent "sightings'' of the late Elvis Presley.[50]

Gramm participated in the ten-day debate on health care reform which occurred on the Senate floor in August 1994. Gramm represented perhaps the leading Republican voice opposing Mitchell's health care reform bill. On August 11 he delivered a scathing attack against the Mitchell bill, charging that it would be too costly and result in health care rationing.

Gramm charged that the Mitchell bill would provide up to 110 million individuals subsidies to purchase their own private health insurance, at an annual cost to the federal government of $194.3 billion. "Do we want to start down a program that has the potential of becoming one of the largest new spending programs in the history of the United States of America?'' Gramm asked the Senate. "Can we really afford to add another burden on the back of the working American family by making them pay part of the health care bills for half the population of the country? I say no.''[51]

Gramm charged that by guaranteeing 95 percent of the public health insurance coverage, Mitchell's health care reform bill would raise patient utilization of medical services, driving up their cost. To contain soaring health care costs, the federal government would have to stringently ration medical services. Gramm argued that by requiring health care rationing, Mitchell's medical reform bill would deprive the 85 percent of the public who are insured of the freedom to secure access to whatever health care services they need, which they have traditionally enjoyed. "When my momma gets sick, I want her to talk to a doctor and not some Government bureaucrat,'' Gramm declared. "I do not want the government to make [health care] decisions for my family, and . . . other American families.''[52]

Gramm concluded by warning that passage of any legislation resembling Clinton's national health insurance plan would be a complete disaster for both the economy and health care system. "If we adopt anything like the Clinton health care plan . . . we will go back and forth between bankrupting the Government and rationing health care.'' Gramm warned. "In the end, we will destroy both the economy and the greatest health care system in history.''[53]

KEMP ATTACKS CLINTON'S NATIONAL HEALTH INSURANCE PLAN

In addition to Dole and Gramm, Clinton's national health insurance plan came under fire from yet another prominent Republican, Jack Kemp, who served as

Secretary of Housing and Urban Development in the Bush Administration. In 1994 Kemp joined Dole and Gramm in attacking Clinton's national health insurance plan. Addressing a meeting of the Republican National Committee in Washington on January 22, Kemp repeated his party's charge that the Clinton plan would result in government control of the health care system. "President Clinton has scared the American people into believing we've got to radically nationalize and have the government control all the decisions in the [health care] marketplace," Kemp claimed.[54]

In an article in the March 20, 1994, edition of the *Los Angeles Times*, Kemp delivered a hard-hitting attack against Clinton's national health insurance plan. He warned that health care costs would soar out of control if the Clinton plan were established, citing a study which unpersuasively argued that the federal government would have to raise taxes by 27 percent to finance the cost of the president's program. He further pointed out that upon the establishment of Medicare in 1965, the Johnson administration had estimated that the cost of the program would rise modestly to $8 billion by 1990; the actual cost that year was $98 billion. "All national health-insurance schemes inevitably cost far more than anyone projected when the programs were adopted," Kemp warned.

Kemp conceded that Clinton's national health insurance plan would reduce health care costs through the imposition of stringent cost-containment measures. However, he warned that such measures would result in severe health care rationing. "Quality will decline because patients and doctors will be forced into more rigid government constraints," Kemp stated. "As in Canada, a model for the Clinton Administration, people will wait months or even years for simple operations, and many will be denied access to treatment because the plan managers judge them too old to benefit, never mind their physicians' opinions."[55] He concluded by charging that the Clinton plan would impose an onerous financial burden upon business, resulting in massive layoffs, and the loss of 1 million jobs.[56]

Two of Kemp's charges against Clinton's national health insurance plan— that it would result in massive tax increases and job losses—are groundless. As we have seen, the Clinton plan would impose stringent cost-containment measures, which would reduce health care costs—both public and private. As a result, no tax increase would be required to finance the Clinton plan.

In addition, Clinton's national health insurance plan would limit private insurance premiums and the share of payroll firms would have to spend on health care, require insurance premiums to be community-rated, and provide subsidies for employers to purchase group plans, allowing them to provide their working families medical benefits on an affordable basis. By making group insurance affordable, the Clinton plan would assure that no firm would suffer a substantial financial burden to pay the health care costs of its working families. As a result, no job losses or business failures would result from the Clinton plan.

Nevertheless, two other charges Kemp made against the Clinton plan—that it would be too costly and result in severe health care rationing—seem convincing, on the surface. As Kemp argued, the cost of Medicare has substantially exceeded the federal government's original estimates when the program was established. However, the reason why Medicare costs have risen out of control is that the federal government has failed to impose any effective cost-containment measures over the program. The absence of such measures is deliberate. To induce health care providers to participate in Medicare, Congress has agreed to generous reimbursements for doctors and hospitals who treat Medicare patients. The willingness of Congress to generously reimburse health care providers under Medicare has precluded the imposition of any effective cost-containment measures to hold down the program's costs.

True, the government has imposed cost-containment measures to limit Medicare and Medicaid spending. The government reimburses doctors and hospitals substantially less under Medicare and Medicaid than private health insurance does. However, health providers have counteracted such measures through cost shifting. Whenever the government reduces hospital and physician reimbursements under Medicare and Medicaid, health care providers recover their losses from treating their Medicare and Medicaid patients by raising their charges for privately insured patients. Cost shifting makes it virtually impossible for the federal government to control health care costs, since health care providers routinely raise their charges for privately insured patients to offset any losses which result from reductions in Medicare and Medicaid reimbursements.[57]

Medicare costs have soared at an uncontrollable rate not because public health insurance is inherently costly, as Kemp argues; but rather, because the program has been designed to serve as a major source of income for the health care industry, which has benefited financially from escalating Medicare costs.[58] Moreover, even if the federal government were to effectively contain Medicare costs, overall health care costs would continue to soar, since medical providers can always offset whatever losses they suffer under Medicare by raising their charges for their privately insured patients. Western Europe, Canada, and Japan have combined the establishment of national health insurance programs with the imposition of cost-containment measures, which have succeeded in holding down their health care costs well below those of the United States. The fact that health care costs are substantially lower in Western Europe, Canada, and Japan—all nations with national health insurance programs—than they are in the United States shows that Kemp's claim that national health insurance is inherently costly cannot be further from the truth. Far from being intrinsically costly, national health insurance is essential to containing health care costs, as international experience shows.

True, the stringent cost-containment measures Western Europe, Canada, and Japan impose have resulted in severe medical rationing, as Kemp noted. However, he failed to acknowledge that the United States also rations health care. Affluent and well-insured individuals have access to all the health care they need. Poor and uninsured individuals have access only to that health care which they can afford or can secure on an uncompensated basis from charitable hospitals.

National health insurance would end the perverse way in which the United States rations health care. Health care would no longer be rationed on the basis of an individual's income and insurance coverage. Rather, health care would be rationed according to its value, as is the case in Western Europe, Canada, and Japan. Individuals in those nations have free access to those health care services that extend normal, healthy, and productive life, especially preventive care; they have restricted access to medical services of only marginal value which do little or nothing to add to normal life, particularly costly medical technology, which are often used by elderly and terminally ill patients to delay their deaths by a few days, weeks, or months.[59]

Western Europe, Canada, and Japan have developed a humane and decent means to ration health care, based upon the benefits that each medical service provides society, not upon how much income and insurance coverage an individual has. The United States needs to adopt the same kind of rationing system. By attacking the way Western Europe, Canada, and Japan ration health care, Kemp places himself in the untenable position of defending America's own perverse and distorted rationing system, which cannot be justified on any grounds of equity.

THE PUBLIC TURNS AGAINST CLINTON'S NATIONAL HEALTH INSURANCE PLAN

As we have seen, Clinton's national health insurance plan was subjected to a withering barrage of attacks by the private insurance industry and the Republican Party in the months after the president introduced his program in his address to a joint session of Congress on September 22, 1993. Those attacks succeeded in turning public opinion against the Clinton plan. During the ten months following Clinton's introduction of his national health insurance plan Yankelovich Partners conducted polls on the president's program for *Time* and CNN. The polls asked their respondents the following question: "Do you favor or oppose President Clinton's health-care plan?" The results of the Time/CNN polls are contained in Table 5.1.

The *Time*/CNN polls show that an overwhelming majority of the public supported Clinton's national health insurance immediately following its introduction by the president on September 22, 1993. However, public support for the Clinton plan fell substantially in the months following Clinton's address, as the president's program was subjected to campaign of blistering attacks from the private insurance industry and the Republican Party. By March 1994, a plurality of the public opposed the Clinton plan for the first time since its introduction. While public support for the Clinton plan rose substantially in April, it fell sharply in June, with a plurality of the population once again opposed. Worse yet, in July public support for the Clinton plan collapsed, falling to its lowest level in the ten months following its introduction.

While a plurality of the public opposed Clinton's national health insurance

Table 5.1
The Results of the *Time*/CNN Polls Measuring Public Opinion on Clinton's
National Health Insurance Plan

Polling Dates	Percent Supporting the Clinton Plan	Percent Opposing the Clinton Plan	Percent Uncertain About the Clinton Plan
September 23, 1993	57	31	12
October 28, 1993	43	36	21
January 17–18, 1994	50	33	17
February 10, 1994	43	42	15
March 2–3, 1994	41	45	14
April 6–7, 1994	48	39	13
June 15–16, 1994	40	43	17
July 20–21, 1994	37	49	14

Sources: Michael Duffy, "Picture of Health," *Time*, October 4, 1993, p. 28; George J. Church, " 'Please Help Us,' " *Time*, November 8, 1993, p. 38; John Greenwald, "Famine—and Feast," *Time*, February 21, 1994, p. 44; George J. Church, "Oh Noooo!" *Time*, March 14, 1994, p. 35; Nina Burleigh, "Bill's Revival Hour," *Time*, April 18, 1994, p. 39; Michael Duffy, "Bending a Promise," *Time*, June 27, 1994, p. 37; James Carney, "Going Flat Out," *Time*, August 1, 1994, p. 17.

plan, they also rejected every alternative to the president's program introduced in Congress. During March 2–3, 1994, Yankelovich Partners conducted a poll of 600 adults for *Time* and CNN. The poll asked its respondents the following question: "Are there other health care reform plans that have been introduced in Congress that are better than Clinton's?" Sixty-two percent of the respondents said that there were no alternatives to the Clinton plan that they could support; only 16 percent stated that there were.[60] While the public remained cool toward the Clinton plan, they liked the alternatives to the president's program even less.

Why had Clinton's national health insurance plan failed to win the support of a majority of the public by July 1994? Because an overwhelming majority of the public accepted the Republican Party's charge that the Clinton plan would drive up health care costs, resulting in an increase in the amount individuals would have to pay for their medical services. Clinton attempted to dispel public fear that his national health insurance plan would raise health care costs. In his address to a joint session of Congress on September 22, 1993, he assured the public that his national health insurance plan would actually reduce health care costs through two means: first, the establishment of health alliances, which would use their collective bargaining power to provide the public the most comprehensive coverage available at the lowest possible premium; and second, the imposition of limits on insurance premiums.[61] "We can find tens of billions of dollars in savings in what is clearly the most costly and most bureaucratic [health care] system in the entire world," Clinton declared. "We have to do it now."[62]

Because Clinton's national health insurance plan would reduce health care costs, there would be no need for the federal government to raise taxes to finance the president's program. Rather, the federal government would use the savings from the reductions in health care costs which would occur under the Clinton plan to finance coverage for the uninsured, without any tax increase. In his address on September 22, 1993, Clinton assured the public that the savings which would result from his national health insurance plan would be sufficient to finance the program without the need for a tax increase: "We can reform the costliest and most wasteful [health care system] on the face of the Earth without enacting new broad-based taxes," he declared.[63]

Clinton was correct in his argument that the establishment of health alliances combined with the imposition of limits on private health insurance premiums would reduce health care costs, with the savings used to finance coverage for the uninsured without the need for any tax increase. However, a plurality of the public did not believe this. The *Newsweek* poll taken immediately following Clinton's address on September 22, 1993, asked its respondents the following question: "Will President Clinton's proposed health-care reform plan mean either real savings on the nation's health-care costs or no real health care savings?" Forty-seven percent of the respondents said that the Clinton plan would result in "no real health care savings"; 36 percent stated that it would lead to "real savings on the nation's health care costs."

Consistent with their belief that Clinton's national health insurance plan would result in no reduction in health care costs, an overwhelming majority of the public feared that the federal government would have to raise taxes to finance the president's program. The *Newsweek* poll asked its respondents the following question: "Will the mixture of cost savings, employer-employee payments and new taxes cover the cost of Clinton's plan, or will it require more taxes than he has proposed?" Seventy-three percent of the respondents said that the Clinton plan would require a tax increase and only 17 percent that it would not.[64]

The fact that an overwhelming majority of the public believed that Clinton's national health insurance plan would result in a tax increase dealt a fatal blow to the president's ability to mobilize popular support for his plan, since only a small fraction of the population was willing to accept a substantial tax increase to finance coverage for the uninsured. During July 20–21, 1994, Yankelovich Partners conducted a poll of 600 adults for *Time* and CNN which asked its respondents the following question: "Under most health reform plans, some Americans would have to pay higher taxes, pay more for insurance, accept wage cuts or forgo future wage increases. Would you be willing to accept any of these changes?" Fifty percent of those polled said they would be willing to pay more in higher taxes and private insurance premiums to provide coverage to the uninsured; 45 percent stated that they would be unwilling to do so.

Those who were willing to pay more in higher taxes and private insurance premiums to provide coverage to the uninsured were then asked the following question: "How much more would you be willing to pay per month in taxes and premiums?'' Forty-three percent of those polled said that they would only be willing to pay less than $30 a month in higher taxes and private insurance premiums; 33 percent stated that they would be willing to pay from $30 to $50; and only 15 percent expressed their willingness to pay over $50.[65]

As we have seen, Clinton's national health insurance plan would not have resulted in a tax increase, since the health care cost-containment measures included in the president's program would have generated sufficient savings to finance coverage for the uninsured. However, as we will see in Chapter 8, in August 1994 Clinton abandoned his national health insurance plan in favor of a health care reform bill introduced by Mitchell in the Senate, which would have raised private insurance premiums by $500 annually for each privately insured individual to finance coverage for the uninsured. That premium increase amounted to a new tax. The *Time*/CNN poll just cited shows that only 50 percent of the public were willing to pay higher taxes to finance coverage for the uninsured; and, among this group, only 48 percent would accept a tax increase of over $30 a month—roughly the amount required to fund health care benefits for the uninsured under the Mitchell bill. As a result, only 24 percent of the public were willing to pay sufficient taxes to finance coverage to the uninsured under the Mitchell bill, the only health care reform plan which received serious consideration in the 103rd Congress. The fact that the health care reform bill sponsored by Mitchell and supported by Clinton and many, if not most, Senate Democrats would result in a substantial tax increase undermined public support for the president's campaign to establish national health insurance, given the unwillingness of the public to accept a significant financial burden in providing coverage to the uninsured.

An overwhelming majority of the public believed that Clinton's national health insurance plan would drive up the amount they would have to pay for medical services, in addition to requiring a tax increase. On October 28, 1993, and March 2–3, 1994, Yankelovich Partners conducted two polls for *Time* and CNN, respectively. The polls asked the following question: ''Under the health-care reforms the Administration is working on, do you think the amount that you pay for medical care will increase, decrease, or remain the same?'' The share of those polled believing that their medical payments would rise under the Clinton plan increased from 58 percent in October 1993 to 70 percent in March 1994. Only 8 percent and 9 percent of those polled in October 1993 and March 1994, respectively, believed their medical payments would decline under the Clinton plan. The share of those polled believing that their medical payments would remain the same under the Clinton plan declined from 23 percent to 17 percent during the same period.[66]

In addition to believing that Clinton's national health insurance plan would raise the amount they would have to pay for their health care, the overwhelming majority of the public felt that their existing coverage would not improve under the president's program. The *Los Angeles Times* poll taken immediately following Clinton's address to a joint session of Congress on September 22, 1993, asked its respondents the following question: "Do you think that you and your immediate family are likely to end up with better health care coverage [under the Clinton plan] than you have right now, or worse, or don't think your health care coverage will change?" Forty-six percent of those polled said that there would be "no change" in their existing coverage; 24 percent believed that it would be "better"; 17 percent felt that it would be "worse"; 9 percent did not know; and 4 percent said that it was "too early to say."[67] The *Los Angeles Times* poll showed that 63 percent of those surveyed believed that their existing coverage would not improve, and might even worsen, under the Clinton plan.

The *Time*/CNN and *Los Angeles Times* polls showed that the overwhelming majority of the public believed that they would pay more for their health care, without any improvement in their coverage under the Clinton plan. As a result, the overwhelming majority believed that they had nothing to gain from the Clinton plan. On October 28, 1993, Yankelovich Partners conducted a poll of 500 adults for *Time* and CNN. The poll asked its respondents the following question: "Do you think, in general, you and your family will be better off, worse off, or about the same [under the Clinton plan]?" Twenty percent said that they would be better off, 29 percent stated that they would be worse off, and 48 believed that they would be about the same.[68] The *Time*/CNN poll showed that 77 percent of those surveyed believed that they would be the same, or worse off, under the Clinton plan.

Consistent with their belief that they would not be better off under Clinton's national health insurance plan, roughly half of the public felt that the president's program would not improve the health care system. During September 16–19, 1993, the *New York Times* and CBS News asked 1,136 individuals what impact the Clinton plan would have on the health care system. Forty-six percent of those polled said that "the Clinton health care reform plan would make U.S. health care better"; 24 percent believed that "it won't have much impact one way or another"; and 20 percent felt that "it would make U.S. health care worse."[69] The poll showed the public evenly divided between those who believed the Clinton plan would improve the health care system and those who felt that the president's program would have no effect on the delivery of medical services, or make it worse.

The *Time*/CNN, *Newsweek*, *Los Angeles Times*, and *New York Times*/CBS News polls showed that at least a plurality of the public rejected Clinton's assurances that his national national health insurance plan would reduce health care costs, with the savings used to finance coverage for the uninsured, without the need for a tax increase. Rather, at least a plurality believed that the Clinton plan would result in no savings in health care costs, require a tax increase to finance coverage for the uninsured, and raise the amount they would have to pay for their medical services, while failing to improve their existing coverage, leaving them no better off than they are under the current health care system, and having no effect on the delivery of medical care or making it worse. As a result, a majority of the public refused to support the Clinton plan, or any other health care reform plan introduced in Congress. With a majority refusing to support the Clinton plan and every alternative to it, Congress saw no immediate and overriding need to establish national health insurance, ending prospects for its establishment.

The collapse of public support for Clinton's national health insurance plan had a substantial effect upon the eagerness of the public for congressional action on health care reform. During April 28–29, 1993, and July 13–14, 1994, Yankelovich Partners conducted two polls for *Time* and CNN, respectively, to determine the degree to which public support for swift congressional action on health care reform existed. The polls asked the following question: "Is it important to reform the U.S. health-care system this year, or can it wait until next year?" The share of those polled who believed that health care reform should be achieved this year declined from 71 percent in April 1993 to 50 percent in July 1994. The share of those polled who believed that health care reform should be delayed until the following year rose from 24 percent to 45 percent during the same period.[70] The *Time*/CNN polls thus showed that public support for swift congressional action on health care reform plunged from 1993 to 1994.

The *Time*/CNN polls indicating a collapse in public support for swift congressional action on health care reform was confirmed by a *Newsweek* survey. During August 4–5, 1994, Princeton Survey Research Associates conducted a poll of 750 adults for *Newsweek* which asked the following question: "Should health-care reform legislation be passed this year, or should Congress take more time to examine the various proposals and start over next year?" Sixty-five percent of those polled said that Congress should "start over next year"; only 31 percent believed that lawmakers should "pass reform this year."[71]

The fact that an overwhelming majority of the public wanted Congress to delay action on national health insurance was consistent with the fear of many, if not most, people that they stood to lose from health care reform. Since Clinton could veto any health care reform bill he objected to, any national health insurance measure passed would have to be acceptable to the President, and represent some version of his program. As we have seen, many, if not most, of the public believed that they stood to lose from Clinton's national health insurance plan. Given their aversion to the Clinton plan, an overwhelming majority of the public wanted Congress to adjourn in October 1994 without taking action on health care reform.

However, the overwhelming majority of the public still supported national health insurance, as we saw in Chapter 1. As a result, the public wanted Congress to reconsider, rather than abandon, the issue of health care reform when lawmakers reconvened in 1995. Given their misgivings about Clinton's national health plan, the overwhelming majority of the public did not want Congress to rush into passing a national health insurance bill in 1994, since any such measure would have to represent some version of the president's program. Rather, the majority wanted a delay in passage of national health insurance legislation in order to give Congress time to produce a better health care reform bill than the Clinton plan.

As the polling data presented in this chapter suggests, the public wanted a national health insurance program which would allow the 85 percent of the population who are insured to keep the coverage they currently have, without raising their taxes or medical bills, and undermining the quality of the existing health care delivery system. The public doubted that Clinton's national health insurance plan could meet those goals; and they wanted a health care reform bill which would do so. However, the public believed that producing such a bill would take time; which is why an overwhelming majority of the people wanted Congress to delay action on health care reform until 1995, at the very earliest.

The public's desire for a national health insurance bill, which guaranteed universal coverage without adversely affecting the coverage of the 85 percent who are currently insured, is an unattainable goal. By reducing financial barriers impeding access to health care among the uninsured, national health insurance will raise patient utilization of medical services, driving up their cost and the overall inflation rate. To the extent that universal coverage is achieved through the federal government, national health insurance will also result in an increase in the already swollen budget deficit. To assure that national health insurance does not add to inflation and the deficit, the federal government would have to impose stringent health care cost-containment measures, which would lead to severe medical rationing. National health insurance would leave those who are currently insured with less access to health care than they currently have, since the program would result in stringent medical rationing.

The public wanted a national health insurance program which guaranteed universal access to unlimited health care, a fiscally and economically impossible goal. The public wanted universal coverage, which contradicted the people's demand that the 85 percent of the population who are currently insured be allowed to keep the coverage they presently have. By demanding the establishment of a national health insurance program, which guaranteed universal coverage, without adversely affecting the coverage of those who are currently insured, the public was asking for the impossible.

By making unrealistic and contradictory demands on the political system concerning the issue of health care reform, the public made it virtually impossible for Congress to overhaul the medical system. Given the public's unrealistic and contradictory demands on the issue of health care reform, it was virtually impossible for Congress to produce a proposal for overhauling the medical system which would satisfy popular expectations concerning the most desirable arrangements for financing the delivery of health care. Clinton failed to produce a national health insurance plan which satisfied public expectations concerning what the people wanted from health care reform; but in fairness to the president, no health care reform plan was possible which could have satisfied public expectations, since the people held unrealistic and contradictory feelings concerning what they wanted from an overhaul of the medical system.

Dole seized upon the collapse of public support for Clinton's national health insurance plan during the Senate debate on health care reform in August 1994. Addressing the Senate floor on August 9, Dole noted that

the American people did not buy the Clinton health plan because it was too complicated, too bureaucratic, too many taxes, too many [government] controls, too many [employer] mandates.... I cannot recall any piece of legislation in my memory that got as much media attention as the President's [national health insurance] bill. It was discussed, debated, and dissected in townhall meetings and kitchen table discussions all across the country.

Despite the fact that the president and first lady had the full use of the White House bully pulpit, and despite the fact that they were both very eloquent, they just did not have a good product. But they tried hard. They went out there every day, but public support went down and down and down.[72]

Dole's remarks concerning the collapse of public support for Clinton's national health insurance plan were echoed by Gramm during the Senate debate on health care reform. Addressing the Senate floor on August 19, Gramm observed that

we have had an opportunity to listen to Bill Clinton ... speak about his health care bill for sixteen months. He has had an opportunity to tell the American people about that health care bill and what it will do.... The President is a great salesman. The First Lady is a great salesman. Their product has not failed to sell because they did not get a chance to sell it. It has not failed to sell because they were not great salesmen. It has failed to sell because it is a bad product....

The President has had an opportunity to be heard, the American people have listened respectfully, but they have come to the conclusion that they do not want [Clinton's national health insurance] plan.[73]

A major reason for the collapse of public support for Clinton's national health insurance plan during the ten months following its introduction was the public relations offensive against the program mounted by the private insurance industry and the Republican Party. As we have seen, the industry and the Republicans argued that the Clinton plan would create a wasteful, costly, inefficient, and bureaucratic health care system operated by the federal government. The polling data show that a majority of the public found this argument at least somewhat convincing.

The private health insurance industry and the Republican Party succeeded in defining the Clinton plan in the most negative light possible, exploiting public suspicion of big government, to argue that any federal intervention in the health care system would result in a reduction in the quality and efficiency of medical care. Since the public tends to believe that the federal government is wasteful and inefficient, they were receptive to the argument that increased federal involvement in the health care system would be harmful. As a result, the insurance industry–Republican argument against federal intrusion into the health care system was sure to strike a responsive chord with the public.

By defining the Clinton plan as an example of harmful federal meddling in the health care marketplace, the private health insurance industry and the Republican Party succeeded in turning public opinion against the president's program, defusing popular pressure for the achievement of comprehensive health care reform. With public support for the Clinton plan sinking, the 103rd Congress saw no immediate and persuasive need to take any action on health care reform. On October 8, 1994, the 103rd Congress adjourned without having taken any action on health care reform. By successfully defining the Clinton plan in the worst possible light, the insurance industry and the Republicans derailed the president's health care reform initiative in the 103rd Congress. With the Republican Party gaining control of both houses of the 104th Congress following the 1994 elections, the failure of the 103rd Congress to pass health care reform legislation destroyed any prospects for the establishment of national health insurance, at least through Clinton's first, and possibly only, term. With the exception of only one Republican, Senator James Jeffords of Vermont, virtually all congressional Republicans are opposed to national health insurance. As a result, national health insurance cannot be established until the Democratic Party regains control of both houses of Congress, making health care reform a political impossibility before 1997.

THE PUBLIC REMAINS SKEPTICAL OF THE NEED FOR HEALTH CARE REFORM

In addition to the arguments made by the private health insurance industry and the Republican Party, the public turned against Clinton's national health insurance plan because a plurality of the population was satisfied with their own coverage and saw no need for a radical overhaul of the health care system. In his speech to a joint session of Congress on September 22, 1993, Clinton attempted to convince the public that the health care system was in a state of disrepair, if not collapse, which required far-reaching reform of the medical system:

Millions of Americans are just one pink slip away from losing their health insurance, and one serious illness away from losing all their savings. Millions more are locked into the jobs they have now just because they or someone in their family has been sick and they have what is called a preexisting condition. And on any given day, over 37 million Americans—most of them working people and their little children—have no health insurance at all.

And in spite of all this, our medical bills are growing at over twice the rate of inflation, and the United States spends over a third more of its income [on health care] than any other nation on Earth. And the gap is growing, causing many of our companies in global competition severe disadvantage.

With the health care system in a severe state of crisis, Clinton urged swift congressional action on medical reform. "There is no excuse for this kind of system," Clinton declared. "We must fix this system and it has to begin with congressional action."[74]

The *USA Today*/CNN/Gallup poll cited earlier showed that an overwhelming majority of the public agreed with Clinton's argument that a health care crisis existed, contrary to Dole's claims that the United States has health care problems, but no crisis. However, despite the fact that an overwhelming majority believed that the health care system was in crisis, less than a third of the public supported a radical overhaul of the medical system, such as that which would result under Clinton's national health insurance plan. The absence of strong public support for the Clinton plan was due to the fact that a substantial share of the population was satisfied with their coverage, and did not see any real and genuine need for comprehensive health care reform.

The *Los Angeles Times* poll cited earlier asked its respondents the following question: "How would you rate the health care coverage for you and your immediate family?" Forty-eight percent of the respondents said their coverage was "essentially good"; 28 percent that it "needs some improvement"; 11 percent that it "needs many improvements"; another 11 percent that it "needs fundamental overhauling"; and 3 percent did not know. The *Los Angeles Times* poll shows that 66 percent of the public were satisfied with their health insurance, and believed, at most, that their coverage needed only some improvement.

In addition to being satisfied, for the most part, with their health insurance, the overwhelming majority of the public did not see any worsening of their coverage. The *Los Angeles Times* poll asked its respondents the following question: "Is the health care coverage you and your family have getting better or worse?" Seventy-one percent of those polled said that their coverage was "staying the same"; 18 percent believed that it was "getting worse"; 8 percent that it was "getting better"; and 3 percent did not know.[75] The *Los Angeles Times* poll shows that 79 percent of the public were enjoying stable, if not improving, coverage.

Because an overwhelming majority of the public was satisfied with their health insurance and did not see their coverage worsening, the population remained skeptical about the need for a radical overhaul of the health care system. During August 31 to September 1, 1994, Yankelovich Partners conducted a poll of 800 adults for *Time* and CNN, who were asked the following question: "What do you think the government should do next regarding health-care reform?" Forty-seven percent of those polled said that the government should "make small changes in our health care system and stop there"; 28 percent believed that the government should "wait [until] next year and try again to make major reforms"; and 20 percent thought that the government should "stop trying to make major reforms, and leave the health system as it is."[76] The *Time*/CNN poll showed that fully 67 percent of the public wanted either modest incremental health care reform, or no reform at all, with only 28 percent still holding out for an overhaul of the medical system.

The *Los Angeles Times* and *Time*/CNN polls show that at least half the public were satisfied with their health insurance, did not believe their coverage was worsening, and while they felt that at least some improvements were needed in the health care system, rejected Clinton's argument that a radical overhaul in the financing of medical services was necessary. As a result, public support for national health insurance was weak, depriving Congress of any urgent and immediate need to establish the program. Unable to convince at least two-thirds of the public of the need for comprehensive health care reform, Clinton's campaign for national health insurance ended up going nowhere.

THE REPUBLICAN PARTY INTRODUCES ITS OWN ALTERNATIVE TO CLINTON'S NATIONAL HEALTH INSURANCE PLAN

In pursuing its campaign against Clinton's national health insurance plan, the Republican Party did not limit itself to simply attacking the president's program. Rather, the Republicans also offered their own alternative to the Clinton plan. On November 22, 1993, Dole joined John Chafee of Rhode Island and eighteen other Republican Senators in introducing a Republican health care reform bill.

The Dole-Chafee bill would have required all uninsured individuals to purchase their own private health insurance by 2005. The federal government would guarantee all uninsured individuals a standard package of health care benefits. It would also impose a financial penalty upon all uninsured individuals by 2005. The penalty would be 20 percent more than the average annual insurance premium in the area in which each uninsured individual resided. Beginning in 1997, the federal government would provide a voucher to all uninsured individuals with incomes of 90 percent below the poverty line to purchase their own private insurance. Additional individuals would qualify for the voucher during 1997– 2005, until it reached all persons with incomes of up to 240 percent of the poverty line. All employers and individuals would be allowed to fully deduct a specified amount of the premiums they pay for private insurance from their taxable income. However, to qualify for a tax deduction, employers and individuals would be required to purchase private plans which provided the federally guaranteed package of health care benefits and extended health care benefits to all persons, regardless of their health status, including coverage for whatever preexisting medical conditions they might suffer from.[77]

The Dole-Chafee bill was a badly flawed measure which stood no chance of passage. The bill failed to include a credible means to finance the purchase of private health insurance for the uninsured, guarantee universal coverage, or contain health care costs.

The Dole-Chafee bill would have financed the cost of vouchers for the uninsured to purchase their own private health insurance through means-testing of premiums under Part B of Medicare and limiting tax subsidies for employer contributions to group plans. Medicare beneficiaries currently pay a flat premium for coverage under Part B of the program. The premium is nonmeans-tested; the rich and nonrich alike pay the same premium.[78] The Dole-Chafee bill would means-test the premium, with wealthy Medicare beneficiaries required to pay a greater premium for their Part B coverage than their poorer counterparts.[79]

Polling data show strong public support for means-testing Medicare premiums. During January 25–26, 1995, the *Los Angeles Times* asked 1,226 adults the following question: "Do you favor or oppose requiring elderly people with above-average incomes to pay a higher Medicare premium than the current $46.10 a month?" Sixty-five percent of those surveyed supported requiring the wealthier elderly to pay higher premiums for their Medicare benefits; 31 percent opposed this; and 4 percent had no opinion.

However, the *Los Angeles Times* poll found that support for means-testing Medicare premiums was greater among the nonelderly than the elderly. Sixty-nine percent of those surveyed aged eighteen to sixty-four supported requiring wealthy elderly individuals to pay more for their Medicare benefits than their poorer counterparts; by contrast, only 50 percent of those questioned aged sixty-five or older supported this. Fully 41 percent of elderly respondents surveyed opposed means-testing Medicare benefits, compared to only 29 percent of the nonelderly.[80]

The elderly are one of the most well organized and politically powerful constituencies in the nation. The major interest group representing the elderly, the American Association of Retired Persons (AARP), is one of the most formidable lobbying organizations in Washington. The AARP has taken a hard line against any reforms in Medicare, such as means-testing any part of the program. In response to Republican congressional efforts to reduce Medicare spending, on April 7, 1995, the AARP announced that it would oppose "severe cuts or . . . dismantling Medicare as we know it."[81]

Through their capacity to form a massive voting bloc, the elderly have the power to defeat any member of Congress who might attempt to means-test any part of Medicare. The fact that over 40 percent of the elderly opposed means-testing Medicare premiums, as called for in the Dole-Chafee bill, rendered such a measure politically impossible. Elderly opponents of means-testing Medicare premiums had the numbers and power to organize and defeat any member of Congress who supported such a measure. While the nonelderly generally supported means-testing Medicare premiums, they lacked the organizational power of the elderly; and they could not serve as an effective counterweight to the opposition to such a measure which was sure to come from a substantial segment of senior citizens. As a result, the provisions in the Dole-Chafee bill requiring the means-testing of Medicare premiums had no chance of passage.

In addition to means-testing part of Medicare, the Dole-Chafee bill would finance the cost of vouchers to low-income uninsured individuals to purchase their own private health insurance by limiting the tax deduction for employer-provided health care benefits. Employer contributions to group insurance for working families are currently fully tax deductible.[82] The Dole-Chafee bill would limit the tax deduction for those contributions to a certain, but unspecified, premium. Any amount employers spend on group insurance in excess of this limit would be taxed as income.[83] In 1994 the federal government spent $74 billion in tax subsidies for employer contributions to group insurance for working families, representing 37.5 percent of the $197.1 billion business spent on health care benefits in 1992.[84] By imposing a limit on the tax deduction employers may receive for the cost of their group insurance, the Dole-Chafee bill would reduce the tax subsidies provided to insured working families, with the savings used to extend coverage to the uninsured.

However, many, if not most, employers take advantage of the tax deduction for group health insurance to provide their working families with generous health care benefits packages. Under the Dole-Chafee bill, those employers would have to reduce the health care benefits they provide their working families to assure that their insurance premiums did not exceed the limit to enable them to qualify for a full tax deduction. Employers would be unlikely to provide their working families any additional health care benefits which would not be fully tax deductible. Accordingly, the Dole-Chafee bill would result in a reduction in health care benefits for working families.

Working families, who represent the overwhelming majority of the electorate, will not accept any reduction in their health care benefits, which would result from the imposition of a limit on the tax deduction for employer-provided health insurance. As a result, substantial public opposition exists to the imposition of any such limit. During May 12–13, 1993, Yankelovich Partners conducted a poll of 1,000 adults for *Time* and CNN. The poll asked its respondents whether they either supported or opposed seven health care reform measures, including "requiring workers who receive health benefits from their employers to pay income tax on those benefits." Sixty-three percent of those polled opposed taxing employer-paid health care benefits; 30 percent supported such a measure. Public opposition to taxing employer-paid health care benefits was stronger than for any of the six other medical reform measures contained in the *Time*/CNN poll, with the exception only of requiring the elderly to pay more for their private health insurance than the nonelderly.[85]

Given the existence of strong public opposition to the imposition of any limit on the tax deduction for employer-provided health insurance, the electorate would be sure to vote out of office any member of Congress who supported legislation, like the Dole-Chafee bill, which included such a measure. As a result, any member of Congress who voted for such a measure would commit political suicide. Accordingly, few, if any, members of Congress were likely to do so, including the Senate Republican cosponsors of the Dole-Chafee bill. Its provision to reduce health care benefits for working families to provide coverage for the uninsured was not a politically serious or realistic proposal to finance an expansion in the insurance system.

Senate Republicans were not the first group to grant serious consideration to limiting the tax deduction for employer-provided health insurance. The president's Task Force on National Health Reform also considered making such a recommendation during the early months of the Clinton administration. However, organized labor rejected the imposition of any limit on the tax deduction for employer-provided health insurance. Unionized workers have among the most generous health care benefits available to the labor force. The imposition of a limit on the tax deduction for employer-provided health insurance would result in a substantial cutback in health care benefits for unionized workers. As a result, organized labor made clear its opposition to the imposition of any such limit to the Clinton administration. As Dan Goodgame notes, organized labor's opposition was sufficient to prevent the administration from granting serious consideration to recommending the imposition of such a limit.

When union bosses, led by AFL-CIO president Lane Kirkland, got wind that the White House was even discussing limits on the tax subsidy for health insurance, they met privately with Mrs. Clinton and told her that labor's support for health reform—deemed essential by the Democrats—was at risk. The First Lady then sent word to her [health care policy advisers]: There's no sense even talking about the tax subsidy. The issue has thus become known as the "third rail" of health care politics—as deadly as a high-voltage train track.[86]

In addition to unionized workers, the imposition of a limit on the tax deduction for employer-provided health insurance would undermine the interests of big business. Large corporations generally provide generous coverage to their working families. Such coverage allows large corporations to attract the best and most highly skilled workers, who see group insurance as an important fringe benefit in determining their place of employment. Large corporations are determined to continue providing their working families attractive health care benefits packages. They insist that the health care benefits they provide be fully tax deductible, and are opposed to paying any taxes on the group insurance they extend, regardless of how extravagant they might be.

As a result, big business opposes any plan, such as that contained in the Dole-Chafee bill, which would limit the tax deduction for employer-provided health insurance. Accordingly, big business made clear its opposition to the imposition of any such limit at the very outset of the Clinton presidency. On February 8, 1993, the Employers Council on Flexible Compensation, an organization representing a number of large corporations, joined the American Federation of Labor–Congress of Industrial Organizations (AFL-CIO) in forming the Coalition to Preserve Health Care Benefits. The purpose of the coalition was to lobby against the imposition of any limit on the tax deduction for employer-provided health insurance which Clinton might recommend.[87]

The Clinton administration was determined to avoid antagonizing business and labor, which jointly exert substantial political clout on Capitol Hill. Business and labor would have used their clout to defeat any health care reform bill which limited the tax deduction for employer-provided health insurance. Since no health care reform bill imposing this limit stood any chance of passage, the Clinton administration quickly dropped any consideration of recommending such a measure.

In addition to lacking a politically viable financing mechanism, the Dole-Chafee bill would not guarantee universal health insurance coverage. True, the bill would provide vouchers for individuals with incomes up to 240 percent of the poverty line to purchase their own private insurance; this upper limit on income was roughly equivalent to $30,000 for a family of four. However, individuals not qualifying for a voucher would likely be unable to purchase private insurance, as is the case now. In 1994 29 percent of the uninsured had annual incomes of $30,000 or over.[88] Since they would not qualify for any vouchers to purchase their own private insurance, and, for the most part, lack the financial means to purchase their own health care benefits, the nearly one-third of the uninsured with incomes of $30,000 or over would remain without coverage under the Dole-Chafee bill.

Perhaps the worst failing of the Dole-Chafee bill is that it included no effective health care cost-containment measures. By reducing financial barriers impeding access to health care among most of the uninsured, the bill would raise patient utilization of medical services, adding to the soaring cost. Since the provision of coverage to the uninsured would be achieved through the extension of vouchers, the bill would raise federal spending for health care, adding to the swollen budget deficit. By failing to include any effective cost-containment measures, the bill would create an economically and fiscally unviable means to provide the uninsured coverage, and it stood no chance of passage.

The only health care cost-containment measure of any kind contained in the Dole-Chafee bill was malpractice insurance reform. The United States has more malpractice suits per physician, its courts provide a higher average malpractice award, and its doctors pay higher average malpractice insurance premiums than in any other nation.[89] To protect themselves against malpractice suits, doctors practice defensive medicine. Many, if not most, doctors provide more services than they otherwise would. This reduces the possibility that they will be sued by failing to provide services their patients may subsequently claim they needed, but were denied.[90]

The high cost of malpractice insurance combined with the widespread practice of defensive medicine drives up health care expenses. Doctors pass on the high cost of malpractice insurance to third-party payers or patients in the form of excessive physician fees. By inflating the amount of services doctors provide, the practice of defensive medicine drives up overall health care costs.

The Dole-Chafee bill would reform the wasteful and inefficient malpractice insurance system by requiring participants in a malpractice case to submit to alternative dispute resolution procedures before going to court. This would serve to avoid the substantial costs associated with malpractice litigation. In addition, doctors following the medical practice guidelines laid down by the newly established Agency for Health Care Policy and Research would be allowed to defend their actions in any malpractice case brought against them. This would make it difficult for patients to win malpractice cases against such doctors. Finally, punitive damage awards for each malpractice case would be limited to $250,000.[91] This would reduce the overall amount paid in malpractice damage awards and curtail the financial incentives for patients and their lawyers to file malpractice suits in the hope that they might win exorbitant settlements.

With fewer malpractice suits going to court, patients having greater difficulty winning their cases, and courts awarding lower damage settlements, the cost of malpractice insurance would decline under the Dole-Chafee bill, allowing doctors to reduce their fees. By making it more difficult to take a malpractice case to court and for patients to win their lawsuits, the bill would relieve doctors of the need to practice defensive medicine. This would result in a reduction in the amount of unnecessary health care services associated with the practice of defensive medicine, leading to a decline in medical costs.

However, the Dole-Chafee bill's emphasis on malpractice insurance reform as a means to contain escalating health care costs is misplaced. The costs associated with the malpractice insurance system are minor and insignificant sources of soaring health care expenses. In 1990 malpractice insurance premiums represented only 0.8 percent of the total cost of health care. The practice of defensive medicine accounted for only 2.3 percent of health care costs.[92] Even if the Dole-Chafee bill eliminated the entire cost of health care associated with the malpractice insurance system, the measure would succeed in reducing America's total medical expenses by only 3.1 percent.

The Dole-Chafee bill promised to address one of the most minor and insignificant sources of rising health care costs—the expenses associated with malpractice insurance—while ignoring the most important inflationary factors. The bill would do nothing to curb the proliferation and excessive utilization of costly medical technology, or to reduce the soaring cost of hospital care, physician services, and prescription drugs. By providing most of the uninsured access to health care, the bill would raise patient utilization of medical services, driving up their cost. And yet, the bill included no effective measures to contain the increase in health care costs which would result from the expansion of public access to medical services.

Given the fact that the Dole-Chafee bill was a badly flawed measure which stood no chance of passage, why did twenty Republican Senators led by their party leader decide to sponsor it? The answer is that the Republican Party recognized that it could not limit itself in the debate on health care reform to simply attacking Clinton's national health insurance plan. The *Los Angeles Times* poll cited earlier shows that a majority of the public wanted at least some improvements in their coverage, with practically the entire population believing that there should also be at least some improvements in the insurance system.

As a result, the Republicans recognized that they could not maintain their credibility with the public by merely voicing their opposition to Clinton's national health insurance plan. Rather, they had to introduce an alternative of their own to the Clinton plan to satisfy the public's desire for at least some reform of the health care system. Republican members of Congress risked defeat the next time they ran for reelection if they appeared to be preventing health care reform altogether. To insulate themselves from the political damage they would suffer from opposing health care reform, the Republicans had to appear to the public to be working for an overhaul of the medical system. Accordingly, Republican senators introduced the Dole-Chafee bill.

However, the Republicans remained opposed to health care reform since any overhaul of the medical system threatened to impose more taxes and restrict access to health care among the party's affluent and well-insured members, as we have seen. As a result, the Dole-Chafee bill was designed to allow the Republicans to represent themselves to the public as a party committed to health care reform, when in fact the opposite was the case. The bill actually gave the Republicans a credible basis to prevent health care reform. They used the bill to attempt to convince the public that they wanted health care reform. In the meantime, the Republicans made clear that they would accept nothing more than the politically and economically unviable bill Dole and Chafee introduced. They opposed the kind of politically and economically feasible health care reform Clinton's national health insurance plan would establish.

In the end, the Dole-Chafee bill allowed the Republican Party to have it both ways. The bill served as a means to identify the Republicans with the politically popular issue of health care reform. In the meantime, they acted to prevent health care reform by refusing to accept anything more than the badly flawed and grossly inadequate bill introduced by Dole and Chafee. The Dole-Chafee bill was nothing more than a cynical and deceptive ploy by the Republicans to develop a credible basis for preventing health care reform by creating the false appearance that the party was actually working to overhaul the medical system, when, in fact, the opposite was the case. By appearing to be sponsoring a health care reform initiative of their own, Republican members of Congress could prevent any overhaul of the medical system without the risk of being voted out of office by an electorate which was now demanding at least some improvements in the financing of health care services.

CONCLUSION

Clinton's national health insurance plan met powerful opposition from the Republican Party, which mounted an intense and unrelenting public relations offensive against the president's program in the months following its introduction. Republicans opposed the Clinton plan because it threatened to impose a tax increase and restrict access to health care among the party's affluent and well-insured membership base. Republicans attempted to mobilize public opposition to the Clinton plan by arguing that it would create a wasteful, inefficient, and bureaucratic health care system operated by the federal government. Clinton attempted to counter this argument by claiming that his national health insurance plan would reduce bureaucracy and paperwork and generate the savings required to provide coverage to the uninsured without any tax increase.

Polling data show that the public was unpersuaded by Clinton's defense of his national health insurance plan. A plurality of the public believed that the Clinton plan would result in additional bureaucracy and paperwork and generate no savings within the health care system. As a result, an overwhelming majority of the public believed that Clinton could only finance coverage for the uninsured through a tax increase. Moreover, roughly half the public was satisfied with their own insurance and rejected Clinton's argument that a radical overhaul of the health care system was necessary, with a plurality of the population opposing the president's program altogether.

By July 1994, the public had become skeptical of the need for health care reform—with a majority of the people satisfied with their insurance, wanting improvements, but no radical overhaul of the health care system, and believing that they would be the same, if not worse off, under Clinton's national health insurance plan. True, a substantial minority of the public were dissatisfied with their coverage, demanded comprehensive health care reform, and were convinced that they stood to gain from the Clinton plan. However, public dissatisfaction with the existing health care system and support for comprehensive medical reform remained weak.

With the public skeptical about the need for health care reform, popular pressure for national health insurance was weak. As a result, Congress saw no clear and compelling need to establish the program. In the end, the Clinton plan fell victim to a variety of political factors: the ability of the Republicans to make false, though effective, arguments against the Clinton plan, which the public found at least somewhat convincing; popular satisfaction with their own coverage; the lack of public support for a radical overhaul of the health care system; and Congress's own reluctance to establish a national health insurance program because it was opposed by the health care industry, which served as an important source of financial support for lawmakers. With both the public and Congress disinclined to support national health insurance, prospects for its establishment rapidly vanished.

By October 1994, Clinton's health care reform initiative had ended in complete failure, with the 103rd Congress having adjourned without taking action on national health insurance. With the 104th Congress under firm Republican control, the failure of the 103rd Congress to pass a national health insurance bill assured that no legislative action on health care reform would be taken during Clinton's first, and possibly only, term. The failure of health care reform—the most important single item on Clinton's domestic policy agenda—was a stinging setback to the president, who had spent much of his time and energy on the issue during the first two years of his first term. It dealt a severe, perhaps fatal, blow to Clinton's carefully cultivated image as a skillful leader in domestic policy, capable of dealing with the most pressing issues on the home front, which had been neglected during the Reagan-Bush era, not the least of which was the health care crisis.

Chapter 6

Business Opposes Clinton's National Health Insurance Plan

[Clinton's national health insurance plan] gives the government bureaucracy the power to choose our doctors for us. It also sacrifices quality. We should be able to make our own choices and pick our own doctors. We would give up [that] freedom under Clinton's plan. Any purported benefit to small business is outweighed by greater negative consequences to our society [under the Clinton plan].[1]

JoAnne Stewart, head of a small business.

With the exception of the health care industry, perhaps no single segment of society had more to gain, or lose, from health care reform than the business community. Business's stake in health care reform derives from one overriding fact: A majority of the public are insured by their employers, most of whom are in the private sector, as we saw in Chapter 2. In 1992 52.6 percent of the public were insured by their employers. Most of the cost of the group health insurance working families receive is financed by their employers. In 1993 78.4 percent of the cost of group insurance was.[2] Because employers provide most of the public group insurance and finance most of its cost, business bears a disproportionate share of the financial burden for the cost of health care. In 1992 business financed 24.7 percent of the cost of health care, with the government funding 43.6 percent, patients 20.8 percent, workers 6.8 percent, and self-insured individuals 4.1 percent.[3] Like the rest of society, business has been hard hit by soaring health care costs. The average group insurance premium per worker financed by contributions from both employers and employees rose from $1,724 in 1985 to $4,000 in 1992.[4]

Because business finances a quarter of the cost of health care, corporations have the potential to play a critical role in influencing the development of medical policy. Should firms choose not to continue providing their working families group health insurance, then employed households would have to find some other means to secure coverage. However, since most working families are nonelderly and able-bodied, they do not qualify for Medicare, which restricts coverage to the elderly and disabled. Similarly, since most working families are middle-class, they would not qualify for Medicaid, which limits coverage to the poor. In addition, most working families cannot afford the cost of private insurance, which is beyond the financial reach of all but the most affluent individuals. Unable to qualify for either Medicare or Medicaid, or to afford the cost of private insurance, most working families would have no alternative but to become uninsured in the absence of group coverage from their employers.

As a result, any termination by firms of the group insurance they provide their working families would add tens of millions of individuals to the ranks of the uninsured. In the absence of any coverage, most of those newly uninsured individuals would be unable to pay the cost of their health care. Accordingly, they would receive uncompensated care from charitable hospitals when they fell ill, resulting in tens of billions of additional dollars the health care system would have to spend on charity care for the uninsured. Many doctors and hospitals would go bankrupt from having to provide uncompensated care to those millions of newly uninsured individuals, leaving thousands of communities without adequate health care facilities and personnel. The termination by firms of the group insurance they provide their working families would result in the collapse of the health care system.

BUSINESS THROWS ITS WEIGHT AGAINST CLINTON'S NATIONAL HEALTH INSURANCE PLAN

Since the survival of the health care system depends upon the willingness of firms to continue providing their working families group health insurance, business has the potential to play a dominant role in influencing the debate on medical reform which has occurred during the 1990s. Business used its influence to defeat Clinton's national health insurance plan. True, business was not united in its opposition to the Clinton plan. Big business was divided over this issue, with some large corporations supporting national health insurance, while others opposed it. In the meantime, small business was practically united in its opposition to the program.

The willingness of at least some large corporations to support national health insurance, coupled with the existence of solid small business opposition to the program, results from the disparity between big and small business in their provision of group coverage to their working families. As we saw in Chapter 2, practically all large corporations provide their working families group insurance, though some of their employees choose not to accept such coverage, since they are required to finance at least some of its cost themselves. By contrast, many, if not most, small businesses do not provide their working families group insurance. This is due to the fact that group insurance is practically unaffordable for small business, for reasons explained in Chapter 2. As a result, while most working families employed by large corporations are insured, many working families employed by small business are not.

Uninsured individuals must often rely upon the uncompensated care they receive from charitable hospitals when they fall ill. Hospitals finance the cost of uncompensated care they provide the uninsured by raising their charges for privately insured patients: They shift the cost of extending health care to the uninsured onto privately insured individuals, which is reflected in higher premiums. In 1994 businesses, mostly large corporations, and their workers paid $30 billion in higher premiums to cover the cost of extending uncompensated care to the uninsured, an amount which represented 11.3 percent of the $265 billion companies and their employees spent on group insurance in 1992.[5]

Cost shifting hurts big business. Large corporations, which finance most of the cost of private insurance, must pay for the uncompensated care received by uninsured individuals, over 40 percent of whom are employed by small business. Accordingly, large corporations finance, not only the cost of private insurance for their working families, but the expense of uncompensated care for the uninsured, who are largely employed by small business. This allows small business to largely escape financial responsibility for providing their working families group insurance.

The health insurance system imposes an onerous financial burden upon large corporations, while allowing small business to escape their responsibilities for financing the cost of private coverage. It shifts the cost of private insurance from small to big business—forcing large corporations to assume responsibility for financing the cost of health care, not only for their own working families, but those employed by small businesses which refuse to provide their employed households group insurance. As a result, many large corporations support, and in some cases are demanding, the establishment of a national health insurance program, in which the federal government requires all employers, especially small businesses, to provide their working families group insurance. By guaranteeing the uninsured coverage, national health insurance would relieve large corporations of the substantial financial burden they currently assume of providing uncompensated care to those with no coverage.

However, national health insurance would require small businesses to assume financial responsibility for providing their working families group coverage, which many of them do not offer. This would add to the business costs of small firms. The mandate Clinton's national health insurance plan would impose requiring employers to provide their working families group insurance would have compelled businesses, most of them small firms which currently do not offer any health care benefits, to spend $29.5 billion in 1993 to do so. Small companies believed that any employer mandate, such as that contained in the Clinton plan, requiring them to provide their working families group insurance would impose a crushing financial burden on small firms, driving many, if not most of them, out of business. As a result, small business was practically united in

their opposition to the Clinton plan or any other national health insurance program which required them to assume financial responsibility for the cost of
health care for their working families.

By relieving large corporations of the financial burden of providing the uninsured uncompensated care, big business stood to gain from national health
insurance, as we have seen. However, many large corporations joined small
business in opposing the program. National health insurance would require employers to provide a minimum package of health care benefits, and finance most
of its cost. As we saw in Chapter 2, Clinton's national health insurance plan
would have required all employers to provide their working families group insurance, extending a minimum package of health care benefits, and to finance
80 percent of its cost.

As we also saw in Chapter 2, businesses acted to reduce their health care
costs during the 1980s by slashing the coverage they provided their working
families, requiring them to shoulder a greater share of the financial burden for
their medical services. Clinton's national health insurance plan would have re-
versed this trend, requiring many businesses which provide their working families group insurance to offer a more generous package of health care benefits
than they currently do. The Clinton plan would have required businesses which
provide group insurance to spend an additional $23 billion in 1993 to pay for
a more comprehensive package of health care benefits mandated by the president's program than they currently extend their working families.[6]

The Clinton plan or any other national health insurance program promised to
require many firms providing group coverage to spend more to extend their
working families a more generous package of health care benefits than they
currently do. This would have required those firms, which were mostly large,
to bear a greater share of the financial burden for the cost of the health care of
their working families than is currently the case, raising their business costs. To
prevent this from occurring, most large corporations broke ranks with big business supporters of national health insurance and joined small firms in opposing
the program.

As a result, the business community was deeply divided over national health
insurance. Big business was split between those large corporations which supported national health insurance as a means to relieve themselves of the financial
burden of providing the uninsured uncompensated care, and those which opposed the program because it would require them to provide a more generous
package of health care benefits than they currently do, raising their business
costs. Small firms remained adamantly opposed to the program because it would
require them to provide their working families group insurance, which many of
them currently fail to do, also raising their business costs.

However, by 1994 most large corporations had concluded that they stood to
lose from health care reform. By requiring employers to provide their working
families group coverage, a national health insurance program would relieve large
corporations of the financial burden of having to finance uncompensated care

for the uninsured. However, a national health insurance program, such as that sponsored by Clinton, would also require large corporations to provide their working families a more generous package of health care benefits than they currently do. Most large corporations concluded that the cost of providing their working families the federally mandated package of health care benefits contained in the Clinton plan would exceed the expense of the uncompensated care for the uninsured they finance under the current medical system.

As a result, large corporations concluded that the current health care system, despite its flaws, was preferable to the national health insurance program which would have been established by Clinton. Accordingly, most large corporations joined a united small business community in opposing Clinton's national health insurance plan. With business determined to continue assuming financial responsibility for providing working families group insurance, and with corporate America almost solidly united against health care reform, Congress saw no urgent need to establish a national health insurance program. With Congress unwilling to establish a national health insurance program in the face of mounting business opposition, Clinton's health care reform initiative quickly collapsed.

THE AUTOMOBILE INDUSTRY THROWS ITS SUPPORT BEHIND NATIONAL HEALTH INSURANCE

As we have seen, businesses were by no means unanimous in their opposition to national health insurance; some bastions of support for the program existed within corporate America. Perhaps the strongest support for national health insurance within the business community came from the automobile industry. Detroit's support for the program was based upon the fact that perhaps no industry bore a greater financial burden for the cost of health care for their working families than the Big Three automakers—General Motors, Ford, and Chrysler. The United Auto Workers (UAW) has made health care benefits a top priority in its collective bargaining with the Big Three automakers. UAW members enjoy among the most comprehensive health care benefits in the labor force. The Big Three automakers provide UAW members comprehensive private insurance coverage, with practically no patient cost-sharing requirements of any kind, including no premiums, deductibles, or coinsurance charges, and only minimal copayments. This differs from other workers, who enjoy far less comprehensive coverage, requiring them to pay substantial patient cost-sharing requirements, in the form of premiums, deductibles, coinsurance charges, and copayments.[7]

Because they generally provide their working families substantially more coverage than other companies do, the Big Three automakers spend a significantly greater share of their payroll on group health insurance than the business community as a whole. In 1993 the automobile industry paid 19 percent of its payroll for group insurance, compared with 6.6 percent for the business community as a whole.[8] General Motors paid $3.7 billion for health care for its working families, representing $1,000 for every car the company manufactured; Ford paid

$1.5 billion, or $900 per car; and Chrysler paid $815 million, or $1,100 per car.[9]

As is the case with all employers who provide their working families group health insurance, much of the cost of health care the Big Three automakers pay for their employed households actually goes to finance the provision of uncompensated care for the uninsured. In 1992 28 percent of the cost of health care the Big Three automakers paid for their working families, representing $1.7 billion, went to finance the cost of uncompensated care.[10] By 1992, cost shifting—in which part of the premiums firms pay to provide group insurance for their working families is used to finance uncompensated care for the uninsured—had become a massive financial burden upon the automobile industry. As a result, the industry became an active supporter of national health insurance. As Harold Poling, chairman and chief executive officer of Ford Motor Company, put it, "If we want to be globally competitive, we can no longer afford to pay for companies that don't cover their workers."[11]

By requiring all employers to provide their working families group coverage, national health insurance would compel all firms to assume financial responsibility for the health care of their employed households. This would relieve businesses which extend their employed households coverage, like the Big Three automakers, of the financial burden of delivering uncompensated care to uninsured individuals who currently do not receive health care benefits from their employers. With all working families insured, the program would eliminate the need for cost shifting, in which part of the premiums firms pay for group insurance for their working families is used to finance uncompensated care for the uninsured. Accordingly, national health insurance promised to relieve the Big Three automakers of the $1.7 billion they pay for uncompensated care, providing the automobile industry a massive financial stake in establishing the program.

The leading voice in the automobile industry's support for national health insurance was Harold Poling. On December 14, 1992, Poling appeared before a conference of experts which Clinton convened in Little Rock to provide him advice on the development of an economic policy the president-elect intended to introduce after he entered the White House. Poling delivered a presentation at the conference in which he appealed to Clinton to make health care reform a top priority of his presidency.

In his presentation, Poling announced his support for national health insurance, declaring that "it's unacceptable that 37 million people have no health care coverage."[12] Poling also urged the establishment of stringent health care cost-containment measures, warning that soaring medical costs were pricing an increasing share of the public out of the insurance market. "With health care costs in the United States approaching $3,000 for every man, woman, and child, neither small nor large companies nor individuals can afford to continue their health care," Poling declared. "Purchasers, providers, and government must cooperate to contain these growing costs."[13]

Poling informed Clinton that Ford's health care costs had risen from 6 percent of payroll in 1970 to 20 percent in 1991, increasing from $144 million to $1.3 billion during the same period.[14] Health care now represented Ford's single largest cost. "Ford spends as much on health care as it does on steel," Poling noted. "Health care is our biggest supplier."[15]

Poling warned Clinton that rising health care costs posed a grave financial and competitive threat to Ford. He noted that America's three major international competitors in the automobile industry—Japan, Germany, and Canada—had substantially lower health care costs than the United States. Because they pay less for the health care of their working families, the Japanese, German, and Canadian automobile industries are able to sell their cars at lower cost than their American competitors, providing the three industrial nations a substantial competitive advantage over the United States in the international automobile market.[16] "We have reached a point where we cannot afford double digit [health care] cost increases," Poling declared. "Our health care costs jeopardize our ability to compete, maintain existing jobs, and create additional jobs."[17]

Poling concluded his presentation by urging Clinton to secure the establishment of a national health insurance program, which would guarantee universal coverage while containing health care costs. He emphasized that health care reform was required, not just to guarantee all Americans health security, but to maintain America's competitiveness in the global marketplace. "We can no longer delay in assuring that [all] Americans have access to affordable health care and we must attack this serious problem [of soaring medical costs which is negatively] impacting U.S. industry's ability to compete globally," Poling declared.[18]

The automobile industry enthusiastically applauded Clinton for introducing his national health insurance plan in his address to a joint session of Congress on September 22, 1993. Following Clinton's address, Poling issued a statement urging quick congressional action on health care reform:

Persistently rising health care costs have eroded the international competitiveness of American business. Credit should go to President Clinton—his [health care reform] plan is the most comprehensive and far-reaching ever offered. Now the President and the Congress, Republicans and Democrats working together, need to pass a plan that provides universal coverage for all Americans, maintains quality, and brings our spiraling health care costs under control. The American people want health-care reform to be analyzed, debated fully and most importantly acted upon promptly. The country cannot wait any longer.[19]

Poling's call for quick congressional action on health care reform was echoed by Jack Smith, chairman and chief executive officer of General Motors Corporation. Following Clinton's address on September 22, 1993, Smith issued a statement of his own urging the establishment of national health insurance. "General Motors commends the President for his health care reform proposal,"

Smith declared. "The country will benefit from having a health care system that covers all of its citizens, reduces the rate of increase in health care costs, and allocates costs fairly throughout our economy."[20]

In their public statements issued following Clinton's address, Poling and Smith urged legislative action on health care reform, but stopped short of specifically endorsing the president's national health insurance program. However, on July 22, 1994, the automobile industry moved closer to an outright endorsement of the Clinton plan by announcing their support of its most controversial element—the requirement that employers provide their working families group insurance.[21] As we have seen, a substantial share of the health care costs paid by the Big Three automakers for their working families is used to finance the provision of uncompensated care for the uninsured, most of whom work for businesses which do not provide their employed households group insurance. By requiring employers to provide their working families group insurance, the federal government would relieve the Big Three automakers of the substantial financial burden they are forced to assume in financing uncompensated care for uninsured working families. As Andrew H. Card, Jr., president of the Automobile Manufacturers Association, put it, in announcing the automobile industry's endorsement of a federal mandate for employers to provide their working families group insurance, "We have moved aggressively to control our health costs, but we cannot control health costs shifted to us because of those [firms] who do not pay their fair share [for health care]."[22]

CLINTON FAILS TO WIN BUSINESS SUPPORT FOR HIS NATIONAL HEALTH INSURANCE PROGRAM

A major element of the Clinton administration's strategy to secure passage of its national health insurance plan was to win business support for the program. By requiring many, if not most, employers to provide their working families a more generous package of health care benefits than they currently do, the Clinton plan would have added to the costs of business, as we have seen, especially among small firms which do not extend their employed households group insurance. By imposing additional costs upon firms, the Clinton plan threatened to provoke opposition from business, which is among the best organized and politically powerful interest groups in Washington.

Business had the power to use its substantial political clout to kill Clinton's national health insurance plan on Capitol Hill. Accordingly, prospects for passage of the Clinton plan were dependent upon the president's ability to win business support for the program. During 1993 to 1994, Clinton worked feverishly to win business support for his national health insurance plan, especially among large corporations.

However, Clinton failed in his campaign to win business support for his national health insurance plan. Support for the Clinton plan, or any other national health insurance program, within the business community was weak, with the notable exception of the automobile industry, which remained one of the few ardent corporate backers of comprehensive health care reform. The overwhelming majority of the business community were adamantly opposed to national health insurance. Most large corporations opposed the program because they feared it would require them to provide their working families a more generous package of health care benefits than they currently do, raising their business costs. Small business remained united in their opposition to national health insurance, since many, if not most, small firms do not provide their working families group coverage but would be required do so under the program, raising their costs substantially.

During 1993 and 1994, the three major interest groups representing the business community—the National Federation of Independent Businesses (NFIB), the Business Roundtable, and the Chamber of Commerce—announced their opposition to Clinton's national health insurance plan. Leading business opposition to the plan was the NFIB, the largest interest group representing small firms, with 600,000 members. On August 16, 1993, John Motley, vice president of the NFIB, addressed a meeting of the National Governors' Association in Tulsa, which Clinton also spoke to afterward. Motley denounced the Clinton plan's mandate that employers provide their working families group health insurance. He warned that employer mandates would force many small businesses, which cannot afford to provide their working families group insurance, into bankruptcy, resulting in massive job losses.[23]

To support Motley's claims, in 1993 the NFIB estimated that a federal mandate requiring employers to provide their working families group health insurance would cost 1.5 million jobs. The NFIB's claim of massive job losses stemming from employer mandates is a familiar charge made by Dole and Gramm in leading the Republican opposition to Clinton's national health insurance plan, as we saw in the previous chapter. However, we showed that those claims were false: that a federal mandate requiring employers to provide their working families group insurance—at least the one which would be imposed under the Clinton plan—would have a neutral effect on the labor market, ranging from marginal job losses to modest job gains. By curbing the growth in health care costs, the Clinton plan would generate substantial savings in medical expenses for businesses, which they could use to hire more workers. Moreover, businesses which currently do not provide their working families group insurance would not go bankrupt if required to assume financial responsibility for the health care of their employed households, as Motley claimed. Rather, as we saw in Chapter 2, those businesses would receive federal subsidies to enable them to afford group insurance for their working families under the Clinton plan.

By curbing the growth of health care costs, Clinton's national health insurance would reduce the financial burden which businesses currently assume in providing their working families group health insurance. In the meantime, the Clinton plan would provide federal subsidies to allow businesses which currently do not extend their working families group insurance to offer such benefits, without having to suffer any financial hardship. Given those facts, it is difficult to find any evidence that a federal mandate requiring employers to provide their working families group insurance, as envisaged under the Clinton plan, would result in the massive job losses which the NFIB and congressional Republicans claim would occur.

The NFIB's opposition to Clinton's national health insurance plan was not unexpected, since the interest group represents small businesses, many of which do not provide their working families group coverage. Among all employers, small business had the most to lose from the Clinton plan, since it was directed against small firms, which would be required to provide their working families group insurance, a financial burden which many small companies were determined to avoid. Indeed, a 1993 Gallup poll found that 85 percent of small business owners surveyed opposed the Clinton plan's requirement that employers provide their working families group insurance and finance 80 percent of its cost.[24] The results of the Gallup poll are consistent with the fact that many, if not most, small businesses did not provide their working families group insurance, and were determined to avoid having to assume this financial responsibility for fear that it might drive them into bankruptcy. As a result, the NFIB's opposition to Clinton's national health insurance plan was hardly a setback to the administration, which fully expected small business to fight the president's program.

Instead, Clinton attempted to mobilize big-business support for his national health insurance plan. Unlike small business, practically all large corporations provide their working families group insurance. Accordingly, large corporations would not be affected by the Clinton plan's requirement that employers provide their working families group insurance.

True, Clinton's national health insurance plan would have required many, if not most, large corporations to provide their working families a more generous package of health care benefits than they currently do, raising their business costs, as we have seen. However, by providing coverage to the uninsured, the Clinton plan would have also relieved large corporations of the burden they currently assume in financing uncompensated care for those without coverage. As a result, the Clinton plan would have imposed little, if any, additional financial costs on big business. Given the fact that the Clinton plan posed no real financial threat to large corporations, the administration hoped that it would be able to win big business's support for the president's program.

Clinton attempted to mobilize big-business support for his national health insurance plan by arguing that, by guaranteeing universal coverage, his program would relieve large corporations of the onerous financial burden they currently assume in funding uncompensated care for the uninsured. The elimination of cost-shifting embedded in the current health care system would result in a substantial reduction in corporate medical costs. In his speech to the Business Roundtable on June 21, 1994, Clinton warned corporate chief executives that, in the absence of comprehensive health care reform, large companies would be saddled with the financial burden of financing the cost of uncompensated care for America's growing uninsured population.

The people . . . who are shifting [health care] costs to you are businesses and employers who do not have health insurance but who get health care. They are shifting costs to you. . . .
Keep in mind, in the last three years, 3 million American workers have lost their health insurance. There are 3 million more Americans without health coverage today than there were three years ago. You are paying for them in cost-shifting.
So unless we have comprehensive reform, you will be put in the position of someday coming to the end of how much you can do managing your health care costs on your own. . . . And you will be facing the cost-shift coming at you . . . from the increasing numbers of employers who don't provide any coverage.[25]

However, Clinton's plea for big-business support for his national health insurance plan fell on deaf ears. On February 2, 1994 Clinton's efforts to win big-business support was dealt a fatal blow when the Business Roundtable announced its opposition to his national health insurance plan. Representing 225 of the largest corporations in the United States, the Business Roundtable is the dominant big-business organization in this nation.[26] By announcing its opposition to the Clinton plan, the Business Roundtable destroyed any prospect that Clinton might win big-business support for his program. Clinton's speech to the Business Roundtable on June 21 represented a last-ditch attempt to persuade the interest group to reverse itself and support his national health insurance plan before Congress took up the issue of health care reform later that summer, as the Senate eventually did in August. However, the Business Roundtable was unconvinced by Clinton's speech and remained firm in its opposition to his national health insurance plan.

With the NFIB and the Business Roundtable announcing their opposition to Clinton's national health insurance plan, the only prospect for the administration to win support for the president's program from a major business interest group lay with the Chamber of Commerce, the largest organization representing corporate America, with 220,000 members, which included both large and small firms.[27] Clinton had every reason to believe that he could win the Chamber of Commerce's endorsement of his national health insurance program. The Chamber of Commerce made it clear that it supported the establishment of a national health insurance program from the very outset of the Clinton presidency. On March 8, 1993, the governing board of the Chamber of Commerce announced its support for the imposition of a federal mandate requiring employers to provide their working families group insurance.[28]

However, the decision by the governing board of the Chamber of Commerce to endorse the imposition of a federal mandate requiring employers to provide their working families group health insurance provoked a storm of opposition among the rank-and-file members of the interest group. As a result, on February 28, 1994, the governing board announced that it was rescinding its support for employer mandates. In explaining the Chamber of Commerce's reversal of its support for employer mandates, Robert Patricelli, chairman of the interest group's health benefits committee, emphasized that the organization was reflecting the opinion of its members. "Last year, we were in favor of [employer mandates]. Today we are rejecting that position. The business community will not in our view support the employer mandate. A very, very substantial portion of our membership rejects the mandate."[29]

Consistent with its rejection of employer mandates, on February 3, 1994, the Chamber of Commerce announced its opposition to Clinton's national health insurance plan, since it would require employers to provide their working families group coverage. In announcing the Chamber of Commerce's opposition to the Clinton plan, Patricelli complained that the president's program would require firms to provide a more generous package of health care benefits than they currently do, raising their business costs. As Patricelli put it, the Clinton plan "proposes such a burden of higher employer premium contributions, rich benefits, and counterproductive regulation [that] it cannot even be used as a starting point" for health care reform.[30]

By February 1994, all three major interest groups representing the business community—the NFIB, the Business Roundtable, and the Chamber of Commerce—had announced their opposition to Clinton's national health insurance plan. This allowed the organized segments of the business community to form a united front in opposing the Clinton plan. With organized business solidly opposed to the Clinton plan, the administration's strategy of mobilizing corporate support for the president's program collapsed. The Clinton administration was left with only a few bastions of support within the business community for the program, most notably the automobile industry.

BUSINESS OPINION ON NATIONAL HEALTH INSURANCE

The fact that an overwhelming majority of the business community opposed national health insurance was consistent with the opinions expressed by the chief executive officers (CEOs) of the nation's largest corporations. Polling data show that at least a plurality of those CEOs opposed national health insurance in general and the Clinton plan in particular.

On September 23, 1993, Clark Martire & Bartolomeo conducted a poll for *Fortune* of eighty-seven CEOs of Fortune 500 companies. The poll asked the Fortune 500 CEOs the following question: "Is [Clinton's national health insurance program] a good health care plan?" Forty-five percent of the CEOs said that the Clinton plan was not good; 28 percent said that it was; and 27 percent were not sure.[31]

Many CEOs of Fortune 500 companies opposed Clinton's national health insurance plan because they feared that it would drive up their health care costs.

As we have seen, the Clinton plan would require many, if not most, employers providing group insurance to extend a more generous package of health care benefits than they currently do, raising business costs. Accordingly, many, if not most, CEOs of Fortune 500 companies opposed the Clinton plan.

The fear among corporate CEOs that Clinton's national health insurance plan would force large companies to assume a greater share of the financial burden for the health care costs of their working families than they currently do was the driving force behind big business opposition to the president's program. As Adam Clymer, Robert Pear, and Robin Toner put it,

Many corporate CEOs had a visceral reaction to the Clinton plan and the expansion of Federal authority that Mr. Clinton was proposing. They said they could control [health care] costs much better than the government could, and they feared that under the Clinton plan they would lose the right to tailor health benefits to their employees' needs.[32]

Fear among corporate CEOs that Clinton's national health insurance plan would drive up health care costs for business was confirmed by the *Fortune* poll. It asked those CEOs of Fortune 500 companies surveyed the following question: "Would the [Clinton] plan result in higher or lower [health care] costs for your company?" Fifty-two percent of the CEOs said that the Clinton plan would result in higher health care costs for their firms; 34 percent were not sure; 8 percent believed that it would result in lower costs; and 6 percent thought that it would lead to no change in their costs.

Because many, if not most, CEOs of Fortune 500 companies believed that Clinton's national health insurance plan would drive up health care costs, they feared that the president's program would damage the economy by making it harder for their firms to compete in the marketplace, hold down costs, and create jobs. This fear was confirmed in the *Fortune* poll, which asked the CEOs of the Fortune 500 companies surveyed the following question: "Would the [Clinton] plan help, hurt, or have no effect on the economy?" Fifty-nine percent of the CEOs said that the Clinton plan would hurt the economy; 22 percent were not sure; 10 percent believed that it would have no effect on the economy; and only 9 percent believed that it would help the economy.[33]

The element of Clinton's national health insurance plan corporate CEOs most objected to was the federal mandate that employers provide their working families group coverage. Corporate CEOs believed that employer mandates would force businesses to provide their working families a more generous package of health care benefits than they currently do, driving up their health care costs. As a result, the overwhelming majority of corporate CEOs opposed employer mandates; by contrast, a majority of the public supported them.

The *New York Times* and CBS News conducted a poll of 484 corporate executives during April 15–29, 1994, and 1,215 average citizens during April 21–23, who were asked the following question: "Should the federal government require companies to provide health insurance for all their workers, or should companies be allowed to decide for themselves whether or not to provide health insurance?'' Seventy-five percent of corporate executives polled opposed the imposition of a federal mandate requiring employers to provide their working families group insurance; by contrast, only 40 percent of the public opposed employer mandates. Only 19 percent of corporate executives supported employer mandates, compared to 53 percent of the public who did so.

Why did an overwhelming majority of corporate executives oppose requiring employers to provide their working families group health insurance, while a majority of the public supported such a federal mandate? The answer lies in differences between the business community and the public over the degree to which the health care system should be overhauled. The *New York Times*/CBS News poll asked its respondents among corporate executives and ordinary citizens, ''What does the health care system in the United States need?'' Forty-nine percent of corporate executives and 52 percent of the public believed that ''fundamental changes'' were needed in the health care system. Thirty-nine percent of corporate executives believed that only ''minor changes'' were needed in the health care system; by contrast, only 9 percent of the public agreed with this view. Only 11 percent of corporate executives believed that the health care system had ''to be completely rebuilt,'' compared to 38 percent of the public who thought so.[34]

The *New York Times*/CBS News poll shows that only a small fraction of the business community supported a radical overhaul of the health care system, in contrast with a substantial minority of the public who supported it. Rather, practically the entire business community supported changes in the health care system which stopped short of a radical overhaul in the financing of medical services. By contrast, a substantially smaller share of the public was willing to accept anything less than a radical overhaul of the health care system.

The business community remained hostile to a radical overhaul of the health care system because corporate executives feared that any sweeping change in the funding of medical services would be made at the financial expense of large corporations, as we have seen. True, a substantial share of the public also believed that a radical overhaul of the health care system would be made at their financial expense, as the previous chapter showed. However, a substantially smaller share of the public believed that they would lose from health care reform than was the case within the business community. As a result, enthusiasm for health care reform remained stronger among the public than within the business community, where support for national health insurance continued to be weak.

CONCLUSION

Business plays a critical role in the politics of health care reform. The overwhelming majority of the public are insured by their employers, most of which are private firms. The voluntary, employment-based health insurance system is dependent upon the willingness of firms to assume financial responsibility for the health care costs of their working families. Should firms refuse to continue to assume this responsibility, then the employment-based insurance system would collapse. The substantial share of the public who are currently insured by business would lose their coverage and become uninsured. Because the very existence of the employment-based insurance system is dependent upon the willingness of firms to provide their working families coverage, business wields enormous influence in determining the course of health care reform. Congress is reluctant to undertake any health care reform which does not have business support.

Given the critical role business plays in the politics of health care reform, Clinton undertook an all-out effort to solicit corporate support for his national health insurance plan. Clinton fully recognized that his national national health insurance plan stood little, if any, chance of passage without business support. However, despite his best efforts, Clinton succeeded in garnering only token business support for his national health insurance plan. The major interest groups representing the business community—the Business Roundtable, Chamber of Commerce, and NFIB—announced their adamant opposition to the Clinton plan.

Business opposed Clinton's national health insurance plan because it would raise the financial burden firms must assume in funding the health care costs of their working families. The Clinton plan would require large corporations to provide their working families a more generous package of health care benefits than they currently do, raising their business costs. It would require small firms, which do not currently provide their working families group insurance, to do so, raising their business costs substantially. As a result, most large corporations joined a united small business community in opposing the Clinton plan.

Business opposition to Clinton's national health insurance plan destroyed prospects for its establishment. Congress was unlikely to establish any national health insurance plan in the absence of business support for the program. As long as firms continued to assume financial responsibility to provide their working families group coverage, the overwhelming majority of the public would remain insured by their employers, depriving Congress of any urgent and compelling need to establish a national health insurance program. By announcing their opposition to the Clinton plan, the major interest groups representing the business community made it clear that firms wanted to continue to assume financial responsibility for the health care costs of their working families on a voluntary basis; they rejected any program, such as that sponsored by the president, which would require them to provide their working families group insurance.

Since most firms provide their working families group insurance on a voluntary basis, Congress saw no clear and overriding need to compel all companies to do so. As a result, the 103rd Congress refused to take any action on health care reform. National health insurance will remain a political impossibility as long as a majority of the public continue to be insured by their employers. With most working families well insured by their employers, public support for national health insurance will remain relatively weak, depriving Congress of any real and immediate need to establish such a program.

Chapter 7

The Division Within the Democratic Party Over National Health Insurance

The Health Security Act lives up to its title. This is a bill to give all Americans [health] security and choice, improve the quality of care, reduce costs and paperwork and make everyone responsible for health care. This bill is good for America.[1]

Senator Barbara Boxer of California, address on the Senate floor, October 28, 1993.

The President has set forth five goals for health care reform: universal coverage, cost-containment, simplicity, choice, and quality. I have real concerns that the [Clinton national health insurance] plan in its current form . . . will not achieve the goals the President himself articulated.[2]

Representative Jim McDermott of Washington, statement issued on October 5, 1993.

The campaign to establish national health insurance during 1993–1994 was led by Clinton and the Democratic Party. National health insurance would not have dominated the political agenda during those two years had it not been for the strong, sustained, and unflinching support the program received from Clinton. Clinton used his power as president to place health care reform at the top of the political agenda.

On September 22, 1993, Clinton introduced his national health insurance plan to a joint session of Congress in a prime-time televised address which succeeded in focusing public attention on health care reform. In his 1994 State of the Union address, Clinton made passage of national health insurance legislation the top priority for the second session of the 103rd Congress, further focusing public attention on health care reform. Clinton attempted to mobilize public support for his national health insurance plan by delivering numerous speeches on his program to meetings of various organized groups and public rallies held throughout the United States.

Clinton worked harder and contributed more to generating public interest in the issue of health care reform than any other president in American history. During 1993–1994, the issue of health care reform received daily coverage in America's major newspapers and was the subject of articles published practically on a weekly basis in the nation's newsmagazines. This issue attracted the particular interest of the television news media, garnering almost daily coverage on the evening news broadcasts of America's five television networks—ABC, CBS, CNN, NBC, and PBS.

The extent of media coverage of the issue of health care reform during 1993–1994 was revealed in a survey conducted by the Times Mirror Center for the People and the Press, in association with the Kaiser Family Foundation and the *Columbia Journalism Review*. Covering the period from September 1 to November 30, 1993, and January 15 to November 13, 1994, the Times/Kaiser/Columbia survey found that America's major newspapers and the five television networks had devoted an astounding combined total of 5,600 stories to the issue of health care reform. Most of those stories came from America's five major newspapers—the *Los Angeles Times, New York Times, Wall Street Journal, Washington Post,* and *USA Today*—which alone devoted a combined total of 3,118 stories to the issue of health care reform during this period.[3] America's five major television networks devoted a combined total of 748 stories to this issue on their news programs.[4]

During 1993–1994, stories on health care reform saturated the television airwaves and print media, generating intense and widespread public interest in this issue. During September and October 1994, the Times Mirror Center polled a representative sample of the public on their interest in the issue of health care reform. A remarkable 32 percent said that they were following media coverage of this issue "very closely."[5]

None of the previous presidents who undertook similar health care initiatives—Harry S. Truman, Richard Nixon, and Jimmy Carter—succeeded in generating anywhere near as much public interest in and media coverage of national health insurance as Clinton did; and this was largely due to Clinton's own energetic and indefatigable determination to keep the public focused on the issue of health care reform, which he succeeded in doing during the first two years of his presidency.

Clinton did not pursue his health care reform initiative alone; rather, national health insurance had the support, not just of the president, but of the overwhelming majority of Democratic members of the 103rd Congress. A combined total of 31 Democratic senators and 145 Democratic House members served as cosponsors of the two national health insurance bills introduced in the 103rd Congress—Clinton's Health Security Act and an alternative measure introduced by Senator Paul Wellstone of Minnesota and Representative Jim McDermott of Washington on March 3, 1993, which would have established a single-payer plan.[6] By contrast, only one Republican lawmaker, Senator James Jeffords of Vermont, served as a cosponsor of national health insurance legislation in the

103rd Congress. Jeffords was the lone Republican congressional cosponsor of the Health Security Act. Virtually every other Republican member of Congress opposed national health insurance.[7] During 1993–1994, national health insurance received serious consideration on Capitol Hill as a result of the support the program received from the overwhelming majority of the Democratic members of the 103rd Congress.

However, despite their general support for national health insurance, Democrats in Washington remained deeply divided over what kind of program should be established. Liberal Democratic members of Congress supported the establishment of a single-payer plan, in which the federal government would guarantee coverage to every individual as an entitlement of American citizenship, and finance the cost of health care through tax revenues. However, single-payer insurance was opposed by Clinton and more moderate Democratic members of Congress. They rejected single-payer insurance as politically unfeasible, given the fact that the program would provide the government a greater role in the health care system than a majority of the public were willing to accept. Instead, Clinton and moderate Democrats supported building upon the current employment-based insurance system. Employers currently provide their working families group coverage on a voluntary basis. Clinton and moderate Democrats wanted to make the provision of such coverage mandatory. By building upon, rather than scrapping and replacing, the current employment-based insurance system with a government program, Clinton and moderate Democrats hoped that their national health insurance plan would be acceptable to the overwhelming majority of the public, who wanted health care reform which stopped short of a radical overhaul of the medical system.

The division among the Democrats between liberal supporters of single-payer insurance and moderate backers of mandatory employment-based insurance prevented the party from forging a consensus behind a single health care reform plan. Plagued by divisions within its ranks over what kind of national health insurance should be established, the Democratic Party was unable to mobilize the political support necessary to pass a health care reform bill. Clinton and moderate Democrats remained adamantly opposed to single-payer insurance, claiming it was politically unfeasible; and liberal Democratic backers of single-payer insurance gave, at best, only grudging support for the president's health care reform plan, since it stopped short of the radical overhaul of the medical system the Left favored. With the Democrats hopelessly divided over what kind of national health insurance should be established, the party was unable to capitalize upon the overwhelming majorities its members had in the 103rd Congress in order to pass a health care reform bill. With Republicans, who are almost unanimously opposed to national health insurance, commanding majorities of both houses of the 104th Congress following the 1994 elections, the failure of the Democratic-controlled 103rd Congress to pass health care reform legislation destroyed prospects for overhauling the medical system during Clinton's first and possibly only term.

THE CASE FOR SINGLE-PAYER HEALTH INSURANCE

Single-payer health insurance represented the most radical among all the approaches to health care reform considered in Washington during 1993–1994. Given this fact, it is surprising that single-payer insurance had so much support among the Democratic majority in the 103rd Congress, especially in the House. Democratic congressional support for single-payer insurance was organized around the health care reform bill introduced by Wellstone and McDermott. The Wellstone-McDermott bill would guarantee universal, comprehensive coverage, financed through federal taxes, and contain health care costs through the imposition of a medical budget on a national and state level.[8] It was cosponsored by five senators and ninety House members, all of whom were Democrats, and the only independent member of Congress, Representative Bernard Sanders of Vermont.[9]

The Wellstone-McDermott bill had surprisingly strong support among the Democratic majority in the 103rd Congress, especially in the House, because of one central, overriding reason: Single-payer health insurance represents the most efficient, not to mention equitable, approach to guarantee universal coverage among all the options for health care reform considered in Washington during 1993–1994. As we saw in Chapter 3, the insurance system is wasteful and inefficient. Fifteen hundred private plans exist, each one with its own bureaucracy to process medical claims and reimburse health care providers, generating a duplication of administrative overhead and paperwork, which adds to medical costs. Private plans spend additional sums on marketing, sales, and advertising to solicit business, and on medical underwriting to limit their financial liabilities by cherry-picking only the healthiest and youngest subscribers, while refusing to insure the oldest and sickest individuals.

Single-payer health insurance would scrap and replace America's mishmash of 1,500 different and competing private plans with a single government program, which would guarantee universal coverage. A single centralized bureaucracy would exist to process medical claims and reimburse health care providers, eliminating the duplication of administrative overhead and paperwork which exists under the current multiple-payer insurance system. In addition, a single-payer plan would provide coverage to every citizen and legal resident on a compulsory basis. The government would not have to spend a dime soliciting any business, eliminating the substantial sums private plans currently spend on marketing, sales, and advertising to attract subscribers, and on medical underwriting to choose only the youngest and healthiest customers. Single-payer insurance would save tens of billions of dollars annually which are currently being wasted by the current insurance system on duplication of administrative overhead and paperwork, as well as on marketing, sales, advertising, and medical underwriting. Those tens of billions of dollars squandered on bureaucratic waste and inefficiency would be used to provide the uninsured coverage.

The fact that single-payer health insurance serves as an efficient means to finance health care is beyond question. Consider a comparison between Canada's single-payer plan and America's multiple-payer insurance system. Each of Canada's ten provinces and two territories maintains a single-payer plan. The fact that only twelve basic plans exist to provide the entire Canadian population coverage allows the nation to finance health care costs with a minimum of bureaucracy and paperwork. In addition, Canada provides each citizen and legal resident coverage on a compulsory basis. Canada's insurance plans do not incur costs soliciting business through marketing, sales, and advertising, or selecting only the youngest and healthiest subscribers through medical underwriting.

Canada's single-payer health insurance plan provides universal coverage through a minimum of bureaucracy and paperwork, and without incurring any marketing, sales, advertising, and medical underwriting costs. By contrast, America's multiple-payer insurance system is plagued by a duplication of administrative overhead and paperwork created by the existence of 1,500 different private plans, each of which maintains a bureaucracy to process medical claims and reimburse health care providers. To solicit business and limit their financial liabilities, those plans generate additional costs for marketing, sales, advertising, and medical underwriting.[10]

Because single-payer insurance is so much more efficient than America's multiple-payer insurance system, the administrative costs of health care in Canada are substantially lower than they are in the United States. Empirical evidence for this came from two highly influential and widely cited studies published during the spring of 1991: the first conducted by Steffie Woolhandler and David U. Himmelstein, and the second by the General Accounting Office (GAO).

Woolhandler and Himmelstein found that in 1987 the administrative costs of health care in the United States were 23.9 percent, compared to only 11 percent in Canada. They concluded that had the health insurance system in the United States been as efficient as it was in Canada in 1987, American health care costs would have been $69 billion to $83.2 billion lower than they actually were, resulting in a 13.8 percent to 16.6 percent reduction in medical spending.[11]

The Woolhandler-Himmelstein study provides irrefutable empirical evidence that a single-payer insurance plan would create a substantially more efficient means to finance health care than the existing multiple-payer insurance system, resulting in tens of billions of dollars in savings annually which could be used to provide the uninsured coverage. As a result, the United States can guarantee universal coverage without spending an additional dime by simply scrapping and replacing the existing private health insurance industry with a single-payer plan. As Woolhandler and Himmelstein put it, "Reducing our administrative costs to Canadian levels would save enough money to fund coverage for all uninsured and underinsured Americans. Universal, comprehensive coverage under a single, publicly administered insurance program is the sine qua non of such administrative simplification."[12]

On June 4, 1991, the GAO released a report entitled *Canada's Health Insurance: Lessons for the United States*, which confirmed Woolhandler and Himmelstein's conclusions concerning the administrative efficiency of the Canadian health care system. The GAO report found that if the United States had a single-payer health insurance plan, similar to the Canadian system, its annual administrative costs for health care would be reduced by $67 billion. The GAO estimated that it would cost $64 billion to provide the uninsured comprehensive coverage, absent any patient cost-sharing requirements.[13] "If the universal coverage and single payer features of the Canadian system were applied to the United States, the savings in administrative costs alone would be sufficient to finance coverage for the millions of Americans who are currently uninsured," the GAO report concluded. "There would be enough [savings] left over to permit a reduction, or possibly elimination, of copayments and deductibles, if that were deemed appropriate."[14]

The studies conducted by Woolhandler and Himmelstein and the GAO provided the empirical evidence liberals needed to argue that the simplest, most straightforward, and efficient means to achieve universal coverage was to scrap and replace the private health insurance industry with a single-payer plan, and use the savings in administrative costs which would result for a government program to provide the uninsured coverage.

CLINTON REJECTS SINGLE-PAYER HEALTH INSURANCE

As the most efficient means available for financing universal coverage, single-payer health insurance makes good economic sense. However, single-payer insurance does not make good political sense, given the fact that there is virtually no chance that Congress would ever pass the program in the foreseeable future. Recognizing this fact, Clinton ruled out recommending a single-payer insurance plan upon entering the White House. As one Clinton aide put it, "The President made a decision early on that . . . he didn't want to go . . . to single payer."[15]

Clinton's rejection of single-payer health insurance was designed to achieve two political objectives: first, to avoid conflict with the private insurance industry; and second, to allow the president to preserve his carefully cultivated image as a moderate Democrat.

Single-payer health insurance would scrap and replace the private health insurance industry with a government program resulting in the wholesale elimination of insurance companies, which are one of the most politically powerful interest groups on Capitol Hill. As we saw in Chapter 3, insurance companies raised their campaign contributions to congressional candidates by a whopping 900 percent during 1991–1992, far exceeding the increase in donations from any other segment of the health care industry. This massive increase in contributions allowed the private insurance industry to become a dominant political force on Capitol Hill during the 1990s. The industry was well positioned to use its massive financial clout to target for defeat any member of Congress willing to defy the wishes of insurance companies and support the establishment of a single-payer plan. Accordingly, single-payer insurance legislation stood no chance of passage. Recognizing that sponsorship of a single-payer plan would embroil him in a politically bruising battle with the private insurance industry on Capitol Hill which he would surely lose, Clinton refused to even consider recommending the establishment of a government program.

By preserving, rather than scrapping and replacing, the private health insurance industry, Clinton hoped that his health care reform plan would not provoke opposition from the politically powerful insurance companies. However, this was not the case. As we saw in Chapter 4, the HIAA sponsored a $14 million public relations campaign which played an instrumental role in the defeat of Clinton's national health insurance plan.

The private health insurance industry had good reason to oppose the Clinton plan, since it would impose stringent controls on insurance premiums, which would result in substantial financial losses for insurance companies. The establishment of health alliances would provide consumers with the bargaining leverage to secure the most comprehensive coverage available at the lowest possible premium, further reducing the income of the industry. By recommending the preservation of the private insurance industry, Clinton believed that he had made the needed political concessions to defuse opposition from insurance companies to his health care reform plan. However, he failed to understand that the industry was opposed to any health care reform plan which promised to undermine the financial position of insurance companies—even a moderate program like his, which posed no threat to their existence.

In addition to his unsuccessful attempt to avoid a politically bruising battle with the private health insurance industry, Clinton could not support single-payer insurance without undermining his image as a moderate Democrat, who shared the public's general desire for limited government. Clinton was determined to present himself to the public as a moderate who avoided complicated, bureaucratic, big-government solutions to social problems which liberal Democrats have traditionally espoused. Single-payer insurance represents the standard approach to health care reform liberal Democrats have traditionally supported. Single-payer insurance can be legitimately seen as a complicated, bureaucratic, big-government solution to the health care crisis, since the program would use the public sector to supplant the marketplace in financing the delivery and containing the cost of medical services.

Consistent with his moderate ideological outlook, Clinton favored market-oriented solutions to social problems. Accordingly, he opposed single-payer insurance because it would give the government a dominant role in financing and containing the cost of health care. Rather, Clinton wanted to build upon, rather than scrap and replace, the existing employment-based insurance system with a government program. As we saw in Chapter 2, Clinton's national health insurance plan would achieve universal coverage and health care cost containment largely through the private sector, rather than the government. Employers would be required to provide their working families group insurance. The public would be organized into health alliances, which would both provide the population health care benefits and use their bargaining power to reduce medical costs.

Clinton's preference for a market-oriented approach to health care reform as an alternative to single-payer health insurance was perhaps best summed up by Elizabeth Drew, who notes that "Clinton didn't want to offer a huge new government-controlled [health care] system, requiring big new taxes." Rather, Clinton favored a market-oriented health care reform plan, which would

inject more competition into the health care system. . . . The concept was to drive down health care costs by organizing insurance purchasers into large groups and have networks of doctors and hospitals compete for their business. The emphasis was on encouraging the spread of health maintenance organizations, which, through grouping practices, generally held their [health care] costs below those of the traditional fee-for-service system.[16]

Speaking before a meeting of the National Governors' Association in Tulsa on August 16, 1993, Clinton officially announced that he was ruling out recommending a single-payer health insurance plan. In explaining his decision, he acknowledged that single-payer insurance was the most efficient means available for financing universal coverage. However, Clinton pointed out that, despite its economic merits, single-payer insurance was politically unfeasible:

[The United States could] go to a single-payer [health insurance] system, like the Canadians do, because it has the least administrative cost. That would require us to replace over $500 billion in private insurance premiums with nearly that in new taxes. I don't think that's a practical option. I don't think that's going to happen.[17]

In lieu of single-payer health insurance, Clinton told the governors that he would seek to achieve universal coverage by requiring employers to provide their working families group coverage. Clinton argued that the only politically feasible means to achieve universal coverage was "to build on the [voluntary, employment-based insurance] system we now have." He pointed out that "most Americans are insured under a system in which employers pay for part of the health insurance and employees pay for part of the insurance, and it's worked pretty well." Given the fact that the current employment-based insurance system has succeeded in providing the overwhelming majority of the public coverage, Clinton believed that the only practical and acceptable means to achieve universal coverage was by preserving the existing arrangements for financing the delivery of health care. As he put it, "Building on the system we have now which works . . . is the fairest way to go" to achieve universal coverage.[18]

PUBLIC OPINION ON HEALTH CARE REFORM

Clinton was correct in deciding to achieve universal coverage by building upon, rather than scrapping and replacing, the current voluntary, employment-based health insurance system with a government program. Polling data show that the overwhelming majority of the public rejected single-payer health insurance, validating Clinton's argument that the program lacked political feasibility. Instead, the public joined him in favoring the achievement of universal coverage by requiring employers to provide their working families group insurance.

Public opposition to single-payer health insurance was revealed in a *Los Angeles Times* poll of 1,682 adults, conducted during April 16–19, 1994. The poll asked its respondents whether they favored maintaining the current private health insurance system or an alternative government-financed and -administered insurance system. Seventy percent of those polled said they favored preserving the current private insurance system; only 21 percent believed that the government should finance and administer the delivery of health care "without private insurance companies."[19]

While the overwhelming majority of the public support the current private health insurance system, the population opposes existing health care arrangements in which employers provide their working families group coverage on a voluntary basis. Rather, like Clinton, the majority believe that the federal government must require employers to extend their working families health care benefits. Public support for mandatory, employment-based insurance was revealed in another *Los Angeles Times* poll of 1,515 adults conducted during July 23–26, 1994. The poll asked its respondents whether they supported a federal mandate requiring employers to provide their working families group insurance. Fifty-eight percent of those polled favored employer mandates; only 31 percent opposed them.[20]

As we saw in Chapter 2, Clinton's national health insurance plan would require employers to finance 80 percent of the cost of group coverage for their working families. A plurality of the public supported the president's policy to require employers to assume most of the cost of the group insurance they provide their working families. During July 14–17, 1994, the *New York Times* and CBS News conducted a poll of 1,339 adults, who were asked the following question: "Should employers be required to pay most of the cost of health insurance for their workers or should they just be required to make available insurance that workers can pay for?" Forty-nine percent of those polled said that "employers should be required to pay most of the cost of health insurance for their workers"; 40 percent believed that they should only "be required to make insurance available that their workers can pay for."[21]

The *Los Angeles Times* and the *New York Times*/CBS News polls show that the overwhelming majority of the public rejected single-payer health insurance in favor of a federal mandate requiring employers to provide their working families group coverage, with a plurality believing that businesses must be compelled to finance most of the cost of the health care benefits they extend their employed households. In building upon, rather than replacing, the current employment-based insurance system with a government program, Clinton's national health insurance plan was consistent with public opinion on health care reform.

However, as we saw in Chapter 5, public support for Clinton's national health insurance collapsed during 1993–1994. By July 1994, a substantial plurality of the public opposed the Clinton plan. Why did the public tend to oppose the Clinton plan, despite the fact that it would have achieved the kind of health care reform the people said they wanted—focusing on a federal mandate requiring employers to provide their working families group insurance, which the over-whelming majority of the public supported? The answer lies in the public's contradictory feeling toward health care reform.

By guaranteeing universal coverage, national health insurance would have reduced the financial barriers impeding public access to health care, raising patient utilization of health care services, driving up their costs and fueling inflation. To the extent that universal coverage was achieved through the federal government, national health insurance would raise the already swollen federal budget deficit. National health insurance cannot be established on a fiscal and economically viable basis without stringent health care cost-containment measures.

The proliferation and utilization of costly medical technology is the major source of spiraling health care costs.[22] Health care cost containment cannot be achieved without restricting public access to medical technology, which would result in a system of health care rationing. However, the public opposes health care rationing, as we will see in the following two chapters, and this is a major reason why people tended to hold contradictory feelings about medical reform: supporting a federal mandate requiring employers to provide their working families group insurance, while opposing the Clinton plan, despite the fact that it would establish such a federal mandate, which is exactly what the public said it wanted. We will return to the role which the specter of health care rationing played in the defeat of the Clinton plan in the following two chapters.

THE DIVISION AMONG LIBERAL DEMOCRATS OVER NATIONAL HEALTH INSURANCE

As we have seen, single-payer health insurance commanded substantial sup-port among the Democratic majority in the 103rd Congress. Fully five senators and ninety-one House members served as cosponsors of the single-payer insur-ance bill introduced by Wellstone and McDermott. Given the substantial support single-payer insurance enjoyed among liberal Democratic members of Congress, Clinton's national health insurance plan, the Health Security Act, stood no chance of passage without the solid support of virtually all ninety-six cosponsors of the Wellstone-McDermott bill.

However, liberal Democratic congressional supporters of single-payer health insurance remained deeply divided in their support for the Health Security Act. One group, led by Representative Henry Waxman of California, urged compro-mise, recommending that congressional supporters of single-payer insurance back the bill as the most comprehensive health care reform plan lawmakers were likely to pass. They were opposed by another group, led by McDermott, who urged that congressional supporters of single-payer insurance reject the bill, since it did not go far enough in achieving comprehensive health care reform.

Waxman Supports the Health Security Act

As chairman of the Subcommittee on Health and the Environment of the Energy and Commerce Committee, which shared jurisdiction over national health insurance with the Ways and Means and Education and Labor Committees in the House, Waxman was one of the most influential players in the politics of health care reform in Congress. Moreover, he was a longtime participant in the politics of health care reform in Congress, having joined Kennedy in cosponsoring an important national health insurance bill in 1979.[23] As a cosponsor of the Wellstone-McDermott bill, Waxman was perhaps the single most powerful supporter of single-payer insurance in Congress.[24] He was among the strongest and most passionate supporters of national health insurance in Congress. "I've been in Congress eighteen years," Waxman noted in an interview published in the October 10, 1993, edition of the *Los Angeles Times*. "All of my legislative career I've felt strongly that we need a national health insurance system to cover everybody."[25]

Waxman shared the concerns of other liberal Democratic members of Congress that the Health Security Act established an unnecessarily complicated means to achieve health care reform. The bill would achieve universal coverage by imposing a federal mandate requiring employers to provide their working families group insurance; and it would contain health care costs through the organization of consumers into health alliances, which would use their bargaining clout to negotiate reductions in private insurance premiums. Like other liberal Democratic members of Congress, Waxman believed that single-payer insurance would establish a more simple and straightforward way to achieve health care reform, through the establishment of a government program to both finance universal coverage and contain medical costs by imposing prospective budgets governing health care spending. However, he recognized that single-payer insurance was politically unfeasible, and that the Health Security Act was the most comprehensive health care reform Congress was likely to pass.

Given the fact that the Health Security Act represented a more politically feasible alternative to achieve health care reform, Waxman attempted to use his substantial influence in Congress to steer Democratic supporters of single-payer health insurance into compromise with Clinton. He argued that the Health Security Act was the most comprehensive health care reform program Congress was likely to pass. Accordingly, supporters of single-payer insurance would have to throw their support behind the bill despite its shortcomings. By failing to do so, supporters of single-payer insurance would destroy any prospects for health care reform in the 103rd Congress, since the Health Security Act stood no chance of passage without the unanimous support of the ninety-six cosponsors of the Wellstone-McDermott bill.

Waxman argued that the real choice the 103rd Congress faced was between passing the Clinton plan and taking no action on health care reform at all. Given this choice, supporters of single-payer insurance would be wise to support the Clinton plan, since it represented a vast improvement over the current health care system, and contained many positive features congressional cosponsors of the Wellstone-McDermott bill could back, the most important of which were universal coverage and medical cost containment. As Waxman put it in his interview with the *Los Angeles Times*,

I personally would prefer a single-payer [health insurance] plan. It is certainly less complicated than what the President is proposing. It would have guaranteed a clear way to a comprehensive, universal benefit and people would have understood it a lot better than they would [the Clinton] plan. . . . But the President made a political decision that the Congress was not ready to pass a single-payer system. And he's come forward with another way of providing the same goals as a single-payer system, which would be a universal, comprehensive [health care] benefit.[26]

Given that the Health Security Act would achieve the same goal of universal coverage as single-payer health insurance, Waxman urged cosponsors of the Wellstone-McDermott bill to back Clinton's health care reform plan. As he put it following Clinton's introduction of his national health insurance plan in his address to a joint session of Congress on September 22, 1993, "When all is said and done, some time next year, the alternatives are going to be pretty much the Clinton proposal and the goals it presents or the status quo . . . I can't believe that those of us who say they'd prefer single payer would rather see no [health care] reform" than the president's program.[27]

However, despite his eagerness to compromise with Clinton, Waxman warned that he would oppose the Health Security Act if the president substantially weakened his bill in order to draw support from conservative Democrats, who favored a more modest and incremental approach to health care reform than the administration's plan. He was especially concerned that Clinton might compromise his commitment to universal coverage in order to win the support of conservative Democratic members of Congress for his bill. His concerns gained credence in October 1993 when Clinton agreed to modify the provisions of his original national health insurance plan relating to universal coverage.

As we saw in Chapter 2, Clinton's national health insurance plan would achieve universal coverage primarily through the provision of federal subsidies to enable employers to purchase health care benefits for their working families. This would allow those businesses which do not currently provide their working families group insurance to be able to afford to do so. However, following his introduction of his national health insurance plan in his address on September 22, 1993, Clinton agreed to modify the provisions of his program relating to the extension of federal subsidies. He agreed that Congress would impose a ceiling on the amount of federal subsidies which would be provided to businesses to enable them to purchase group insurance for their working families. Should the cost of that group insurance exceed the amount of federal subsidies allotted, then Clinton would have to ask Congress for an additional appropriation which would be made available to businesses for the purchase of health care benefits for their working families. This concession was designed to assure conservative Democrats that the achievement of universal coverage would not add to the already swollen federal budget deficit. By making his national health insurance plan deficit-neutral, Clinton hoped that he could win the support of conservative Democratic members of Congress for the Health Security Act.

However, Clinton's compromise on federal subsidies made it possible, if not probable, that universal coverage insurance would not be achieved under the Health Security Act. Congress might be unwilling to appropriate sufficient federal subsidies to allow all businesses to purchase group insurance for their working families, even if urged to do so by Clinton. This would leave some working families uninsured, assuring that the president would fall short of his goal of achieving universal coverage.

Waxman responded to Clinton's introduction of the Health Security Act on October 27, 1993, by making it clear he would reject any health care reform bill which fell short of guaranteeing universal coverage. He was especially critical of Clinton's bill, charging that the concessions the president had made on federal subsidies had compromised the administration's commitment to universal coverage. "It's a serious problem, a serious flaw in the administration's proposal," Waxman declared in condemning those concessions. "It undermines the credibility of the administration promise of universal coverage—health care security that will always be there—because it won't be there if they run out of money."

Waxman saw Clinton's concessions on federal subsidies as part of a broader pattern of compromises on health care reform the president had made in order to win the support of conservative Democratic and even moderate Republican members of Congress for the Health Security Act. "They've made a number of accommodations to conservative Democrats and Republicans as well as some of the [medical] interest groups too early," Waxman complained. "They've made a lot of changes in the bill to try to accommodate groups that are still against them."[28]

While urging support of the Health Security Act, Waxman warned that he would abandon his backing of the bill if Clinton made any further compromises in his health care reform plan which prevented the president from honoring his commitment to achieve universal health insurance coverage. "I think if we don't get a bill that provides universal coverage, comprehensive health-care benefits, that's fair to the elderly and poor, as some Republicans and conservative Democrats are proposing, I would have to reach the conclusion that we lost the fight [for national health insurance] and that it's not worth voting for," Waxman warned in his interview with the *Los Angeles Times*.[29]

Waxman's position on national health insurance posed a dilemma for Clinton. The president needed the unanimous support of congressional Democratic supporters of single-payer insurance if he was to have any hope that the lawmakers would pass the Health Security Act. Waxman made it clear that he and other supporters of single-payer insurance were willing to support the Health Security Act—but only if Clinton agreed not to make any concessions which would prevent him from honoring his pledge to guarantee universal coverage.

However, as we saw in Chapter 5, public support for Clinton's national health insurance plan had collapsed by July 1994. An overwhelming majority of the public favored more modest and incremental health care reform than that contained in the Clinton plan. To win public support for his national health insurance plan, Clinton needed to pursue more limited health care reform than that contained in the Health Security Act, which necessarily meant that his bill would have to fall short of guaranteeing universal coverage. However, Waxman made it clear that he and other supporters of single-payer insurance would reject any health care reform bill which fell short of guaranteeing universal coverage.

As a result, Clinton was caught in a no-win situation. If he demanded the radical overhaul of the health care system which included a guarantee of universal health insurance coverage, as contained in the Health Security Act, his bill would stand no chance of passage, since it would lack public support. However, if he agreed to more limited and incremental health care reform which fell short of guaranteeing universal coverage, his campaign to secure the establishment of national health insurance would lose the support of Democratic congressional backers of single-payer insurance. Since fully ninety-six members of Congress supported single-payer insurance, no national health insurance bill could be passed without support from backers of a government-financed and-administered insurance system. In the end, by refusing to accept any bill which fell short of universal coverage, Waxman and other congressional supporters of single-payer insurance who backed the Health Security Act derailed any chance that Clinton might come up with a health care reform plan which could command public support, and be passed.

Waxman was wrong when he stated that the choice before the 103rd Congress was between Clinton's national health insurance plan and no health care reform at all. Given its lack of public support, the Clinton plan stood no chance of passage. Rather, the real choice before the 103rd Congress was between a scaled-down version of the Clinton plan, which fell short of universal coverage, and no health care reform at all. By ruling out support for modest and incremental health care reform, Waxman and other supporters of single-payer insurance effectively destroyed any prospects for health care reform in the 103rd Congress.

McDermott Opposes the Health Security Act

As the primary House cosponsor of the Wellstone-McDermott bill, Mc-Dermott was perhaps the single most influential supporter of single-payer health insurance in the 103rd Congress. As we have seen, of the ninety-six congressional cosponsors of the bill, ninety-one were House members, all but one Democrats. As a result, House Democrats represented a substantial and practically the sole source of support for single-payer insurance in the 103rd Congress.

As primary House cosponsor of the Wellstone-McDermott bill, McDermott led the Democratic faction supporting single-payer health insurance in the House. As a result, he exerted influence over House Democratic supporters of single-payer insurance in shaping the congressional bargaining over health care legislation during 1993 and 1994. Since no national health insurance bill was possible without the support of House cosponsors of the Wellstone-McDermott bill, McDermott was well positioned to use his influence to determine the ultimate outcome of the politics of health care reform in the 103rd Congress, and he steered House supporters of single-payer insurance to reject any compromise with Clinton.

McDermott urged congressional supporters to take a hard line against Clinton's health care reform initiative and reject the Health Security Act. He argued that congressional supporters of single-payer insurance should accept nothing less than the scrapping and replacement of the current employment-based insurance system with a government-financed and -administered insurance program. Since the Health Security Act would preserve, rather than eliminate, the employment-based insurance system, McDermott argued that the bill fell short of the radical overhaul of the health care system congressional supporters of single-payer insurance favored.

On October 5, 1993, McDermott issued a statement outlining his objections to the Health Security Act. He charged that the bill would fall short of Clinton's goal of guaranteeing universal coverage, jeopardize the health care benefits of Medicare and Medicaid beneficiaries, and preserve waste and inefficiency in the health care system.

As we saw in Chapter 2, the Health Security Act would require working families to pay 20 percent of the cost of their group health insurance, with the remaining 80 percent financed by their employers. However, McDermott argued that many working families would be unable to afford paying 20 percent of the cost of their group insurance. True, the bill would provide federal subsidies for members of a regional health alliance to pay for their own group insurance, but only for families with incomes below 150 percent of the poverty line. Many middle-class families not eligible for subsidies would be unable to afford paying their 20 percent share of cost of group insurance, and would opt to remain uninsured.

McDermott was sharply critical of the means which the Health Security Act would use to finance coverage for the uninsured. As we saw in Chapter 2, the bill would finance coverage for the uninsured largely by reducing Medicare and Medicaid spending by $238 billion from 1994 to 2000. McDermott charged that reductions in Medicare and Medicaid spending of that magnitude could only be achieved by severely curtailing access to the health care currently provided to beneficiaries of the two programs.

McDermott argued that the only viable means to finance coverage for the uninsured was not to sharply reduce Medicare and Medicaid spending, but to eliminate the administrative waste and inefficiency associated with the private health insurance industry. As we saw, the private insurance industry represents a major source of administrative waste and inefficiency, which stems from the duplication of administrative overhead and paperwork associated with the existence of 1,500 separate and competing voluntary plans. By establishing a single government program for managing the insurance system, single-payer insurance would create a more efficient means to finance the delivery of health care, resulting in substantial administrative savings.

However, the Health Security Act would do nothing to generate administrative savings, since the bill would preserve the wasteful and inefficient private health insurance industry. By contrast, McDermott claimed, by scrapping and replacing the private insurance industry with a government-financed and -administered insurance program, the Wellstone-McDermott bill would reduce insurance administrative costs by $70 billion annually. Those administrative savings would be used to finance coverage for the uninsured without any debilitating reductions in Medicare and Medicaid spending.[30]

McDermott concluded that the Health Security Act could not serve as a credible basis for health care reform because the bill would preserve the private health insurance industry as the primary source for financing and administering the delivery of medical services. Given the administrative waste and inefficiency generated by the industry, McDermott charged that a humane and rational health care system could not be established until insurance companies were replaced by a government program to guarantee universal, comprehensive coverage. In delivering his attack against the Health Security Act, McDermott declared that

I have great concerns about a plan [which would] preserve a [health care] financing system all agree has been a disaster. It is hard to believe that placing insurance companies in charge of the [health care] delivery system will provide rational and humane cost-containment or a commitment to universal care. Certainly, there is no evidence that it will improve [health care] quality. Insurance companies simply have no mandate to protect the public good. . . .

I will continue to fight for a solution that changes our system of financing . . . health care, preserves free choice of provider, achieves cost-containment on the basis of beneficial results and the public good, yields substantial administrative savings, and enhances quality. . . . The single-payer approach unequivocally achieves all these goals.[31]

A major problem McDermott had with the Health Security Act was that it created an overly cumbersome and complicated means to achieve health care reform. Employers would provide their working families group health insurance. The federal government would provide employers subsidies to purchase group insurance if its cost exceeded 7.9 percent of payroll. Each state would establish a health alliance in every region, which would contract with private health insurance plans to provide coverage to the public. Health alliances would hold open enrollment periods during which each individual would have the opportunity to select a private plan offered by the alliance. Regional health alliances would use their collective bargaining power to reduce health care costs by restraining the growth in their insurance premiums. However, if this failed, then a National Health Board would impose limits of its own on insurance premiums paid by each health alliance.

McDermott argued that the single-payer health insurance plan contained in the Wellstone-McDermott bill would provide a much simpler and more straightforward means to achieve health care reform. The federal government would provide health insurance to every citizen and legal resident, financed through taxes. A budget would be imposed to contain health care costs at the national and state level. Under the Wellstone-McDermott bill universal, comprehensive coverage would be achieved in a simple, straightforward manner, without the need for federal subsidies for employers, health alliances, private insurance, or limits on insurance premiums, all of which would be complicating factors in realizing health care reform through the Health Security Act. McDermott believed that the Wellstone-McDermott bill was the only viable means for achieving universal coverage, since the Health Security Act resembled a Rube Goldberg contraption, which was too complicated and convoluted to comprehend, let alone pass. Indeed, McDermott predicted that support for the Wellstone-McDermott bill would grow, once "people see that Clinton's proposal, with all of its Rube Goldberg stuff, can't fly."[32]

The reason why the Health Security Act was so complicated and cumbersome was that Clinton had made too many compromises and concessions to win support for the bill among conservative Democratic members of Congress, who opposed single-payer health insurance. Due to conservative opposition to single-payer insurance, Clinton could not recommend a health care reform plan which would guarantee universal coverage through the federal government; rather, he had to achieve this goal by building upon the current employment-based insurance system. Any attempt to achieve universal coverage through the employment-based insurance system required a number of federal regulations to assure that national health insurance could be established on a fiscally and economically viable basis. Federal subsidies would have to be provided employers to assure that they could afford to purchase group insurance for their working families; health alliances would have to be established to give consumers both a choice of private plans and the collective bargaining clout to restrain the growth in insurance premiums; the federal government would have to impose limits on insurance premiums if the market failed to do so. All the complications written into the Health Security Act stemmed from the fact that Clinton had rejected single-payer insurance in favor of building upon the current employment-based insurance system, which necessitated the imposition of a complicated array of federal regulations to assure that universal coverage could be achieved on a fiscally and economically viable basis. All those regulations could have been dispensed with had Clinton opted to guarantee universal coverage through a simple, straightforward single-payer insurance plan.

McDermott believed that the compromises and concessions Clinton had made to win support for the Health Security Act among conservative Democratic members of Congress had rendered the bill unviable as a means to achieve universal health insurance coverage. He made this clear following Clinton's introduction of the Health Security Act on October 27, 1993. McDermott responded to the introduction of the Health Security Act by charging that the administration had compromised too much in order to find a middle ground in health care reform and design a national health insurance bill which would appeal to conservative Democrats. "[Clinton aides] have gone nuts to find what the middle is" in health care reform, McDermott claimed. "They have made a lot of very carefully contrived decisions to try to find the exact middle, and I don't think they can do it that way."[33]

McDermott's efforts to steer House supporters of single-payer health insurance into opposing the Health Security Act were successful. Only forty-six of the ninety-one House cosponsors of the Wellstone-McDermott bill agreed to also cosponsor the Health Security Act.[34] With fully half of all House cosponsors of the Wellstone-McDermott bill refusing to support the Health Security Act, Clinton's national health insurance plan stood no chance of passage. Indeed, the Health Security Act succeeded in garnering the support of only 32 senators and 101 House members in the 103rd Congress, well short of the majority needed for passage of the bill in both houses of the legislative branch.[35] With the exception of Senator Jeffords, virtually all congressional cosponsors of the bill were Democrats.

Clinton fully recognized that McDermott and the more liberal factions of House supporters of single-payer health insurance had the capacity and the will to prevent health care reform altogether. In an effort to secure the support of this liberal faction for the Health Security Act, Clinton agreed to make a major concession to congressional supporters of single-payer insurance. The bill provided each state the option of replacing its private insurance industry with a government program.[36]

However, McDermott rejected this concession because the Health Security Act did not require the states to establish a single-payer health insurance plan; rather, each state was free to decide on its own whether to do so.[37] However, few if any states were likely to avail themselves of the option of establishing a single-payer plan. As a result, the option the states would have under the Health Security Act to establish single-payer plans represented an empty gesture by

Clinton, designed more to secure the support of congressional backers of single-payer insurance for the bill than to develop a meaningful basis for instituting a government program. Accordingly, Clinton's decision to provide states the option of establishing their own single-payer insurance plans under the Health Security Act failed to secure the support of McDermott and the more liberal Democratic House faction backing single-payer insurance for the bill.

McDermott succeeded in having the more liberal Democratic House supporters of single-payer health insurance take a hard line on health care reform. They would accept nothing less than the scrapping and replacement of the private insurance industry with a government program. Any national health insurance plan, like the Health Security Act, which fell short of this goal would be unacceptable.

In effect, McDermott steered half of all House supporters of single-payer insurance to take an all-or-nothing approach to health care reform: either Congress established a single-payer plan, or there would be no health care reform at all. Since Congress was not about to establish a single-payer plan, and half of all House cosponsors of the Wellstone-McDermott bill refused to accept anything less than a government program, no basis existed for the passage of any health care reform legislation in the 103rd Congress. By taking a hard and intransigent line on health care reform, and refusing to compromise on their goal, McDermott and the more liberal House faction supporting single-payer insurance effectively destroyed any prospects for passage of a health care reform bill in the 103rd Congress.

Wellstone Joins McDermott in Opposing the Health Security Act

In pursuing his campaign in Congress against the Health Security Act, McDermott received valuable support from Wellstone, the lead cosponsor of the Wellstone-McDermott bill in the Senate. Unlike in the House, practically no support existed for single-payer health insurance in the Senate. As we saw, only five senators served as cosponsors for the Wellstone-McDermott bill, as opposed to ninety-one House members. As a result, no substantial bloc of senators supporting single-payer insurance existed which Wellstone could lead. Given the almost complete absence of support for single-payer insurance in the Senate, Wellstone had little, if any, influence to exert in the congressional bargaining over the final outcome of national health insurance legislation. This differed from the House, where McDermott wielded influence over a substantial bloc of Democratic House members who supported single-payer insurance, giving the representative significant clout in the congressional maneuvering over the final outcome of national health insurance legislation.

Despite his lack of influence in the Senate, Wellstone remained an outspoken voice in support of single-payer health insurance in Congress. Like McDermott, he rejected the Health Security Act, arguing that it failed to provide a fair and equitable basis for guaranteeing universal coverage. In an article published in 1994, Wellstone charged that the bill was inequitable. By imposing substantial patient cost-sharing requirements, of up to $3,000 annually for each family, the bill would do little to ease the onerous financial burdens households currently assume in having to meet their health care expenses. The Health Security Act would impose financial hardship upon small businesses, self-employed workers, and the unemployed, all of whom would have difficulty purchasing their own private insurance, as required under the bill.

Wellstone was particularly critical of the Health Security Act for its failure to require all individuals to enroll in a regional health alliance. As we saw in Chapter 2, the bill would have exempted all employers with over 5,000 workers from the requirement of having to enroll in a regional health alliance. Large corporations and government entities tend to employ younger and healthier workers. By contrast, regional health alliances would represent entire communities, which have many older and sicker residents. As a result, health care costs for large employers would be lower than those of regional health alliances.

By allowing large employers to opt out of regional health alliances, the Health Security Act would permit large employers to take advantage of their lower health care costs to provide their working families the most comprehensive coverage available at the lowest possible premiums. Given the fact that they would be left with older and sicker members, regional health alliances would have to pay higher premiums for comparable coverage provided to large employers. As a result, the Health Security Act would allow younger and healthier workers employed with either large corporations or the government to negotiate more favorable terms for their private insurance than would have been the case with the older and sicker members of regional health alliances. Accordingly, the bill would preserve the inequities of the current health care market which allows firms employing young and healthy working families to take advantage of their lower health care costs to purchase private insurance at lower premiums than comparable coverage secured by their older and sicker counterparts.

Wellstone charged that by building upon, rather than scrapping and replacing, the current employment-based insurance system, Clinton's national health insurance plan would rely too heavily upon market forces for achieving health care reform, perpetuating all the inequities which persist in the delivery of medical services:

The Clinton plan fails because it gives markets one more chance to solve America's health care problems. Markets by definition create inequality. When market forces are dominant [in the health care system], they construct elaborate administrative mechanisms to distinguish the healthy from the sick. The public sector is then faced with the task of constructing bureaucracies to control discrimination. Such a system is not conducive to either controlling costs or providing quality care.[38]

Wellstone agreed with Waxman and McDermott that the inadequacies of Clinton's national health insurance plan were the result of the president's determination to make concessions to interest groups traditionally opposed to health care reform in order to win their support for his program to overhaul the medical system. Those concessions resulted in Clinton producing a much weaker and more ineffective national health insurance plan than supporters of single-payer insurance were capable of backing:

The Clinton Administration's strategy has been to build a broad coalition for health care reform—perhaps too broad—including providers, businesses, consumers, and some insurance companies. It bowed to pressure from business to permit large employers to opt out of the [health alliance] system, opening the door to continued cost-shifting, administrative nightmares, and discrimination. The President is inclined to agree with providers that rate-setting should be avoided unless the market fails. This is bad news for one-tier, universal coverage, for effective cost containment, and thus for the viability of the [health care] system.[39]

Wellstone argued that by replacing the wasteful and inefficient private health insurance industry with a more efficient government program, the Wellstone-McDermott bill would reduce annual administrative costs in the health care system by $107 billion.[40] Those savings would be used to finance coverage for the uninsured, without adding a dime to health care costs. The public would be covered by a single insurance plan, providing the same benefits to all individuals, regardless of their employment or income status. The plan would be financed on a progressive basis, through taxes; the wealthier the individual, the more taxes he or she would pay for their insurance. Single-payer insurance represents the most efficient and equitable means available for guaranteeing universal coverage. As a result, Wellstone made it clear that he would reject anything short of the single-payer health insurance plan contained in the Wellstone-McDermott bill:

[The Wellstone-McDermott bill] faces some tough issues head on. It would sharply limit the role of the health insurance industry. It would finance the [health care] system progressively through public funds. . . . [Under the Wellstone-McDermott bill], health care . . . will be vastly more affordable and accessible, more responsive to human need, and a great improvement over the status quo.[41]

As we will see in Chapter 8, on August 2, 1994, Clinton retreated from his insistence on universal health insurance coverage, endorsing a scaled-back health care reform bill sponsored by Mitchell which would have guaranteed health care benefits to only 95 percent of the public. By August 1994, it was clear that the Senate would not pass legislation to guarantee universal coverage. As a result, Mitchell had no alternative but to craft a compromise bill which would expand private insurance while stopping short of universal coverage. Clinton and Mitchell hoped that this compromise would be sufficient to build a Democratic majority in the Senate in favor of more modest health care reform legislation than the president's original national health insurance plan. Senate Democratic sponsors of Clinton's national health insurance plan were almost unanimous in their acceptance of Mitchell's health care reform bill, conceding that the achievement of universal coverage was politically unfeasible.

However, Wellstone refused to join his Senate Democratic colleagues in agreeing to compromise legislation which would expand private insurance while stopping short of universal coverage. Wellstone insisted that Senate Democrats must not compromise on their goal of achieving universal coverage. Addressing the Senate floor on August 13, 1994, Wellstone noted that the Mitchell bill goal of guaranteeing 95 percent of the public coverage would still leave millions of individuals uninsured. "The Mitchell bill . . . leaves out some 14 million Americans," Wellstone noted. "It is not universal coverage. Most people . . . understand that when 14 million people are left out, that could very well be them."[42] Wellstone concluded his address by urging that there be no retreat on Clinton's original goal of universal coverage. "[The Mitchell bill] does not live up to the commitment which we began with, which is: We ought to make sure that . . . each and every man, woman, and child can afford humane, decent health care for themselves, their loved ones, and their children," Wellstone declared.[43]

Wellstone reinforced the hard line against the Health Security Act taken by McDermott. Wellstone and McDermott both agreed on pursuing an all-or-nothing strategy on health care reform, rejecting anything which fell short of the single-payer health insurance plan contained in the Wellstone-McDermott bill. By steering half of all House supporters of single-payer insurance into rejecting the Health Security Act, Wellstone and McDermott assured the defeat of Clinton's national health insurance plan in the 103rd Congress, derailing the president's health care initiative.

Moreover, by representing the Senate's lone liberal voice against Mitchell's health care reform bill, Wellstone derailed the Senate majority leader's last-ditch attempt to craft compromise legislation to overhaul the medical system in the 103rd Congress. By opposing the Mitchell bill, Wellstone served notice that congressional liberal Democrats, who remained a formidable voting bloc in the House, would reject any legislation which fell short of universal coverage. This scuttled Clinton and Mitchell's last-minute efforts in August 1994 to build a consensus among congressional Democrats for more modest health care reform, further dooming the president's initiative to overhaul the medical system.

CONCLUSION

During 1993–1994, national health insurance dominated the political agenda as a result of the Democratic Party's commitment, under Clinton's leadership, to achieve health care reform. The fact that both the White House and Congress were controlled by the Democrats during those two years gave the party a unique opportunity to fulfill its commitment to establish national health insurance. However, the Democrats were badly divided and weakened in pursuing their health care reform initiative. The weakness of the Democrats on health care reform was due to their failure to forge a consensus concerning what kind of national health insurance should be established. Rather, Democrats were deeply divided on the issue of health care reform between two sharply opposing groups: liberals, who favored single-payer insurance; and moderates, led by Clinton, who favored building upon, rather than scrapping and replacing, the current employment-based insurance system.

Single-payer health insurance commanded substantial support among House Democrats. Without the unanimous backing of House Democratic supporters of single-payer insurance, the Health Security Act stood no chance of passage. Recognizing this, Clinton attempted to secure the support of the House Democrats by including an option within the bill which would have permitted the states to establish their own single-payer insurance plans, in lieu of private insurance. However, this was not enough for more liberal House Democratic supporters of single-payer insurance, led by McDermott, who insisted on an all-or-nothing strategy on health care reform: Either Congress would pass a single-payer insurance plan, or there would be no health care reform plan at all.

By taking a completely intransigent position on health care reform, McDermott and the more liberal House Democratic supporters of single-payer health insurance, backed by Senator Wellstone, assured the defeat of the Health Security Act in the 103rd Congress. With the Republican Party, which strongly opposes national health insurance, maintaining majorities in both houses of the 104th Congress, the failure of the 103rd Congress to pass health care reform legislation killed any chance for achieving an overhaul of the medical system during Clinton's first, and possibly only, term. As a result, by maintaining an inflexible position on health care reform, the more liberal Democratic supporters of single-payer insurance assured that no national health insurance legislation would be passed before 1997, at the very earliest. The collapse of Clinton's health care reform initiative during 1993–1994 was as much due to the weakness of the Democratic Party and divisions between its liberal and moderate wings, as it was to opposition from the Republicans and the private insurance industry.

Chapter 8

The Collapse of Clinton's Health Care Reform Initiative

> The Clinton health plan is dead and no additional powder on its lifeless,
> puffed-up face is going to make it attractive to the American people.[1]
> > Senator Phil Gramm of Texas, address on the Senate
> > floor, August 19, 1994.

During 1993–1994, Clinton faced a formidable task in pursuing his health care reform initiative. To secure the establishment of national health insurance, Clinton and his Democratic congressional allies had to advance his health care reform legislation through the maze of legislative committees exercising jurisdiction over medical policy before it could go to the floor of either house for debate. Clinton was more successful in advancing national health insurance through Congress than any previous presidential supporter of health care reform. In the half century since health care reform was first considered by Congress in 1945, national health insurance legislation had been approved by only a single congressional committee—the Senate Labor and Human Resources Committee, which passed a comprehensive health care reform bill in the 102nd Congress.[2]

By contrast, slightly modified versions of Clinton's national health insurance plan were approved by three of the five congressional committees in the 103rd Congress exercising jurisdiction over health care reform. A fourth committee, the Senate Finance Committee, approved a scaled-down version of the Clinton plan. Never in history had national health insurance legislation won approval by practically all the committees exercising jurisdiction over health care reform in a single Congress. Approval of health care reform legislation by the Labor and Human Resources and Finance Committees cleared the way for Mitchell to bring a scaled-down version of the Clinton plan to the Senate floor for debate. The ten-day Senate debate on health care reform, which took place during August 9–19, 1994, marks the first time in American history that either house of Congress undertook a formal debate on national health insurance.

However, despite the progress Clinton made in advancing his national health insurance plan through the 103rd Congress, the Senate failed to take any action on health care reform following the conclusion of its floor debate on this issue on August 19. As a result, while Clinton succeeded in pushing national health insurance further through Congress than any previous presidential supporter of health care reform, his campaign to overhaul the medical system ended like all similar efforts undertaken by previous chief executives—in failure.

CLINTON'S NATIONAL HEALTH INSURANCE PLAN
WORKS ITS WAY THROUGH CONGRESS

During spring and summer of 1994, Clinton made substantial progress in advancing his national health insurance plan through Congress. Before the Clinton plan could go to either house of Congress for debate, the president's program needed to be approved by two Senate and at least two of the three House committees exercising jurisdiction over health care reform. In June slightly modified versions of the Clinton plan were approved by one Senate and two House committees.

On June 9 Clinton's national health insurance plan cleared its first full congressional committee when the Senate Labor and Human Resources Committee approved its own slightly modified version of the president's program by a vote of eleven to six. All ten Democratic members of the committee voted to approve the Clinton plan. Senator Jeffords, the lone congressional Republican cosponsor of the Clinton plan, joined Democratic members of the committee in voting to approve the president's program. The remaining six Republican members of the committee voted to reject the Clinton plan.[3]

On June 23 Clinton's national health insurance plan mounted another congressional hurdle when the House Education and Labor Committee approved another slightly modified version of the president's program by a vote of twenty-six to seventeen. Twenty-six Democratic members of the committee voted to approve the Clinton plan; all fifteen Republican and two Democratic members of the committee voted to reject it.[4]

On June 30 the House Ways and Means Committee became the third and final congressional committee to take favorable action on Clinton's national health insurance plan, approving a slightly modified version of the president's program by the narrowest of margins: twenty to eighteen. Twenty Democratic members of the committee voted to approve the Clinton plan; all fourteen Republican and four Democratic members of the committee voted to reject it.[5]

The national health insurance bills approved by the Senate Labor and Human Resources and House Education and Labor and Ways and Means Committees followed the same basic approach to guaranteeing universal coverage contained in the Clinton plan. Employers would have been required to provide their working families group insurance and finance 80 percent of its cost. The House Ways and Means Committee would establish a new federal insurance program, Medicare Part C. Employers with under 100 workers would have the option of enrolling their working families in Medicare Part C in lieu of providing them group insurance. The federal government would provide low-income families subsidies for the purchase of private insurance. Small and medium-size businesses would be provided the option of purchasing their group insurance through a health alliance, which they would be allowed to join on a voluntary basis. Insurance premiums for members of a health alliance would be community-rated. Private plans would be prohibited from denying health care benefits to any individual due to chronic ailments he or she may suffer from; or to exclude preexisting medical conditions from the coverage they provide their subscribers. The federal government would impose limits to control the growth of health care costs. The Senate Labor and Human Resources and House Education and Labor Committees would have contained health care costs by imposing limits on the annual growth in insurance premiums, requiring that they not increase more than the CPI beginning in 2000; the House Ways and Means Committee would have done the same by placing a ceiling requiring that the annual increase in medical spending not exceed that of the GDP beginning in 2001.[6]

With two of the three House committees exercising jurisdiction over health care reform—Ways and Means and Education and Labor—having approved national health insurance bills, the House Democratic leadership was now free to bring health care reform legislation to the House floor. Accordingly, on July 29 House Majority Leader Richard Gephardt of Missouri outlined the details of national health insurance legislation which he intended to bring to the House floor.[7] Gephardt's national health insurance bill most closely resembled legislation approved by the House Ways and Means Committee. Like the committee's bill, the Gephardt plan would have provided employers with under 100 workers the option of enrolling them and their families in Medicare Part C in lieu of extending them group insurance.[8]

The House was originally scheduled to begin floor debate on Gephardt's national health insurance plan on August 15.[9] However, on August 11 House Democratic leaders announced that they would not undertake a floor debate on the Gephardt plan until the Senate, which, at the time was pursuing a floor debate of its own, completed action on health care reform.[10] As a result, the political spotlight on national health insurance quickly moved to the Senate, where the fate of Clinton's health care reform now rested.

THE SENATE FINANCE COMMITTEE APPROVES A HEALTH CARE REFORM BILL

Even as the House Ways and Means Committee approved a slightly modified version of Clinton's national health insurance plan, the president's program ran into its first major obstacle in the Senate Finance Committee. On June 9 Moynihan introduced his national health insurance bill to the committee which, like the Clinton plan, would require employers to provide their working families group coverage.[11] However, on June 30 the committee voted to reject the employer mandates contained in the Moynihan bill by a margin of fourteen to six. Nine Republicans joined five Democrats in voting to kill employer mandates; the remaining six Democrats voted for employer mandates.[12] In lieu of the Moynihan bill, on July 2 the Senate Finance Committee voted by a margin of twelve to eight to approve more modest legislation designed to expand public access to private insurance, while stopping short of guaranteeing universal coverage.[13]

Senate Finance's health care reform bill was similar to national health insurance legislation approved by three other congressional committees in June, except in two important respects. First, the Senate Finance Committee's bill would have expanded public access to private insurance, but stopped well short of guaranteeing universal coverage; and second, it would have discouraged, but not prevented, substantial increases in private insurance premiums. By contrast, the health care reform legislation approved by the three other congressional committees would have guaranteed universal coverage; and imposed firm ceilings to control the growth in private insurance premiums.

The Senate Labor and Human Resources and House Education and Labor and Ways and Means Committees would have guaranteed universal health insurance coverage by imposing a federal mandate requiring employers to provide their working families health care benefits. The Senate Finance Committee's health care reform bill contained no such employer mandate. Instead, the bill would provide federal subsidies to low-income families for the purchase of private insurance. The goal of those subsidies would be to guarantee that 95 percent of the public would be insured by 2002. A Health Commission would be established to determine whether that goal had been reached. If the commission determined that the federal subsidies to low-income families for the purchase of private insurance fell short of guaranteeing 95 percent of the public coverage by 2002, then the body would be required to propose recommendations to Congress to achieve this goal. However, Congress would be free to either act upon or ignore the commission's recommendations.

The Senate Labor and Human Resources and House Education and Labor Committees would have contained health care costs by imposing limits on the growth in private health insurance premiums. The Senate Finance Committee's health care reform bill contained no such limits. Instead, the bill would impose punitive measures to discourage substantial increases in insurance premiums. The Internal Revenue Service would set a target premium for private insurance in each area. If a private plan's premium exceeded the target, then a 25 percent tax would be imposed on the difference between the actual premium and the target premium.[14]

By failing to guarantee universal health insurance coverage, while imposing only weak, and possibly ineffective, health care cost-containment measures, the Senate Finance Committee's health care reform bill fell far short of the goal of providing universal access to affordable medical services, which served as the bedrock principles of Clinton's health care reform initiative. However, despite its shortcomings, the Finance Committee's bill was the only health care reform legislation the Senate was likely to pass. The Senate was not about to pass the far more sweeping health care reforms contained in Clinton's national health insurance plan and in the various versions of the president's program offered by the Senate Labor and Human Resources Committee and the House Democratic leadership. As a result, the only health care reform bill which Mitchell could conceivably bring to the Senate floor was legislation which closely resembled the Finance Committee's measure.

CLINTON WEIGHS IN ON HEALTH CARE REFORM

However, the Senate Finance Committee's health care reform bill still fell far short of the goals Clinton hoped to achieve in pursuing his health care reform initiative. True, in his 1994 State of the Union address, Clinton stressed that he was open to compromise on the final version of health care reform legislation Congress might pass. "I am open . . . to the best ideas of members of both parties," Clinton told Congress. "I have no special brief for any specific approach, even in our own bill."

However, Clinton also stressed in his State of the Union address that universal health insurance coverage was the one goal that he would not compromise on. Clinton emphasized that any health care reform bill Congress passed must guarantee universal coverage. Waving his veto pen, Clinton went so far as to threaten to veto any health care reform bill which failed to guarantee universal coverage. "If you send me legislation that does not guarantee every American private health insurance that can never be taken away, you will force me to take this pen, veto the legislation, and we'll come right back here and start over again," Clinton warned Congress.[15]

Clinton's intransigent insistence that he would accept nothing less than universal health insurance coverage in any health care reform bill Congress passed presented the president and Senate Democrats with a dilemma. The Finance Committee's bill, which stopped well short of universal coverage, was the only health care reform legislation the Senate was likely to pass. And yet, Clinton had warned that he would veto such legislation, foreclosing any possibility of passage of a health care reform bill in the 103rd Congress. Since the Senate would not pass any bill guaranteeing universal coverage, no prospects for enactment of health care reform legislation in the 103rd Congress existed unless Clinton agreed to accept a measure which fell short of universal coverage.

Clinton desperately needed the 103rd Congress to pass a health care reform bill. The Democratic Party maintained overwhelming majorities in both houses of Congress. As a result, the best chance for passage of health care legislation was in the 103rd Congress. The party in power almost always loses seats in midterm congressional elections, assuring that there would be fewer Democrats in the 104th Congress, making passage of health care reform legislation highly unlikely during 1995–1996.

As a result, if health care reform legislation was to be passed during Clinton's first, and possibly only, term, such action needed to be taken by the 103rd Congress. To guarantee such action, Clinton needed to compromise with Senate Democrats, and drop his insistence on universal health insurance coverage, in order to permit passage of a more modest bill resembling the Finance Committee's legislation. Clinton was better off with passage of a health care bill which fell short of universal coverage than with no legislation at all. Having invested the first two years of his presidency in an ambitious and relentless effort to secure the establishment of national health insurance, Clinton could not politically afford to have the 103rd Congress adjourn in October 1994 without having taken any action on health care reform.

Accordingly, on August 2 Clinton dropped his insistence on universal health insurance coverage by endorsing a health care reform bill Mitchell introduced in the Senate the same day.[16] The Mitchell bill represented a last-ditch attempt by the Senate majority leader to craft compromise legislation which would expand private insurance while stopping short of universal coverage. As a result, the Mitchell bill represented a more modest version of Clinton's original national health insurance plan. Clinton and Mitchell hoped that the Senate majority leader's bill was sufficiently modest and practical to allow them to build a Democratic majority in the 103rd Congress behind the legislation before lawmakers adjourned in October.

By agreeing to abandon the lofty goal of universal coverage in favor of Mitchell's last-minute compromise legislation, Clinton hoped to secure passage of a scaled-back version of his original national health insurance plan and salvage his flagging health care reform initiative before the adjournment of the 103rd Congress. Clinton knew all too well that the window of opportunity for health care reform would close with the end of the 103rd Congress; and the president had no choice but to abandon his once solid commitment to universal coverage if he was to have any hope of success in securing passage of legislation to overhaul the medical system during his first, and possibly only, term.

MITCHELL INTRODUCES HIS HEALTH CARE REFORM BILL

With the two Senate committees exercising jurisdiction over health care reform—the Labor and Human Resources and Finance Committees—having approved legislation to overhaul the medical system, the way was now clear for Mitchell to bring a bill to the floor. On August 2, 1994, Mitchell introduced his health care reform bill, which closely resembled the Finance Committee's measure. The Mitchell bill would provide low-income families subsidies to assist them in purchasing their own private insurance beginning in 1997. The federal government and states would fully subsidize the cost of private insurance for poor families in lieu of Medicaid. The provision of private insurance for families earning annual incomes from over 100 percent to 200 percent of the poverty line would be partially subsidized on an income-related basis; the lower a family's income, the greater the federal subsidy it would receive.

The government would provide additional subsidies to finance the cost of private insurance for pregnant women and children under the age of nineteen. The federal government and states would fully subsidize the cost of private insurance for pregnant women and children in families earning annual incomes of up to 185 percent of the poverty line. The provision of private insurance for pregnant women and children in families earning annual incomes of from over 185 percent to 300 percent would be partially subsidized on an income-related basis.[17] In addition to subsidizing private insurance for low-income families, Mitchell's health care reform bill would expand Medicare to include coverage for home health care and prescription drugs.[18]

Most of the cost of private health insurance for working families is financed by employers, making coverage affordable for households who have employers. However, this is not the case with self-employed families, who must pay the entire cost of their private insurance, making coverage practically unaffordable for them. Accordingly, many, if not most, self-employed families are uninsured. To make private insurance more affordable, Mitchell's health care reform bill would raise the federal deduction provided to self-employed families for the purchase of coverage from 25 percent to 50 percent of the cost of coverage.[19]

The goal of the government subsidies provided for under Mitchell's health care reform bill would be to guarantee that 95 percent of the public was insured by 2000. A National Health Care Cost and Coverage Commission would be established to determine whether 95 percent of the public is insured by 2000. If the commission determined that the federal subsidies provided to low-income individuals had fallen short of guaranteeing 95 percent of the public private health insurance coverage, then the body would be required to propose recommendations to Congress concerning how to achieve this goal.

If Congress failed to take action to guarantee 95 percent of the public coverage by the end of 2000, then an employer mandate would take effect. Employers with twenty-five or more workers would be required to provide their working families group health insurance in those states where less than 95 percent of residents are insured, and finance 50 percent of its cost. Employers with less than twenty-five workers would not be required to provide their working families group insurance.

The federal government would provide income-related subsidies to assist working families earning annual incomes under 200 percent of the poverty line to purchase their group health insurance, should the employer mandate take effect; the lower the income, the greater the federal subsidy each low-income household would receive. Poor working families would pay no more than 4 percent of their income for group insurance. Families earning annual incomes of 200 percent of the poverty line would pay no more than 8 percent of their income for group insurance. The federal subsidies provided to low-income individuals for the purchase of private insurance would be financed through deep cuts in Medicare and Medicaid spending, which will be discussed later.

Mitchell's health care reform bill would have used a combination of market and regulatory mechanisms to contain health care costs and make group health insurance more affordable for small business. A major objective of the bill was to give small business the same kind of bargaining clout in the insurance market big business currently enjoys.

Each large corporation represents a substantial share of the private health insurance market in a given area. Private plans aggressively compete to sell group coverage to each large corporation, since it represents a substantial share of the insurance market. Given their importance in the insurance market, large corporations have the bargaining clout to negotiate with the private insurance industry in securing the most comprehensive coverage at the lowest possible premium for their working families.

By contrast, each small business represents only an insignificant share of the private health insurance market in a given area. Private plans do not place a high priority on the sale of group coverage to any given small business, since it represents only a small fraction of the insurance market in its area. Given their weak position in the insurance market, small businesses lack the bargaining clout to negotiate with the private insurance industry in securing the most comprehensive coverage at the lowest premium possible for their working families. The lack of bargaining clout in the insurance market is a major reason why small businesses must pay an average of 35 percent higher premiums for the same group coverage offered to large corporations, as we saw.

Mitchell's health care reform bill would have required the states to establish a health alliance in each area. Employers with under 500 workers would be required to join a health alliance. All other individuals would be allowed to voluntarily join a health alliance. Health alliances would be required to provide their members a choice of at least three private plans, including one fee-for-service plan and one HMO.

To survive, private health insurance plans would have to negotiate contracts with health alliances; many, if not most, consumers in each area would be enrolled in those organizations. Private plans which failed to negotiate such contracts would be excluded from a substantial share of the insurance market, resulting in a significant loss of business, and the possibility of bankruptcy. To secure such contracts, private plans would have to offer members of health alliances the most comprehensive coverage at the lowest premium possible. As a result, by joining health alliances, small businesses would gain the bargaining clout in the insurance market to provide their working families more comprehensive coverage at lower premiums than they currently do.

In addition to restructuring the private health insurance market to the advantage of consumers, Mitchell's health care reform bill would attempt to further reduce medical costs by imposing punitive measures to discourage substantial increases in premiums. The federal government would impose an insurance premium target equal to the CPI plus 3 percent for 1997, 2.5 percent for 1998, and 2 percent thereafter. A 25 percent tax would be imposed on high-cost private insurance plans, equal to the difference between the actual premium and the target premium. Revenues from this tax would represent an additional source of financing for the federal subsidies provided to low-income individuals for the purchase of private insurance.

A major obstacle impeding the ability of small businesses to purchase group health insurance for their working families is the way premiums are rated. Group insurance premiums are experience-rated to reflect the cost of providing health care to each group. Because the cost of health care is spread among a large number of individuals, the premiums large corporations pay to finance the provision of medical services for their working families is sufficient to fund treatment for any employee or member of his or her household who suffers a catastrophic illness or injury. This assures that insurance premiums for large corporations will not be subject to any sudden or substantial increase. By contrast, because the cost of health care is spread among a small number of individuals, the premiums small businesses pay to finance the provision of medical services for their working families is usually insufficient to fund treatment for any employee or a member of his or her household who suffers a catastrophic illness or injury. As a result, small businesses face the prospect of a sudden and substantial increase in their premiums should any of their workers or members of their families suffer a catastrophic illness or injury. In addition to their lack of bargaining clout in the insurance market, the experience-rating of premiums is another major reason why small businesses must pay 35 percent higher premiums for the same group coverage offered to large corporations.

Mitchell's health care reform bill would make group health insurance more affordable for small business by requiring that premiums be community-rated for employers with fewer than 500 workers. Employers with more than 500 workers would be able to purchase private insurance based upon experience-rated premiums. Community-rated premiums reflect the cost of providing health care for entire communities. Since community-rated premiums spread the cost of health care over entire communities, no group need face a sudden and substantial increase in their premiums should one of its members suffer a catastrophic illness or injury. The premiums each community pays to finance the cost of health care for its members is sufficient to fund the medical services required to treat any catastrophic illness or injury any member may suffer. As a result, community-rating assures that increases in premiums will be modest and predictable, making group coverage more affordable for small business.

Private health insurance is a business, rather than a social service. Private plans are not primarily interested in providing residents of the communities they serve access to health care. Rather, private plans are mostly committed to limiting their financial liabilities.

Private health insurance plans cherry-pick their members by limiting coverage to younger and healthier individuals, while denying health care benefits to their older and sicker counterparts. To further limit their financial liabilities, insurance companies refuse to provide coverage for preexisting medical conditions members suffer upon their enrollment in a private plan. By refusing to provide coverage for older and sicker individuals and for preexisting medical conditions their members suffer upon their enrollment in a private plan, insurance companies limit their financial liabilities, guaranteeing a high level of revenues. Mitchell's health care reform bill would prohibit private plans from cherry-picking their members. Private plans would be required to enroll all individuals who wish to purchase insurance, regardless of their age and health status, and exclude coverage for preexisting medical conditions only during the first six months of membership in a plan.[20]

Mitchell's health care reform bill would have achieved its goal of guaranteeing 95 percent of the public health insurance coverage without adding to the swollen federal budget deficit. On August 9, 1994 the Congressional Budget Office (CBO) released its report on the Mitchell bill. The CBO estimated that in the absence of congressional action, the number of uninsured individuals would rise from 40 million in 1997 to 44 million in 2004. The share of the population who were uninsured would increase from 15.2 percent to 15.8 percent during the same period.

Upon taking effect in 1997, Mitchell's health care reform bill would provide coverage to 27 million uninsured individuals, leaving 13 million persons, representing 4.9 percent of the population, without health care benefits. By 2004, 14 million individuals, representing 5 percent of the population, would remain without coverage. As a result, the Mitchell bill would immediately achieve its goal of guaranteeing 95 percent of the public coverage; and that objective would be sustained through the foreseeable future. Should the bill fail to achieve this goal, then employers with twenty-five or more workers would be required to provide their working families group insurance in those states in which less than 95 percent of the residents have coverage, beginning in 2000. The CBO projected that the imposition of such an employer mandate would result in universal coverage during 2000 to 2004, and presumably beyond.[21]

Mitchell's health care reform bill would have financed coverage for the uninsured by reducing Medicare and Medicaid spending, guaranteeing that the legislation would not add to the swollen federal budget deficit. As Table 8.1 shows, the CBO projected that the cost of federal subsidies to assist low-income individuals to purchase their own private health insurance under the Mitchell bill would be $194.3 billion in 2004, assuming no employer mandate took effect under the provisions of the legislation. The bill would subsidize the purchase of private insurance for the poor in lieu of Medicaid, practically eliminating the program. This would result in $138.3 billion in reduced Medicaid spending in 2004. An additional $48.4 billion in savings from Medicare would be achieved that same year. As a result, a total of $186.7 billion in savings from Medicare and Medicaid would be achieved in 2004, almost sufficient to finance the $194.3 billion in subsidies the federal government would spend that year to assist low-

Table 8.1
The CBO's Projections of the Fiscal Effects of Mitchell's Health Care Reform Bill in 2004 Both With and Without an Employer Mandate in Billions of Dollars

	Without Employer Mandate	With Employer Mandate
Medicaid Savings	−138.3	−138.3
Medicare Savings	−48.4	−48.4
Total Health Care Savings	−186.7	−186.7
Subsidies For Low-Income Individuals	194.3	165.5
Additional Health Care Spending	25.4	27.5
Total Additional Health Care Spending	219.7	193.0
Net Additional Health Care Spending	33.0	6.3
Additional Revenues	51.2	33.5
Net Fiscal Effect	−18.2	−27.2

Source: Congressional Record, 103rd Congress, 2nd Session, pp. S11215–24.

income individuals in purchasing their own private insurance. When additional health care spending is balanced by extra taxes, the Mitchell bill would result in net additional revenues of $18.2 billion in 2004, guaranteeing that the legislation would not contribute to the bloated federal budget deficit.

As we have seen, Mitchell's health care bill would impose an employer mandate, should the legislation fail to guarantee 95 percent of the public coverage by 2000. However, even if the employer mandate went into effect, the bill still would not add to the federal budget deficit, as Table 8.1 shows. Indeed, by requiring employers to provide their working families group health insurance, the employer mandate would shift the financial burden of extending the public coverage from the federal government to business. As a result, the federal government would spend less subsidizing the cost of private insurance for low-income families under an employer mandate than without one. Accordingly, the Mitchell bill would result in net additional revenues of $27.2 billion in 2004 with an employer mandate, compared with $18.2 billion without one.

As we have seen, the CBO projected that Mitchell's health care reform bill would succeed in its goal of guaranteeing 95 percent of the public coverage by 2000. However, under the provisions of the bill, no employer mandate would go into effect unless the legislation fell short of this goal. As a result, no employer mandate would likely go into effect; and the CBO projections contained in the first column of Table 8.1 more accurately reflect the fiscal effects of the bill, since they assume no employer mandate.

Despite the fact that Mitchell's health care reform bill would expand private health insurance coverage, without adding to the enlarged federal budget deficit, the legislation was by no means perfect. The greatest flaw in Mitchell's health care reform bill was its lack of effective health care cost-containment measures. True, the bill did impose a 25 percent tax on high-cost private health insurance plans. However, the effectiveness the 25 percent tax would have in deterring private plans from substantially raising their premiums is questionable. Private plans might be better off financially raising their premiums substantially, and paying the 25 percent tax. If this were true, then the 25 percent tax would be ineffective as a deterrent to rising private insurance premiums.

The incentive for private health insurance plans to increase their premiums would be especially great, given the fact that Mitchell's health care bill would provide federal subsidies to millions of low-income individuals to assist them in purchasing their own coverage. By expanding access to health care among low-income individuals, the Mitchell bill would result in increased patient utilization of medical services, raising their cost. Private insurance premiums would have to rise to reflect rising health care costs. Given the increased health care costs which would result from the Mitchell bill, it is doubtful that the 25 percent tax on high-cost private plans would be sufficient to deter substantial increases in insurance premiums.

DOLE INTRODUCES A REPUBLICAN ALTERNATIVE TO MITCHELL'S HEALTH CARE REFORM BILL

Mitchell's health care reform bill was almost unanimously opposed by Senate Republicans, despite the fact that the majority leader's legislation closely resembled the Dole-Chafee bill. As we saw in Chapter 5, the Dole-Chafee bill would require all individuals to purchase their own private health insurance, with the federal government providing subsidies to low-income persons to do so, much as Mitchell's legislation would do. However, by the summer of 1994 Senate Republicans had abandoned the Dole-Chafee bill, believing that it was no longer politically feasible. With public support for Clinton's national health insurance plan having collapsed by the summer of 1994, Senate Republicans no longer felt the need to sponsor health care reform legislation to guarantee universal coverage, as the Dole-Chafee bill would do.

Indeed, by August Clinton and Senate Democrats had abandoned their goal of achieving universal coverage, with Mitchell's health care reform bill guaranteeing only 95 percent of the public coverage. With Clinton and Senate Democrats conceding that passage of legislation guaranteeing universal coverage was no longer politically feasible, Senate Republicans decided to abandon the Dole-Chafee bill in favor of a new measure which, like Mitchell's health care reform legislation, would expand public access to private insurance, while stopping short of assuring that every individual receive health care benefits.

Accordingly, on August 9 Dole joined Senator Bob Packwood of Oregon in introducing a new health care reform bill, cosponsored by forty of the forty-four Republican members of the Senate.[22] The Dole-Packwood bill would provide federal subsidies to low-income individuals to assist them in purchasing their own private insurance. The federal government and states would fully subsidize the cost of private insurance for poor families in lieu of Medicaid. The provision of private insurance for families earning annual incomes of from 100 percent to 150 percent of the poverty line would be partially subsidized on an income-related basis; the lower the income, the greater the federal subsidy a household would receive. Self-employed families are currently allowed to deduct 25 percent of the cost of private insurance from their taxable income. The Dole-Packwood bill would make the cost of private insurance for self-employed families fully tax deductible. Private plans would be required to provide coverage to all individuals wishing to purchase insurance. Exclusions in coverage for preexisting medical conditions would be limited to the first twelve months of enrollment in a private plan for illnesses diagnosed during six months prior to an individual's purchase of insurance.[23]

The Dole-Packwood bill was a badly flawed health care reform measure. In all likelihood, the bill would not achieve its goal of expanding public access to health care by subsidizing the purchase of private health insurance for low-income individuals. It provided federal subsidies for low-income individuals to purchase their own private insurance—but only if these subsidies did not add to the budget deficit. The federal government would be required to either cut back or eliminate its subsidies altogether if they contributed to the deficit. The bill would finance those subsidies through reductions in Medicare and Medicaid spending.[24] However, it failed to specify whether its reductions in Medicare and Medicaid would be sufficient to finance those subsidies. Given the enormous cost the government would have to incur in financing the purchase of private insurance by low-income individuals, there is no reason to believe that the reductions in Medicare and Medicaid spending would, in fact, be sufficient to fund those subsidies.

As a result, the Dole-Packwood bill would, in all likelihood, add to the budget deficit, assuring that either little or no federal subsidies would be provided for low-income individuals to purchase their own private insurance. Accordingly, the bill was nothing more than a political sham, which promised to provide low-income individuals access to health care, while containing provisions which would prevent this from occurring. Its promise to provide low-income individuals access to health care was probably fraudulent.

Even if the Dole-Packwood bill succeeded in providing low-income individuals access to health care, the measure was still badly flawed for two reasons: First, it would do little to provide the uninsured coverage; and second, it represented a fiscally and economically unfeasible means to achieve medical reform, since it included no health care cost-containment measures.

Unlike the Mitchell bill, the Dole-Packwood bill failed to provide low-income families sufficient federal subsidies to enable them to purchase their own private health insurance. True, both bills would fully subsidize the purchase of private

Table 8.2
The Percentage of Earnings Spent by Families With Children With Annual
Incomes of From 100 Percent to 300 Percent of the Poverty Line on Private
Health Insurance Under the Mitchell and Dole-Packwood Bills

Annual Income	The Percentage of Income Spent on Private Health Insurance Under the Mitchell Bill	The Percent of Income Spent on Private Health Insurance Under the Dole-Packwood Bill
$14,000	0	0
$22,000	0	26
$29,000	1	20
$36,000	3	16
$44,000	4	13

Source: Congressional Record, 103rd Congress, 2nd Session, p. 11682.

insurance for poor families, extending coverage to all indigent individuals. However, the Mitchell bill would guarantee access to health care for all nonpoor
families; the Dole-Packwood bill would not.

Mitchell's health care reform bill would provide generous federal subsidies
to assist families with children earning annual incomes of from 100 to 300
percent of the poverty line to purchase their own private insurance. As Table
8.2 shows, the subsidies would be sufficiently generous under the Mitchell bill
to make private insurance affordable for all nonpoor families. No nonpoor family earning an annual income of $44,000 would have to pay more than 4 percent
of its earnings, or $1,700 annually, for private insurance under the Mitchell bill.

By contrast, the Dole-Packwood bill would provide inadequate federal subsidies to assist families earning annual incomes of from 100 percent to 150
percent of the poverty line to purchase their own private insurance. Moreover,
families earning annual incomes of over 150 percent of the poverty line would
be ineligible for any subsidies. As a result, the Dole-Packwood bill failed to
make private insurance affordable for nonpoor families. As Table 8.2 shows, a
family earning an annual income of $22,000, equivalent to 150 percent of the
poverty line, would have to pay 26 percent of its earnings, or $5,883 annually,
for private insurance.[25] Since families earning annual incomes of over 150 percent of the poverty line would receive no federal subsidies, the cost of private
insurance would remain prohibitive for middle-class families under the Dole-
Packwood bill. Families earning annual incomes of over $22,000 to $44,000
would have to pay from 26 percent to 13 percent of their earnings for private
insurance, respectively; the lower the income, the more a family would have to
pay, making coverage especially costly for lower-income households.

In 1993 32 percent of the uninsured were members of families earning annual
incomes of from 100 to 200 percent of the poverty line; 27 percent earned

incomes from over 200 percent to 400 percent of the poverty line; and 13 percent earned incomes of over 400 percent of the poverty line. Those middle- and upper-class families would receive few, if any, federal subsidies to assist them in purchasing private health insurance under the Dole-Packwood bill. In all likelihood, they would remain uninsured.

Relatively few uninsured middle- and even upper-class families would be able to afford the massive amount they would be required to pay for private health insurance under the Dole-Packwood bill. Rather, the only segment of the uninsured population which would have access to health care under the bill would be the poor, whose purchase of private insurance would be fully subsidized. However, in 1993 only 28 percent of the uninsured were poor.[26]

As a result, only that quarter of the uninsured who are poor would be able to secure coverage under the Dole-Packwood bill. The remaining three-quarters of the uninsured population who are nonpoor would have remained without coverage. Indeed, Lewin VHI, a private consulting firm, estimated that the Dole-Packwood bill would leave 30 million individuals uninsured in 2000, compared to 40.9 million persons who were uninsured in 1993.[27] Accordingly, the bill would reduce the number of individuals who are uninsured by only a quarter, extending coverage only to poor individuals without coverage. Middle-class individuals would represent practically all the 30 million persons who would remain uninsured under the bill.

In addition to its failure to reduce the number of uninsured individuals by more than a token amount, the Dole-Packwood bill would not impose any effective health care cost-containment measures. The bill would reduce financial barriers impeding public access to health care by subsidizing the provision of private insurance for low-income families, resulting in increased patient utilization of medical services, raising their cost and the overall inflation rate. Federal spending on health care would increase to finance those subsidies, resulting in a rise in the mounting budget deficit.

As we have seen, the Dole-Packwood bill required that federal subsidies to assist low-income individuals to purchase their own private insurance be either scaled back or eliminated if they increased the deficit. As a result, the federal government would have had to renege on its commitment to provide coverage to low-income uninsured individuals under the bill once it began to increase the deficit. By promising to raise already soaring health care costs, the overall inflation rate, and the federal deficit, and by failing to fulfill its commitment to provide coverage to low-income uninsured individuals, the Dole-Packwood bill represented a legally, fiscally, and economically unviable means to achieve health care reform, and stood no chance of passage.

The fact that the Dole-Packwood bill was a badly flawed means to provide the uninsured coverage was perhaps best expressed by Senator Tom Daschle of South Dakota. Addressing the Senate floor on August 15, 1994, Daschle declared that

Seventy-five percent of those who are uninsured today will be uninsured under the Dole bill in the year 2000. . . .

If we enacted the Dole bill today, 30 million Americans would still not have health insurance six years from now. . . .

There is no cost containment anywhere to be found in the Dole bill. . . . And for that reason alone, I think you should call the Dole bill the Insurance Industry Protection Act. . . .

There is nothing in the Dole bill to control insurance company premiums. . . .

The Dole plan says, "Go ahead, insurance companies, continue to increase your premiums at 15 or 20 percent; we're not going to stop you."[28]

As Daschle correctly pointed out, the Dole-Packwood bill did not represent a serious effort by Senate Republicans to achieve health care reform. Rather, the bill served as a means for the Republican Party to continue to oppose health care reform without losing credibility with the public. Despite the collapse of public support for Clinton's national health insurance plan, the people continued to be concerned, if not alarmed, over the increase in the number of uninsured individuals and overall health care costs.

The public still generally wanted Congress to take some action on health care reform, as we saw in Chapter 5. As a result, Republicans needed to convince the public that the party was committed to health care reform. The Dole-Packwood bill was designed to do just that. The bill would create the false public impression that Republicans were committed to health care reform, while allowing the party to oppose every meaningful effort to overhaul the medical system, such as that provided for in Mitchell's legislation. By allowing Republicans to identify themselves with the politically popular cause of health care reform, the Dole-Packwood bill was designed to give the party the political credibility it needed to defeat Mitchell's legislation, and every other meaningful effort to overhaul the medical system. The public would not oppose the Republican effort to defeat the Mitchell bill, and every other serious effort to achieve health care reform, as long as the party continued to commit itself, however disingenuously, to the politically popular goal of overhauling the medical system.

The fact that the Dole-Packwood bill did not represent a serious effort to achieve health care reform became clear in the 104th Congress. Despite maintaining firm majorities in both houses of Congress, Senate Republicans did not even bother to reintroduce the Dole-Packwood bill. Senate Republicans knew full well that the bill represented a fiscally and economically unfeasible means to achieve health care reform, and had no intention of passing it. The bill was a cynical political ploy to give the Republican Party the credibility to pursue its opposition to meaningful health care reform.

With the collapse of Clinton's health care reform initiative in August 1994, the issue of national health insurance quickly faded from the political agenda. As a result, the Republican Party did not need to address the issue of health care reform in the 104th Congress with legislative ploys like the Dole-Packwood bill. No longer serving any useful political purpose, the Dole-Packwood bill was quickly buried and forgotten following the collapse of Clinton's health care reform initiative.[29]

WHY THE SENATE FAILED TO TAKE ACTION ON HEALTH CARE REFORM IN AUGUST 1994

Following the introduction of the Mitchell and Dole-Packwood bills, the Senate undertook a historic and unprecedented ten-day debate on health care reform during August 9–19, 1994. The Senate concluded its debate by taking no action on health care reform, ending Clinton's hopes of securing passage of a national health insurance bill in the 103rd Congress. The Senate debate on health care reform was the only time in the half century since the issue first emerged on the political agenda that either house of Congress gave serious consideration to the passage of legislation to overhaul the medical system.

The Senate failed to take advantage of the unique opportunity which existed in August 1994 to pass a health care reform bill for two major reasons: First, any legislation to provide the uninsured coverage would impose a substantial increase in taxes and premiums on privately insured individuals to finance coverage for the uninsured; and second, any bill to enlarge public access to health care would result in the imposition of stringent medical cost-containment measures, leading to the rationing of medical services. The Senate failed to take action on health care reform because it would require middle-class insured individuals to pay more for less coverage than exists under the current health care system. Health care reform would leave the overwhelming majority of the public who are insured worse off than they currently are, guaranteeing a popular backlash against Congress for any action that its members might take to overhaul the medical system. As a result, senators concluded that it was in their rational interest to take no action on health care reform.

The Politics of Health Care Reform: Raising Taxes and Insurance Premiums

A major reason why the Senate failed to take action on health care reform was that any plan to overhaul the medical system, such as that contained in Mitchell's health care reform bill, would result in a substantial increase in taxes and premiums on the privately insured. The additional taxes and insurance premiums which would result from health care reform was a major reason why Republican lawmakers almost unanimously voiced opposition to any sweeping overhaul of the medical system during the Senate debate on the Mitchell bill. Republican Senators argued that Mitchell's health care reform bill was politically unfeasible because it would impose a massive financial burden on the privately insured, in the form of higher taxes and premiums, in order to provide coverage to the uninsured.

To guarantee 95 percent of the public health insurance, Mitchell's health care reform bill would provide federal subsidies to 57 million low-income individuals to assist them in purchasing their own private plans, in addition to the 60 million elderly, disabled, and poor persons covered by either Medicare or Medicaid.[30] The provision of those subsidies would result in $1.235 trillion in additional federal spending on medical services during 1995–2004 with no employer mandate, and $1.170 trillion during the same period with an employer mandate. The Mitchell bill would finance this additional federal health care spending by reducing federal outlays on Medicaid by $768.4 billion and on Medicare by $198.8 billion during 1995–2004.[31] State spending on Medicaid would be reduced by an additional $40.4 billion during the same period.[32]

In addition to reducing Medicare and Medicaid spending, Mitchell's health care reform plan would impose eighteen new taxes, most of which would be assessed on private plans, including a 1.75 percent tax on insurance premiums, a 25 percent tax on high-cost private plans, an increase in Medicare premiums for high-income beneficiaries, and a repeal of the tax deductibility of employer contributions to some types of group plans.[33] The Mitchell bill would raise taxes by $261.8 billion during 1995–2004 with no employer mandate, and $220.6 billion during the same period with an employer mandate.

The financial burden of the tax increases imposed by Mitchell's health care reform bill would be shouldered by privately insured individuals. During 1995–2004, the Mitchell bill would impose $156.8 billion in taxes on private plans with no employer mandate, and $115.6 billion with an employer mandate.[34] Private plans would pass the cost of those taxes on to their subscribers in the form of higher insurance premiums. As a result, the tax increases imposed on private plans by the Mitchell bill would be paid by privately insured individuals.

In addition to tax increases, Mitchell's health care reform bill would be financed through substantial reductions in Medicare and Medicaid spending, as we have seen. Those spending reductions would result in substantial slashes in Medicare and Medicaid reimbursements to health care providers. Health care providers would respond to those reductions in their Medicare and Medicaid reimbursements by raising their charges for privately insured patients. Those increased charges would be reflected in higher insurance premiums.

As a result, the Mitchell bill would shift a substantial share of the financial burden for providing health care to Medicare and Medicaid beneficiaries from the federal government to the private health insurance system—a process known as cost shifting. Senate Republicans cited figures on the cost-shifting impact of the Mitchell bill provided by Martin Feldstein, who served as chairman of President Ronald Reagan's Council of Economic Advisers from 1982 to 1984. In an article published in the August 9, 1994, edition of the *Wall Street Journal*, Feldstein estimated that the cost shifting resulting from reductions in Medicaid spending under the Mitchell bill would increase private insurance premiums by

$29 billion in 1994. An additional $13 billion increase in private insurance premiums in 1994 would result from the cost shifting related to reductions in Medicare spending.[35]

In 1994 Mitchell's health care reform bill would impose $42 billion in increased private health insurance premiums resulting from cost shifting related to reductions in Medicare and Medicaid spending. By 2004, the Mitchell bill would impose an additional $36.6 billion increase in taxes on private insurance with no employer mandate, and $16.9 billion with an employer mandate.[36] Those tax increases would be reflected in higher insurance premiums. As a result, by the time it became fully effective at the turn of the twenty-first century, the Mitchell bill would have raised private insurance premiums by $80 billion annually.

As we have seen, the Mitchell bill would impose a mandate requiring employers to provide their working families group health insurance if the legislation had failed to achieve its goal of guaranteeing 95 percent of the public coverage by 2002 through voluntary means. However, the bill would most likely have achieved this goal without the need to resort to an employer mandate, as we also have seen. Accordingly, by the time it became fully effective at the turn of the twenty-first century, the Mitchell bill would have raised private insurance premiums by $80 billion annually, assuming the absence of an employer mandate.

Senate Republicans denounced the tax increases and cost-shifting contained in Mitchell's health care reform bill, which would result in higher private health insurance premiums. They warned that the cost of the Mitchell bill would be borne by the middle class, who represent the overwhelming majority of privately-insured individuals. Privately-insured, mostly middle-class, individuals would have to pay higher premiums in order to subsidize coverage for low-income individuals. Accordingly, the Mitchell bill would result in a substantial redistribution of income from middle- to low-income individuals. As Feldstein put it, "it's clear that most of the tax dollars in [the Mitchell] plan are for income redistribution rather than the expansion of insurance coverage."[37]

Senate Republicans had good reason to attack Mitchell's health care reform bill as a financial threat to the middle class. During 1993–1994, Clinton had attempted to mobilize public support for health care reform by pointing out the benefits it would provide the middle class. Clinton knew that he could only build popular support for health care reform if he could convince the public that the middle class stood to gain from an overhaul of the medical system.

Clinton's support for national health insurance was largely based upon the fact that the era of job security, when individuals could expect lifetime employment with either a large corporation or the government, was over by the 1990s. In lieu of lifetime employment, individuals would have to change jobs several times during their careers or establish businesses of their own in order to survive financially. However, individuals lacked the flexibility to change jobs or establish businesses because of the difficulty involved in securing private health insurance. Many individuals were locked into jobs which provided them private insurance, and unable to change jobs or establish businesses because this would have resulted in the loss of their coverage; they were unable to find another employer willing to provide them health care benefits and lacked the financial means to purchase their own private insurance. As a result, they had to stay in the same jobs, if they wanted to remain insured. By fostering job lock and impeding the ability of workers to change jobs, the insurance system represents a major roadblock in the ability of the middle class to adapt to an economy based upon increased job insecurity.

As a result, the health insurance system represents an economic threat to the middle class. Needed was a national health insurance program which would guarantee the middle class access to health care, regardless of their employment status. This would give the middle class the flexibility to change jobs or establish businesses of their own, without fear that they might lose their private insurance.

In his radio address on June 25, 1994, Clinton explained why the middle class needed national health insurance:

Our strength in the world has always been the imaginative ingenuity of our middle class. But the lack of security about health coverage is putting a roadblock in the way of middle-class Americans as more and more people have to change jobs more often. Today, eighty-one million Americans live in families with preexisting conditions that could keep them from taking better jobs or creating new businesses and already mean that millions of them either don't have health insurance or pay too much for it. If middle-class Americans are held back by worries about their health care and the health of their families, they often don't do what they must to succeed.

To provide the middle class the flexibility to change jobs or establish businesses of their own, Clinton argued that the federal government must guarantee universal health insurance coverage. "Unless we provide coverage for all Americans, our economy will continue to suffer and more and more Americans will lack the [health] security they need to take advantage of the opportunities that lie ahead," Clinton declared.[38]

Clinton's argument that national health insurance would benefit the middle class had validity. Many middle-class individuals find themselves stuck in jobs they do not like, and unable to take advantage of new economic opportunities, because they need the insurance which comes with their employment. Universal coverage would allow the middle class to leave their jobs and take advantage of new economic opportunities, without the fear that this would result in the loss of their access to health care.

Congressional Republicans recognized that national health insurance had appeal with the middle class. If they were to defuse public support for national health insurance, congressional Republicans needed to counter Clinton's claims that the middle class stood to gain from health care reform. Senate Republicans needed to show that Clinton's claims regarding the benefits to the middle class from national health insurance were deceptive, and that middle-class Americans actually stood to lose, more than they would gain, from health care reform.

The Republican argument that health care reform hurt, rather than benefited, the middle class was perhaps best expressed by Senator Pete Domenici of New Mexico. Addressing the Senate floor on August 10, 1994, Domenici pointed to the substantial tax increase Mitchell's health care reform plan would impose on privately insured, middle-class individuals:

I have heard a lot ... that we ought to pass [Mitchell's health care] reform package because it is good for the middle class. Right? Let me talk about the new taxes in this bill. If the middle class feels put upon by previous taxes they better hold on to their wallets. This proposal has massive new taxes. ... Between 1995 and 2004, nearly $300 billion. ... I find it very hard to believe that these new taxes will help middle-class Americans as the President has indicated. ...

For middle-class Americans these taxes add up. ... For most middle-class Americans their taxes will go up at least an additional $500 a year in very short order.[39]

In addition to tax increases, Mitchell's health care reform bill would result in substantial reductions in Medicare and Medicaid spending, as we have seen. Health care providers would act to offset their losses sustained through those reductions in Medicare and Medicaid spending by raising their charges for privately insured patients, adding to the financial burdens the middle class would suffer under the Mitchell bill. Addressing the Senate floor on August 16, 1994, Malcolm Wallop of Wyoming warned that the substantial reductions in Medicare spending imposed under the Mitchell bill would result in a shift of the financial burden for providing health care to the elderly and disabled from the federal government to the private insurance system, resulting in increased premiums for privately insured, middle-class individuals:

The Clinton-Mitchell bill proposes to cut Medicare by $200 billion over ten years with all of the costs ... falling on the [health care] provider. ... [Health care providers are not] going to pick up $200 billion all onto themselves when they have the option of spreading it out [to their privately insured patients]. Guess who gets it when they do that? Middle-class America.[40]

As we have seen, Mitchell's health care reform bill would impose an $80 billion annual increase in taxes and cost shifting, which would be reflected in higher premiums for the 155 million individuals who were privately insured in 1994.[41] As a result, the Mitchell bill would raise premiums by $500 annually for each privately insured individual. Polling data presented in Chapter 5 show that only a small minority of the public were willing to pay over $30 a month to finance coverage for the uninsured—the amount they would have to pay to fund the Mitchell bill. Accordingly, the Mitchell bill would impose higher taxes to finance coverage for the uninsured than the overwhelming majority of the public were willing to bear.

The Politics of Health Care Reform: Medical Rationing

In addition to its resistance to increasing premiums for the privately insured, another major reason why the Senate took no action on health care reform in August 1994 was that any overhaul of the medical system would result in stringent health care rationing. By reducing financial barriers impeding public access to health care, any expansion in private health insurance, such as provided for under the Mitchell bill, would raise patient utilization of medical services, especially costly hospital technology. To prevent a massive increase in health care costs resulting from expanded public utilization of medical services, the federal government would have to impose stringent health care cost-containment measures. In the absence of such measures, health care costs would soar even further, fueling inflation. To the extent that expanded private insurance coverage was subsidized by the federal government, any increase in health care costs would result in an increase in the already swollen budget deficit.

The provision of private health insurance coverage to most of the uninsured, as the Mitchell bill would do, could not be achieved on an economically and fiscally viable basis without the imposition of stringent health care cost-containment measures. By restricting public and private health care spending, those measures would force doctors to ration the medical services they provide. Patient utilization of costly medical technology would have to be severely restricted. Virtually every advanced industrial democracy guarantees universal health insurance, and rations medical services in order to contain their cost.[42] The United States would have to do the same under any plan to expand public access to health care, such as the Mitchell bill.

The 85 percent of the public who are insured have virtually unlimited access to health care. That access would have to be restricted, if the federal government were to establish an economically and fiscally viable basis for extending coverage to most of the uninsured, as provided for under Mitchell's health care reform bill. In their campaign against the Mitchell bill, congressional Republicans pointed out that any attempt to expand coverage to the uninsured would lead to rationing, restricting access to health care among the 85 percent of the public who are insured. By emphasizing that the overwhelming majority of the public who are insured would have less access to health care under the Mitchell bill than they currently do, congressional Republicans hoped to mobilize popular opposition to Clinton's campaign to overhaul the medical system. Few insured individuals would be likely to support health care reform once they realized that they would have less access to medical services than is currently the case; and that the federal government might deny either them or their loved ones the medical technology that they might someday need in undergoing treatment for a catastrophic or life-threatening illness or injury.

The Republican Party's strategy in derailing Clinton's health care reform initiative was based upon a twofold argument: first, the United States has the best health care system in the world; and second, the establishment of national health insurance would undermine the quality of American health care by requiring the United States to emulate Western Europe and Canada in rationing medical services.

The Republican Party views the American health care system as the envy of the world. Insured Americans have access to all the health care they need to treat any illness or injury, no matter how life-threatening. When foreigners become ill they come to the United States for medical treatment. Given the vast superiority of the American health care system, the United States should avoid the establishment of a national health insurance program. Any comprehensive health care reform would result in stringent rationing in which Americans would have to face long waiting lines or be denied access to life-sustaining medical technology, as is routinely the case in the other advanced industrial democracies, which have national health insurance programs. From the Republican viewpoint, it simply makes no sense to reform the American health care system, which provides access to the best medical services in the world, in order to require the United States to emulate the Western European and Canadian systems, which serve as models for the delivery of inferior health care.

The Republican argument that the establishment of national health insurance would undermine the quality of American health care was perhaps best expressed by Lieutenant Governor Elizabeth McCaughey of New York. Prior to her election to the lieutenant governorship of New York in 1994, McCaughey wrote a devastating critique of Clinton's national health insurance plan, which appeared in the February 7, 1994, issue of the *New Republic*. In her article, McCaughey warned that the Clinton plan would substantially undermine the quality of health care in the United States by imposing the same kind of stringent medical rationing existing in Canada:

If you are seriously ill, the best place to be is in the United States. Among all industrialized nations, the United States has the highest cure rates for stomach, cervical, and uterine cancers, the second highest cure rate for breast cancer and is second to none in treating heart disease. In other countries that spend less, people who are sick get less care, are less likely to survive, and have poorer quality of life after major illness. Consider what happens in Canada, whose health care system is often held up as a model for the United States. In Canada medical technology is rationed to dangerously low levels. The United States has 3.26 open-heart surgery units per million people; Canada has only 1.23 units per million. Cardiovascular disease is Canada's number one health problem, yet open-heart surgery units and catheterization equipment are kept in such short supply that the average wait for urgent (not elective) surgery is eight weeks. The shocking result is that in Canada, a cardiac patient is ten times as likely to die waiting in line for surgery as on the operating table. In the United States, there is no wait.[43]

The fact that a country like Canada would deny critically ill patients access to life-sustaining medical technology gave the Republican Party ample ammunition to argue that national health insurance has established a cruel and inhumane system of health care in the other advanced industrial nations where such programs exist, in contrast to the United States, which humanely allows all insured individuals to secure the medical services they need. Addressing the Senate floor on August 11, 1994, Gramm attacked Senate Democrats who argued that the United States has a morally inferior health care system because this nation is the only advanced industrial democracy which fails to guarantee its citizens universal coverage. Rather, Gramm argued, the United States has a morally superior health care system precisely because all insured individuals can secure the medical services they need, in contrast to Western Europe and Canada, where critically ill patients are routinely denied access to life-sustaining medical technology:

I can hardly believe my ears when the health care system of the United States of America is compared unfavorably to the health care systems of Canada, Great Britain, and Germany. Last year, more heart attack patients died in Canada waiting to get into the operating room than died on the operating table. People all over the world under government-dominated systems are dying because health care that is readily available in America is not available in those countries. . . .

We have in the United States of America the greatest health care system in the history of the world. In the past twenty-five years, 90 percent of all the pharmaceuticals, 95 percent of all the medical procedures, 90 percent of the routine miracles that we expect every time we go to the doctor and every time we go to the hospital have been developed by Americans.

It is very interesting to me that so many of my colleagues, when they think of medical perfection, look to the north, to Canada, and yet I notice that when [Americans] and the people they love get sick, they never go to Canada to try to get well. Yet, on any given day in America, in any referral hospital . . . those referral wards are full of rich or politically powerful Canadians. They are full of people who have had an opportunity to look socialized medicine in the face in Great Britain, or Germany, or elsewhere and they have seen an ugly, uncaring face, and they have come to the United States of America to get health care. . . .

I am not going to support tearing down the greatest medical care system in the history of the world to rebuild it in the image of the Post Office.

For the Republican Party, the battle against Clinton's health care reform initiative represented more than just a legislative fight for the future of the American medical system. Rather, the battle against Clinton's initiative represented an epic struggle by the Republicans to prevent the president from overhauling and transforming the best health care system in the world and requiring this nation to adopt the kind of second-rate, inferior model for delivering medical services which operates in Western Europe and Canada. Given the enormous stakes involved in the health care debate, the Republicans were determined to defeat Clinton's initiative at all costs. As Gramm put it during his address on the Senate floor, "We have a lot to lose in this debate as well as a lot to gain."[44]

During the Senate debate on health care reform in August 1994, Republican lawmakers repeatedly warned that the quality of American health care would be undermined by the medical rationing which would result from the Mitchell bill. Senator Connie Mack of Florida argued that "we have the highest quality of [health] care and lead the world in innovation. These are the defining features which make our [health care] system second to none. The quality of our system attracts patients from all over the world, whose own health care system has failed them."[45]

Mack charged that the 25 percent tax on high-cost private health insurance plans contained in the Mitchell bill amounted to premium caps designed to deter private plans from exceeding the medical spending targets provided for by the legislation. Mack warned that private plans would restrict their provision of health care to their members in order to avoid having to pay the tax, resulting in medical rationing:

If we put a cap on how much is spent [on health care] . . . the number of medical procedures will decline and rationing of services will occur. Specialty services will be terminated and consolidated, with fewer services available to people. Research and education will be slashed as a means to meet the cap. Development of new drugs will come to a standstill. The quality of our health care will be dramatically affected.

Mack read from a letter to Clinton signed by 562 economists, which warned that health care cost-containment measures provided for in the president's own national health insurance "will produce shortages, black markets, and reduced quality" of health care. The economists warned that

in countries that have imposed these types of regulations, patients face delays of months and years for surgery, government bureaucrats decide treatment options instead of doctors or patients, and innovations in medical techniques and pharmaceuticals are drastically reduced.

Caps, fee schedules, and other government regulations may appear to reduce medical spending, but such gains are illusory. We will instead end up with lower-quality medical care, reduced medical innovation, and expensive new bureaucracies to monitor compliance.[46]

The economists concluded their letter by warning Clinton that "the threat of price controls on medicines has already decreased research and development at drug companies, which will lead to reduced discoveries and loss of life in the future."[47]

Mack's charge that the Mitchell bill would result in health care rationing was supported by Senator Charles Grassley of Iowa. Grassley argued that the 25 percent tax imposed on high-cost private health insurance plans provided for in the Mitchell bill amounted to premium caps which would result in health care rationing:

If the Clinton-style global [health care] budgets and [insurance] premium caps go into effect . . . health plans will have to strenuously economize in order to remain profitable.

Economizing means that the quality of care could decline, access to care could be reduced and rationing could result. . . .

I fear for those with costly and life-threatening or handicapping illness. I do not want to see a state of affairs come about in which such people find that their care is delayed, or their access to advanced diagnostics is put off, or their access to the best specialists is restricted.

Grassley read from a study conducted by Rudolph Penner, former director of the CBO, which warned that the imposition of health care cost-containment measures, such as those found in the Mitchell bill, would result in medical rationing:

In the process of changing the present health care system to achieve greater control over costs, some of the desirable features of the current health care system would be adversely affected. In particular: less spending on research and development, longer waiting times for access to new technology, and limitations on our existing choices of providers, health insurance coverage, and treatment alternatives.[48]

SENATE REPUBLICANS SPEAK OUT AGAINST THE CANADIAN HEALTH CARE SYSTEM

A major argument made by Republicans to defeat the Mitchell bill during the Senate debate on health care reform in August 1994 was that the legislation would give the government the same kind of control over public access to health care as currently exists in Canada. Republican senators pointed to the experience of Canada, which like all advanced industrial democracies with national health insurance programs rations health care, as an example of the restrictions on public access to medical services Americans would have to suffer under the Mitchell bill. Senator Kay Bailey Hutchison of Texas warned that the United States would have to adopt the Canadian practice of rationing health care if the Mitchell bill were passed:

We are patterning [the Mitchell bill] after what we have seen in Canada. In fact, President Clinton said in the [1992 presidential] campaign that he was looking at the Canadian system as the model for his [national health insurance] plan.

But I wish you would talk with someone who has lived in Canada and lived under their health care system. If someone is well in the Canadian system, they do fine. But if you are sick in the Canadian system, you have a problem. There is rationed health care because there is a limit on what can be spent [on medical services] and that causes rationing. You wait six months for heart bypass surgery; [and] hope you have that luxury. A lot of people who can afford it will go to the United States to have surgery because they cannot wait nine months for cataract surgery or three months for a mammogram.

I read an article by a woman who had just had a baby in Canada. She said that she thought she would have anesthesia. But there was only one anesthetist in the hospital there and the anesthetist was taken up with emergency surgery, and by the time he could get to her it was too late.

That would not happen in America. No woman has a baby without anesthesia if she wants it, regardless of whether she can pay or not. That is because we have the quality of health care ... that we do. I do not think we want to give up that quality for a system that is not working in Canada, and we certainly do not want to put that kind of a system in place in America where we do have the quality.[49]

Hutchison's attacks against the Canadian health care system were supported by Senators Don Nickles of Oklahoma, Dan Coats of Indiana and Alphonse D'Amato of New York. Nickles repeated the familiar Republican argument that national health insurance posed a threat to the quality of American health care:

We have quality health care in this country. I know every person in ... America today ... has been the beneficiary to some extent of the best quality health care in the world. . . . Let us try to make sure we do no harm to this quality health care system. . . .

We have a real quality health care system in this country. Let us not emulate countries that do not have quality health care.

Nickles focused on Canada as a particularly bad model for the United States to emulate in redesigning its health care system. He pointed out that many Canadians are dissatisfied with the shortages in health care resources existing in their nation. Desperate for access to medical technology they have been denied in their own nation, those dissatisfied Canadians have crossed the border to secure health care in the United States:

Some people say, "Let us emulate ... Canada." ... They have [health] care. They have a government program that covers everybody. But I venture to say if you looked at the waiting lists, if you look at the government rationing, if you look at the delays that are involved ... you find many of those people are coming to the United States as a last resort to get quality health care. . . .

The Canadians are coming south ... into the United States to get health care if they really need it.

The [Canadian] doctor says, "You need a bypass but we have already had our quota. . . . We cannot do it in this province now. This is the fourth quarter of the year and, frankly, we are out of money. So, elective surgery, we have said, in this province in Canada, we are going to postpone until next year."

A lot of [Canadians] might not be willing to take that risk so they come to the United States. If we [adopt the Canadian health care system] where would Americans go [for medical services]?[50]

Coats joined his Republican colleagues in urging the Senate to refrain from any far-reaching restructuring of the American health care system, which he called "the most effective health care system in the world, that provides more quality care to more people than any other system."[51] Coats claimed that the United States was experiencing a massive influx of Canadians who were entering this nation to take advantage of its superior health care system. Coats pointed out that a major entry point for Canadians seeking health care in the United States is the American border city of Buffalo:

I have a good friend who is a Congressman from . . . Buffalo, just across the line from Canada. He said, "Our number one industry in Buffalo is the provision of health care services by Americans for Canadians. They stream across the border because they do not want to wait for [medical] procedures and because they believe that the United States gives them . . . better quality [health care]."[52]

Echoing the pleas of his Republican colleagues, D'Amato urged the Senate to avoid imposing any sweeping overhaul of the American health care system, which, in the senator's words, remained "the best health care system in the world, bar none." "We were sent here to bring about a better [health care] system if possible," D'Amato told his Senate colleagues. "But not to destroy the best [health care] system that exists in the world."[53]

As a senator from New York, D'Amato was all too familiar with the exodus of Canadians to Buffalo to secure access to health care. D'Amato pointed to this exodus in disputing the arguments of liberal medical policy experts, who have traditionally extolled the virtues of Canada as a model for American medical reform. Rather, D'Amato saw this exodus as evidence that the health care system of the United States was far superior to that of Canada. "I hear about this great Canadian [national health insurance] plan," D'Amato sarcastically remarked. "Is that why so many [Canadians] come over to use the hospitals in Buffalo, because they do not want to wait six months, eight months, a year, a year and a half, for some of the optional services that here in this country our people get when they are sick or in pain?[54]

CANADA AND THE POLITICS OF HEALTH CARE REFORM IN THE UNITED STATES

As we have seen, a major element in the Republican Party's campaign to derail Clinton's health care reform initiative was to point to Canada as an example of the kind of medical system the United States would face if it established a national health insurance program. The United States could not have established national health insurance on an economically and fiscally viable basis without imposing a stringent system of health care rationing, similar to that existing in Canada. Canada imposes stringent hospital budgets, which results in severe limits on the amount of medical technology available. As a result, many Canadians suffering from catastrophic or terminal illnesses or injuries are denied access to medical technology due to shortages of hospital resources.

The Republican Party saw Canada as an example of a cruel and inhumane health care system which denies terminally ill individuals access to the medical technology they need to sustain their lives, and leaves them to die. As Speaker of the House Newt Gingrich charged, "The Canadian model controls [health care] costs by letting people die."[55] The Republican Party successfully derailed Clinton's health care reform initiative by advancing the credible argument that the president's program for expanding private health insurance coverage and containing medical costs would force the United States to adopt a Canadian-style health care system, in which stringent medical rationing would occur. Canada served as an example of a health care system in which individuals with catastrophic or terminal illnesses and injuries receive inferior medical services due to the lack of medical technology available. This lies in sharp contrast to the United States, where an abundance of medical technology exists to treat individuals with catastrophic or terminal illnesses and injuries. The Republican Party successfully used Canada as a model of an inferior health care system which the United States must not adopt.

The Republicans' use of Canada to discredit and defeat Clinton's health care reform initiative was nothing new. Opponents of health care reform have routinely used Canada as an example of the kind of inferior medical services Americans would receive under a national health insurance program. Supporters of health care reform argue that American conservatives have deliberately distorted and exaggerated the shortages in medical resources existing in Canada in order to unfairly discredit and malign efforts by liberals to establish a national health insurance program in the United States. One such supporter of national health insurance who charges that American opponents of national health insurance have concocted a false and distorted image of the Canadian health care system is Robert G. Evans, an economist at the University of British Columbia:

In the United States, a richly financed lobby throws its weight against publicly financed health care for all citizens (known as the "Canadian model"). Defending the American status quo by attacking the alternatives, these threatened interests fabricate and market an image of Canada—endless queues, merciless rationing, primitive technology, physicians (and patients) fleeing for the [American] border—which ranges from grossly distorted to blatantly false. Such claims may be effective interest group politics in the United States—but they have little to do with health care . . . in Canada.[56]

However, despite his claim that American opponents of national health insurance have advanced a false and distorted image of the Canadian health care system, Evans concedes that shortages in medical resources do indeed exist in Canada, much as American conservatives claim:

[Canadian] provincial governments limit the proliferation of hospital capacity and particularly of expensive diagnostic equipment, by funding them through hospital and capital operating budgets, not through fees per item of service. A hospital which wishes to acquire an MRI machine, for example, or a lithotripter, must not only receive planning approval from its provincial ministry of health, it must also convince the ministry to supply the capital funds. Private physicians can in principle purchase and use such equipment, but if there is no corresponding procedural item in the fee schedule, they cannot be reimbursed (by government or patient) for its use.

The result is that [Canadian] physicians claim a shortage of [hospital] capacity, while in the United States beds and facilities are in surplus. . . . And it is certainly true that per capita availability and use of major diagnostic equipment is much greater in the United States [than in Canada].[57]

Evans concedes that the imposition of stringent hospital budgets in Canada has resulted in

a steady decline in acute care utilization . . . and a much less rapid proliferation of new and very expensive, high-technology interventions. Canadian provinces do acquire the most recent technology, but such equipment tends to be confined to teaching hospital centers and does not proliferate to the regional hospital system or free-standing facilities. Thus the availability per capita of such equipment tends to be lower [in Canada] than in . . . the United States.[58]

Evans concedes that Canada rations medical services due to the existence of health care shortages: "The control of hospital costs through global budgets has been associated with a slower rate of increase in the number of [medical] procedures performed [in Canada] . . . than in the United States."[59] Unable to secure access to the health care they need in their own nation, many Canadians cross the American border to secure access to medical services in the United States. "[Canadian] physicians . . . can, and do, sometimes refer patients to the United States and then energetically publicize the incident as part of a continuing struggle with provincial governments over the availability of health resources," Evans acknowledges.[60]

Evans is not the only supporter of national health insurance to concede that Canada rations health care. Two other such supporters are Arnold Birenbaum, a professor at the Albert Einstein College of Medicine, and Theodore R. Marmor, a political scientist at Yale University. Birenbaum agrees with Evans that American conservatives have produced a false and distorted image of the Canadian medical system in order to unfairly discredit efforts by health care reformers to establish a national health insurance program in the United States. He denounces those American conservatives for having "made outrageous and untrue claims about Canadian health, the costs of care north of the border, and how it was the first step on the road to serfdom."[61]

However, Birenbaum concedes that American opponents of national health insurance are correct in their primary criticism of the Canadian health care system: that it has resulted in stringent medical rationing.

Canadian health planners in each province . . . allocate less for high-technology equipment such as magnetic resonance imaging (MRI), a technique for looking in detail at soft tissue. Access to this equipment in American cities is quite easy, and often [Canadian health care] providers refer patients [to the United States]. While the equipment does obviate the need to do invasive or exploratory procedures on patients, it is also very expensive. Canada has managed to do without imaging, and the city of Seattle has more MRI units than the entire Dominion.[62]

Birenbaum concedes that the severe limits Canada imposes on hospital acquisition of medical technology has resulted in a stringent system of health care rationing:

Waiting lists are established for some specialty care, particularly if the condition is not life-threatening. Those without priority status have sometimes waited a long time for surgery, and the number of people with elective status, rather than urgent or emergent, was substantial. Waitlisted are those patients considered in urgent need of open-heart surgery and lithotripsy—a medical procedure that uses sound-waves to destroy kidney and gallbladder stones. . . .

Queues or lines are established for expensive state-of-the are procedures. These are the grim facts of living with a system that rations high-technology medicine, something that Canadians would like to see changed.[63]

Marmor joins Evans and Birenbaum in charging that American conservatives have created a false and distorted image of the Canadian health care system:

Led by the AMA . . . the critics of Canada's "socialized medicine" [use] the full arsenal of propagandistic techniques to question both Canada's performance and its relevance to the United States. The HIAA came to take the lead role here, shamelessly blasting a favorable report [of the Canadian health care system] by the Government Accounting Office in 1991 as "partisan."

Marmor concludes that "the growth of a vigorous . . . anti-Canada lobby took its toll" on the campaign by health care reformers to establish a national health insurance program in the United States during the 1990s.[64]

Like Evans and Birenbaum, Marmor flatly concedes the fact noted by American opponents of national health insurance that "Canada does ration health care," admitting that "at certain times and in some places, substantial waiting lists for certain surgical and diagnostic procedures occur:"[65]

There is no question that some expensive, high-technology items are not as available in Canada as they are in the United States. Canada has a full range of high-technology facilities, but in considerably less abundance and with little competition for market share. Expensive capital equipment is first approved only for highly specialized centers, and subsequent diffusion is closely controlled by provincial ministries of health. This control results in lower rates of use for some technologies in Canada—cardiac surgery, magnetic resonance imaging, lithoscopy, and so on [than in the United States].[66]

Consistent with the claims made by Evans, Birenbaum, and Marmor, Table 8.3 shows that a number of key medical technologies are available in substantially smaller quantities in Canada than they are in the United States.

Table 8.3
The Comparative Availability of Selected Medical Technologies in the
United States and Canada Measured in Units per Million Individuals

Medical Technology	United States	Canada	Ratio Between the United States and Canada
Open-heart surgery	3.26	1.23	2.7:1
Cardiac catheterization	5.06	1.50	3.4:1
Organ transplantation	1.31	1.08	1.2:1
Radiation therapy	3.97	0.54	7.4:1
Extracorporeal shock wave lithoscopy	0.94	0.16	5.9:1
Magnetic resonance imaging	3.69	0.46	8.0:1

Source: Theodore R. Marmor, *Understanding Health Care Reform* (New Haven, Conn.: Yale University Press, 1994), p. 188.

THE PUBLIC, CONGRESS, AND THE POLITICS OF HEALTH CARE RATIONING

National health insurance cannot be established on an economically and fiscally viable basis without a stringent system of health care rationing. Indeed, every advanced industrial democracy with a national health insurance program stringently rations health care. Canada spends the third largest share of its GDP on health care of any nation in the world, behind the United States and Sweden. Per capita health care spending in Canada ranks second among the nations of the world, trailing only the United States.[67] And yet, despite its generous spending on health care, even Canada must ration medical services in order to maintain the economic and fiscal viability of its national health insurance program, as we have seen.

The public fully understood that the establishment of national health insurance would require health care rationing. On June 17, 1994 Princeton Survey Research Associates conducted a poll for *Newsweek* of 499 adults, who were asked the following question: "Will health care reform lead to rationing, in which some forms of medical care will not be covered by basic insurance because they are too costly, too much of a long shot, or not essential?" Seventy-four percent of those polled said that health care reform would result in rationing; and only 16 percent believed it would not.[68]

As the *Newsweek* poll shows, the overwhelming majority of the public accepted the Republican agrument that any health care reform plan which provided coverage to the uninsured would require stringent medical rationing. True, the actual legislation introduced by the Senate Democratic leadership in August 1994, the Mitchell bill, would neither guarantee universal coverage, nor establish stringent hospital budgets, which have given rise to the kind of health care rationing existing in Canada and other advanced industrial democracies. As we have seen, the Mitchell bill would fall short of universal coverage, and deprive the federal government of any effective means to contain health care costs.

Nevertheless, the Mitchell bill would guarantee 95 percent of the public coverage, extending private insurance to 30 million uninsured individuals by 2004.[69] By imposing a substantial expansion in the number of privately insured individuals, the Mitchell bill would result in a significant increase in patient utilization of health care, driving up its cost, and the overall inflation rate. The Mitchell bill would require the federal government to subsidize the purchase of private insurance by low-income individuals, resulting in an increase in the swollen budget deficit. To contain the increase in inflation and the deficit which would result from providing low-income uninsured individuals access to health care, the federal government would have to adopt the same kind of stringent medical cost-containment measures existing in Canada, leading to the imposition of severe health care rationing.

Senate Republicans succeeded in discrediting and defeating the Mitchell bill by correctly arguing that there was no way that the federal government could provide private health insurance to most of the uninsured, as the legislation would have required, without imposing stringent health care rationing. The Republican Party's strategy against the Mitchell bill was based upon the premise that the public would not accept health care rationing, however much they favored medical reform. The Republicans assumed that popular aversion to rationing was so great that the public would not accept any health care reform bill which restricted their access to medical services.

The *Newsweek* poll just cited shows that the Republicans were correct; only a minority of the public were willing to accept health care rationing. The *Newsweek* poll asked its respondents the following question: "If it would bring down health care costs or permit universal coverage, would you be willing to limit your use of medical specialists or the latest high technology?" Only 40 percent of those polled said that they would be willing to limit their use of either medical specialists or technology in order to contain health care costs.[70] Table 8.4 shows that only a minority of the public was willing to limit medical research and their utilization of either specialists or any one of a number of costly, high-technology medical procedures.

By the time the Senate opened debate on health care reform in August 1994, public support for Clinton's national health insurance plan had already collapsed, as we saw in Chapter 5. The collapse of popular support for the Clinton plan was due in large part to the public's recognition that the establishment of national health insurance would require the imposition of health care rationing, which only a minority of the population were willing to accept, as the *Newsweek* poll shows. By warning that the Mitchell bill would result in the imposition of stringent health care rationing, Republican senators succeeded in reinforcing public opposition to comprehensive health care reform.

Senate Republicans acted to create a negative public image of national health insurance by pointing to the Canadian health care system. They effectively ar-

Table 8.4
The Results of a *Newsweek* Poll on Public Opinion on Health Care Rationing Taken on June 17, 1994

Medical Service	Percent of the Public Willing to Minimize Their Utilization of This Medical Service in Order to Reduce Health Care Costs
Elective surgery for nonlife-threatening illnesses	46
Health care for patients likely to remain comatose	44
Expensive, long-odds operations	39
Heroic care for the very old	34
Consulting medical specialists	31
High-technology diagnostic procedures	30
Heroic care for tiny preemies	28
Experimental health care	24
Medical research	17

Source: Melinda Beck, "Rationing Health Care," *Newsweek*, June 27, 1994, p. 35.

gued that if the Mitchell bill passed, Americans would face the same kind of barriers in their access to health care Canadians have long endured. Canada, where terminally and catastrophically ill individuals are routinely denied access to the life-sustaining medical technology they need, provided Republicans a fitting image of the kind of inferior medical services Americans would receive under the Mitchell bill, or any other legislation to achieve comprehensive medical reform. The specter of Canadian-style health care rationing in the United States only served to solidify public opposition to national health insurance.

Senate Republicans were disingenuous in their argument that a comprehensive health care reform plan, like the Mitchell bill, would result in medical rationing. In making this argument, Senate Republicans conveniently neglected to mention that the United States already rations health care. As we saw in Chapter 2, the uninsured receive substantially less health care than their insured counterparts. As a result of their lack of access to health care, the uninsured tend to be sicker and more prone to death than their insured counterparts. The purpose of national health insurance is to extend the same access to health care among the uninsured currently enjoyed by their insured counterparts; and to guarantee health security to all individuals to assure that they will be able to receive medical services when needed.

However, by extending access to health care among at least some of the uninsured, the Mitchell bill, or any other comprehensive health care reform plan which might have been established, would have raised patient utilization of medical services, driving up their cost. The federal government would have had to impose stringent health care cost-containment measures to assure the fiscal and economic viability of its medical reform plan, resulting in rationing. The 85 percent of the public who are insured have access to all the available health care they may need. Their access to health care, especially costly medical technology, would have been severely curtailed under a comprehensive health care reform plan, like the Mitchell bill.

The Mitchell bill would have extended the health care rationing, which is currently limited only to the uninsured, to practically the entire population. The only segment of society which would have escaped health care rationing would have been the relative handful of individuals sufficiently wealthy to pay for their medical services out of pocket. The rest of the public, who rely on health insurance to maintain their access to health care, would have had their medical services severely curtailed under the Mitchell bill.

By opposing health care rationing, Senate Republicans were defending the privilege the 85 percent of the public, who are insured currently, have of enjoying virtually unlimited access to all the health care they may need. Senate Republicans succeeded in derailing Clinton's health care reform initiative precisely because it threatened to severely curtail the provision of medical services for the insured. By opposing Clinton's initiative, Senate Republicans could represent themselves as defenders of interests of the 85 percent of the public who are insured. Because the insured represent such an overwhelming majority of the population, Senate Republicans were assured that they could defeat Clinton's initiative. Most of the 85 percent of the public who are insured were not about to see their access to health care severely curtailed in order to extend medical benefits to the remainder of the population who have no coverage. Senate Republicans succeeded in derailing Clinton's health care reform initiative precisely because they were representing the interests of the overwhelming majority of the public who are insured.

True, Clinton's health care reform initiative represented a decent and humane attempt to extend access to medical services among the uninsured, who receive either little or no health care. However, the interests of the uninsured were ignored on Capitol Hill, since they represent only 15 percent of the public. Members of Congress can only be reelected by serving the interests of the majority; and the interests of the 85 percent of the public who are insured, not the remainder of the public who have no coverage, dictated the outcome of the debate on health care reform.

True, the most decent and humane action Congress could have taken on health care reform was to extend coverage to the uninsured, who have either little or no access to medical services. However, Congress could not take such action, since it would have undermined the virtually unlimited access to medical services enjoyed by the overwhelming majority of the public who are insured. Politics, not morality, drives the legislative process on Capitol Hill, and in taking no action on health care reform Congress was behaving in an entirely rational manner.

The fact that national health insurance could not be established without stringent health care rationing effectively prevented Congress from taking any action on health care reform in August 1994. Had Congress passed health care reform legislation, like the Mitchell bill, then lawmakers would have had to impose a stringent hospital budget, such as that existing in Canada. To prevent health care spending from exceeding that budget, hospitals would have had to ration health care. Terminally or catastrophically ill patients would have had to be denied access to life-sustaining medical technology.

Angry relatives of terminally or catastrophically ill patients denied access to life-sustaining medical technology would have contacted their senators and representatives in Congress. They would have pleaded with members of Congress to lift the health care cost-containment measures imposed as part of the medical reform bill passed by lawmakers. Any member of Congress refusing to lift those measures would have appeared to be cruel and heartless to his or her constituents. No member of Congress could have justified denying terminally ill constituents access to the life-sustaining medical technology they needed in order to contain health care costs. Constituents were sure to organize and defeat any member of Congress willing to do this.

Passage of legislation guaranteeing near universal health insurance coverage, like the Mitchell bill, would place members of Congress in a politically vulnerable position. In order to assure that near universal coverage could be achieved on an economically and fiscally viable basis, Congress would have to couple passage of health care reform legislation with the imposition of stringent medical cost-containment measures, resulting in rationing. Members of Congress would have to take political responsibility for those terminally ill constituents who would be denied access to life-sustaining medical technology. Angry relatives of those constituents would be expected to organize and defeat any member of Congress who was willing to sustain the health care cost-containment measures which resulted in the denial of needed medical services.

By passing health care reform legislation, members of Congress would become directly involved in the politically explosive issue of determining who lives and who dies under the medical rationing which would accompany an overhaul of the health care system. By imposing health care cost-containment measures which would result in denying hundreds of thousands of terminally and catastrophically ill individuals access to life-sustaining medical technology annually, members of Congress would have to take responsibility for the premature deaths of large numbers of sick and elderly constituents. This assured that members of Congress would be targeted for defeat by the relatives of those constituents. Fearing that they too might be denied access to needed life-sustaining medical technology sometime in the future, other voters would join relatives of terminally or catastrophically ill patients in targeting for defeat those members of Congress who support health care rationing as a means to contain medical costs.

Members of Congress win reelection by avoiding difficult political choices, in order not to alienate organized constituencies. Health care reform would directly involve members of Congress in the most difficult political choice of all: deciding who lives and who dies. Members of Congress were unwilling to involve themselves in making this choice: they were not about to impose health care cost-containment measures, which would result in rationing; to face the angry relatives of those who would be denied access to medical technology under the health care rationing which would result from medical reform; and to alienate those relatives as well as other voters, risking defeat the next time they ran for reelection. Unwilling to impose any health care cost-containment measures, which would result in rationing, Congress was unable to pass any medical reform legislation in August 1994, even one as modest as the Mitchell bill. In the absence of such measures, any legislation to achieve near universal coverage, such as the Mitchell bill, would be economically and fiscally unviable. Given the politically explosive issues involved in health care reform, the best option available to Congress during the closing months of 1994 was to adjourn without taking any action to overhaul the medical system—and that is exactly what lawmakers did.

CONCLUSION

During the spring and summer of 1994, Clinton and congressional Democrats made substantial progress in advancing health care reform legislation through Capitol Hill. In August Mitchell succeeded in moving health care reform legislation out of committee and onto the Senate floor for debate, marking the first time in the half century since national health insurance has been on the political agenda that a bill to overhaul the medical system was granted serious consideration in either house of Congress. However, despite the historic strides made by Clinton in shepherding health care reform legislation through Congress, the president's campaign to establish national health insurance ended the same way all previous such efforts have—in failure. The Senate failed to take action on health care reform for two reasons: First, any legislation to provide coverage to the uninsured would impose higher taxes than the public was willing to accept; and second, the extension of health care benefits to the uninsured could not be established on an economically and fiscally viable basis without the imposition of stringent medical cost-containment measures, which would result in severe rationing.

In effect, comprehensive health care reform would require the 85 percent of the public who are insured to pay more for less coverage than they currently do, leaving them worse off than they are now. With health care reform threatening to undermine the interests of the overwhelming majority of the public who are insured, Congress had no rational interest in overhauling the medical system. Any such overhaul would antagonize large segments of the insured population, who would find themselves worse off under health care reform.

Those insured individuals would organize to defeat those members of Congress supporting health care reform the next time they ran for reelection.

Given the political risks associated with health care reform, the best course of action for members of Congress was to take no action on overhauling the medical system—which is exactly what they did. By leaving the current health care system intact, members of Congress spared themselves the political retribution they would have suffered had they taken any action which would have undermined the interests of the overwhelming majority of the public who are insured, and basically satisfied with their coverage. With health care reform threatening to leave the insured worse off than they are now, and expose members of Congress to the risk of defeat the next time they ran for reelection, lawmakers came to the sensible conclusion that the only course available to them was to avoid any overhaul of the medical system.

Why did Clinton's health care reform initiative, which began so promisingly following the president's inauguration, end so miserably in August 1994? This book has been devoted to answering this question. We will summarize our answer in the following, final chapter.

Chapter 9

Why Did Clinton's Health Care Reform Initiative Fail?

> Universal [health insurance] coverage is not in the soul of the American people, or at least in those who represent them. We are a hard-hearted nation. . . . We have all this money for you and me . . . but we can't help these [uninsured] low-income working stiffs. We're writing off the [uninsured] lower middle class. . . . We're basically telling them: "Take a walk." That's hard-hearted.[1]
>
> Uwe Reinhardt, health economist, Princeton University.

> You were always dealing with a fundamental underlying dynamic [governing Clinton's health care reform initiative]: The American people want change [in the health care system] as long as it does not cost them too much or affect them too much personally. The problem [with the failure of Clinton's health care reform initiative] was not Harry and Louise. The problem was us.[2]
>
> Drew E. Altman, President, The Henry J. Kaiser Family Foundation.

As we noted at the outset of this book, Clinton was by no means the first president to launch a campaign to establish national health insurance. Similar campaigns were undertaken by Truman, Nixon, and Carter. However, national health insurance was only a minor element in the domestic policy agendas of those three presidents. Neither Truman, Nixon, nor Carter suffered politically as a result of the failure of their health care reform initiatives because none of those three presidents pursued a full-fledged and aggressive campaign to establish national health insurance. Rather, all three were halfhearted and reluctant supporters of national health insurance, consistent with the fact that they did not regard the program as among the most important issues on their agendas.

By contrast, Clinton made health care reform the central element of his domestic policy agenda, consistent with his passionate and deep commitment to national health insurance, and his single-minded determination to secure its establishment. During 1993–1994, Clinton tirelessly worked to secure passage of his national health insurance plan, delivering numerous speeches on the need for health care reform, including two prime-time television addresses.[3] As a result of his efforts, Clinton generated more public and congressional interest in health care reform than any president in history. Polling data show that the public had well-defined and coherent, if not always consistent, views on health care reform, evidence that the people played close attention to the debate on national health insurance during 1993–1994. The public had a clear opportunity to focus on health care reform, given the extensive coverage the issue received in the media.

Prior to the Clinton presidency, national health insurance legislation had been approved by only a single committee—the Senate Labor and Human Resources Committee, which passed a comprehensive health care reform bill in 1992. However, as we have seen, in June and July 1994 slightly modified versions of Clinton's national health insurance plan were approved by three of the five congressional committees exercising jurisdiction over health care reform, with a fourth committee, Senate Finance, passing a more modest variation of the president's program. With national health insurance legislation having been approved by the necessary congressional committees, Mitchell was able to bring a health care reform bill to the Senate floor. The Senate debate on the Mitchell bill in August 1994 marked the first time in American history that either house of Congress granted formal consideration to comprehensive health care reform legislation. Clinton's success in moving national health insurance legislation all the way to the Senate floor was truly a historic achievement, not duplicated by any other president in America's long, arduous, half-century debate on health care reform.

However, despite his success in moving national health insurance legislation further down the legislative process than any other president, Clinton health care reform initiative ended the same way all previous such campaigns have—in failure. The Senate concluded its debate on the Mitchell bill by taking no action on health care reform. Until the Senate debate on health care reform got formally under way, few would have predicted that the 103rd Congress would adjourn in October 1994 without taking any action on health care reform. Certainly, Clinton himself could not have conceived such a disastrous outcome to his health care reform initiative. Given his success in generating so much public and congressional interest in and, to a lesser extent, support for health care reform, he had every reason to believe that he would prevail in his campaign to secure the establishment of a national health insurance program, despite the failure of similar efforts undertaken by previous presidents. In remarks to reporters in the Roosevelt Room on January 3, 1994, Clinton confidently predicted that his health care reform initiative would end in success. "I believe that 1994 will go down in history as the year when, after decades and decades of false starts and lame excuses and being overcome by special interests, the American people finally, finally had health care security for all,'' Clinton confidently declared.[4]

Polling data revealed strong public anxiety over the security of their health insurance coverage and the costs of their health care. With growing public concern over the health care crisis and a president demanding medical reform, it seemed difficult to believe that the 103rd Congress would adjourn without taking action on overhauling the health care system. And yet, that is precisely what happened.

THE REASONS FOR THE FAILURE OF CLINTON'S HEALTH CARE REFORM INITIATIVE

Why did Clinton's health care initiative end in failure, despite the president's success in generating such massive public and congressional interest in and, to a lesser extent, support for national health insurance during 1993–1994? There are four major reasons why Clinton's initiative, which began so promisingly, ended in such dismal failure: First, the health care industry had the political resources to prevent the establishment of national health insurance, which threatened to undermine the financial interest of practically every segment of the medical system; second, the public turned against the Clinton plan when it became clear that privately insured, middle-class individuals, who represent the overwhelming majority of the population, stood more to lose than to gain from comprehensive health care reform; third, the sweeping changes in the health care financing system the Clinton plan would have imposed threatened to raise corporate medical costs, provoking business opposition to the president's program; and fourth, the Democratic Party remained deeply divided over what kind of national health insurance program should be established, dealing a fatal blow to Clinton's ability to build a Democratic majority in the 103rd Congress behind any single health care reform plan.

The Health Care Industry Opposes Clinton's National Health Insurance Plan

In retrospect, it seems hard to understand how Clinton's health care reform initiative could have succeeded, given the fact that there were so many interest groups which had a stake in preserving the current medical system and stood to lose from the establishment of a national health insurance program. The primary interest group which had a stake in preserving the current health care system was the medical industry itself. The industry earns huge sums from the current health care system. Health care providers are free to extend as many medical services as they wish, guaranteeing doctors, hospitals, and nursing homes a substantial stream of income. The private insurance and pharmaceutical industries earn gigantic sums from the sale of their products—insurance coverage and prescription drugs.

Health care is a trillion-dollar industry, which consumes 14 percent of GDP. With so much money at stake in the current health care system, the medical industry stood to lose hundreds of billions of dollars from national health insurance. By guaranteeing universal coverage, national health insurance would have reduced financial barriers impeding public access to health care, raising patient utilization of medical services, and driving up their cost and the overall inflation rate. To the extent that universal coverage was achieved through federal subsidies, national health insurance would have also driven up the already swollen budget deficit.

To assure that national health insurance was established on an economically and fiscally viable basis, the federal government would have had to impose stringent health care cost-containment measures. Hospital and nursing-home rates, physician fees, and drug prices would have had to be reduced. Patient utilization of medical technology would have had to be stringently rationed, further reducing hospital and physician incomes. The private insurance industry would have had to be streamlined to reduce bureaucratic waste and inefficiency. National health insurance represented a financial threat to practically every segment of the health care industry. As a result, with few exceptions, the industry was united in opposition to the program.

The health care industry had ample political resources to derail Clinton's medical reform initiative. The industry had established strong political ties to members of Congress through the tens of millions of dollars in campaign contributions medical interest group PACs had provided to incumbent lawmakers. As we saw in Chapter 3, medical PACs provided $26.4 million in campaign contributions to congressional candidates, mostly incumbent lawmakers, during January 1, 1993 to May 31, 1994, guaranteeing medical interest groups substantial influence over the 103rd Congress, which considered Clinton's national health insurance plan.

Given the substantial financial influence the health care industry exerts on Capitol Hill, members of Congress had no rational interest in passing a national health insurance bill. The industry would have retaliated against members of Congress who voted for a national health insurance bill by targeting them for defeat the next time they ran for reelection. As we have seen, Republicans were practically united in their opposition to national health insurance; support for the program came almost exclusively from Democrats. As a result, the health care industry could have easily targeted for defeat Democratic members of Congress who supported national health insurance the next time they ran for reelection by making campaign contributions to their Republican opponents.

The Democratic Party's support for national health insurance is consistent with the fact that the socioeconomic group most in need of health care reform is the middle class. The wealthy have the financial means to purchase their own private insurance, and the poor are covered by Medicaid. However, many, if not most, middle-class families are too poor to purchase their own private insurance and too "rich" to be eligible for Medicaid. If they cannot find employers willing to provide them private insurance, middle-class families usually have no alternative but to become uninsured. Indeed, in 1993 fully 59 percent of the uninsured were middle-class, earning annual incomes of from the poverty line to four times the poverty line.[5] Much of the growth of the uninsured population during the 1990s is due to corporate and government downsizing, which has resulted in the layoffs of millions of middle-class workers. As corporate and government downsizing continue, the ranks of the middle-class uninsured are certain to grow.

The Democrats see themselves as the party of the middle class, committed to protecting such Americans from job, economic, and health insecurity through social welfare programs like Social Security, Medicare, Medicaid-financed nursing-home insurance, and unemployment insurance. Given that the overwhelming majority of the uninsured are middle-class, who are the socioeconomic group most vulnerable to losing their coverage under the current voluntary, employment-based insurance system, the Democratic Party is committed to guaranteeing access to health care through national health insurance. Given the failure of the insurance system to provide health security for the middle class, the Democrats saw their support for national health insurance as vital to maintaining their commitment to guaranteeing the social welfare of middle-class Americans.

However, support for national health insurance placed the Democratic Party in a particularly vexing dilemma. While support for national health insurance was vital to the Democratic commitment to the health security of the middle class, the party's sponsorship of health care reform also risked antagonizing the medical industry, a major source of financial support for congressional Democrats. Given the political risks they would take in supporting national health insurance, Democratic members of Congress were reluctant to back Clinton's national health insurance initiative. True, health care reform legislation was approved by most of the Democrats serving on the various congressional committees exercising jurisdiction over national health insurance. However, no vote was taken on health care reform legislation in either house of the 103rd Congress. By failing to take such a vote, congressional Democrats avoided having to go on record as supporting national health insurance, assuring that they would not antagonize the national health insurance industry. The political influence of the industry was sufficient that medical interest groups succeeded in intimidating congressional Democrats into silence on the issue of health care reform. In order to deter the industry from targeting them for defeat the next time they ran for reelection, congressional Democrats were determined not to bring health care reform legislation to vote in either house of the 103rd Congress. In the absence of such a vote, congressional Democrats could continue to support health care reform in principle, as they generally did, without having to vote in support of national health insurance legislation which was sure to expose them to political retaliation from the medical industry. Given Democratic reluctance to bring health care reform legislation to a vote in the 103rd Congress, passage of a national health insurance bill remained a political impossibility during 1993–1994.

In addition to PACs, the health care industry was well represented on Capitol Hill by a number of highly influential lobbyists with solid connections to members of Congress. Those lobbyists conveyed the industry's opposition to health care reform directly to members of Congress. Given the massive campaign contributions made by the industry to members of Congress, lobbyists representing medical interest groups had no difficulty directly reaching lawmakers.

The health care industry was well positioned to derail Clinton's medical reform initiative precisely because medical interest groups maintain excellent access to members of Congress. They have lobbyists among the best in Washington, who work as hired guns for the industry. Given its superior access to members of Congress and formidable lobbying power, the industry was able to take its case against Clinton's health care reform initiative directly to lawmakers. This gave the industry the influence it needed to steer Congress against Clinton's initiative. The health care industry's enormous influence on Capitol Hill was perhaps best summed up by Uwe Reinhardt, a health economist at Princeton University: "What the head of the AMA thinks in the shower in the morning is more important than the aspirations of 10 million Americans."[6]

Business Opposes the Clinton Plan

In addition to the health care industry, Clinton's medical reform initiative confronted strong opposition from business. In many ways, opposition from business to Clinton's health care reform initiative was even more devastating than that from the medical industry. A major purpose of Clinton's national health insurance plan was to relieve large corporations of the financial burden of the growing cost of health care. Practically all large corporations provide their working families group insurance, while many, if not most, small firms do not. As a result, large corporations must bear the financial burden of cost shifting; health care providers finance the cost of uncompensated care to the uninsured, most of whom work for small business, by raising their charges for privately insured patients, most of whom are employed in large corporations. Cost shifting represents a major part of the cost of group insurance for large corporations.

Clinton's national health insurance plan would have required all employers not providing their working families group coverage to do so. With all employers providing their working families group coverage, cost shifting would end. Health care providers would no longer finance uncompensated care for the uninsured by raising their charges for privately insured patients, since the Clinton plan would achieve universal coverage. The elimination of cost shifting would relieve large corporations of the financial burden of having to pay higher group insurance premiums in order to finance uncompensated care for the uninsured, who mostly work for small business. With the elimination of cost shifting, group insurance premiums for large corporations would decline.

In addition to eliminating cost shifting, Clinton's national health insurance plan was designed to relieve large corporations of the financial burden of growing health care costs by imposing stringent limits on medical expenses and the share of payroll business would be required to pay for group coverage for its working families. As we have seen, the Clinton plan would have required consumers to join health alliances, which would have had the bargaining power to secure the most comprehensive coverage at the lowest possible premiums for their members. The federal government would have imposed stringent limits on private insurance premiums, tying their growth to that of the consumer price index. Federal subsidies would have been provided to assure that no employers spent more than 7.9 percent of their payroll on group insurance.

Clinton's national health insurance plan would have benefited large corporations by eliminating cost shifting, containing health care costs through market and regulatory means, and limiting the share of payroll employers would have had to spend on group coverage. As a result, Clinton had every reason to believe that big business would embrace his program and lobby for its passage. Instead, on February 3, 1994, the major interest group representing large corporations, the Business Roundtable, announced its opposition to the Clinton plan, as we have seen. Making matters worse for Clinton, the Chamber of Commerce, which had earlier endorsed the heart of the president's program, employer mandates, joined the Business Roundtable in its opposition to the Clinton plan.

Why did large corporations, which stood to benefit from Clinton's national health insurance plan, oppose it? The answer lies in the fact that, on balance, large corporations stood to lose more than they would gain from the Clinton plan. The president's program would have required large corporations as a whole to provide more health care benefits to their working families than they currently do, raising business costs.

Employers are currently free to provide whatever health care benefits to their working families they wish. They can easily reduce their health care costs by cutting the medical benefits they provide their working families. However, Clinton's national health insurance plan would have mandated that employers provide a minimum package of health care benefits and prohibited them from reducing their health care costs by cutting the medical benefits they provide. By depriving employers of the flexibility they currently have to reduce the health care benefits they provide their working families, the Clinton plan would have raised business costs even further.

Clinton's national health insurance plan would have required large corporations as a whole to provide their working families more health care benefits than they currently do; and would have deprived employers of the right they currently have to reduce their medical costs by shrinking the group coverage they extend to their employed households. As a result, the plan represented a costly federal mandate on business; big business had a rational interest in defeating it.

Joining big business in its opposition to Clinton's national health insurance plan was small business. As mentioned, many, if not most, small firms do not provide their working families group insurance. The Clinton plan would have required them to do so, raising their costs substantially. The Clinton plan would have imposed an onerous financial burden on small business by requiring small firms which currently do not provide their working families group insurance to assume the enormous expense of doing so. To prevent its members from having to assume this burden, the largest interest group representing small business, the NFIB, constituted a particularly active and vociferous opponent of the Clinton plan.

Perhaps no single actor in American politics had greater power to determine the outcome of the debate on health care reform during 1993–1994 than business. Most individuals are insured through their families' employers, most of which are private firms. Any action by even a small segment of the business community to terminate the group health insurance provided to working families would raise the number of uninsured individuals by tens of millions. To assure that the overwhelming majority of the public remain insured, the federal government needs businesses to continue assuming their responsibility of providing group insurance to their working families.

The stability of America's employment-based health insurance system rests upon the willingness of businesses to provide their working families group coverage. As a result, Congress must be especially sensitive to business opinion on health care reform. Should business become dissatisfied with the financial burden employers currently assume in providing group insurance for their working families, corporations could register their unhappiness with the current health care financing system by terminating the coverage they extend their employed households, increasing the number of uninsured individuals by tens of millions. To assure that business continues to assume its responsibility of providing their working families group insurance, Congress needs to make sure that corporations are satisfied with the current health care financing system.

In February 1994 business made clear its satisfaction with the current health care financing system by rejecting Clinton's national health insurance plan. Despite the financial burdens imposed upon business by the current health care financing system, the Clinton plan would have added to corporate medical costs by requiring firms to provide their working families a more generous package of health care benefits than they currently do. As a result, business had every reason to oppose the Clinton plan. By rejecting the Clinton plan, business made clear its willingness to continue assuming responsibility for providing most working families group insurance. Congress is only likely to establish a national health insurance program should business renege on its responsibility to provide most working families coverage, requiring the federal government to assume this obligation. Given business's willingness to continue this responsibility, Congress had no urgent and compelling need to establish a national health insurance program. Congress simply saw no need for the federal government to guarantee universal coverage, as long as most individuals continue to be insured by their employers.

Clinton hoped that business would conceive his national health insurance plan as a means to relieve corporations of the financial burden of financing health care for their working families, and that business would use its enormous influence on Capitol Hill to press Congress to pass his program. Instead, business believed that the Clinton plan would add to corporate health care costs, and organized to defeat the president's program. Clinton gravely miscalculated in his assumption that his national health insurance plan would win business support; this miscalculation cost the president the vital corporate backing that he needed to secure passage of his health care reform program.

Public Opinion Turns Against Clinton's National Health Insurance Plan

Opposition from the health care industry and business represented formidable obstacles preventing Clinton from prevailing in his campaign to secure the establishment of national health insurance. However, such opposition was not sufficient to derail Clinton's health care initiative. Rather, Clinton could have overcome opposition from the health care industry and business to his national health insurance plan, albeit with great difficulty, had he succeeded in mobilizing public support for his program. Congress would have been highly unlikely to ignore Clinton's demands for action on health care reform had lawmakers perceived a groundswell of public support for national health insurance.

In the final analysis, Clinton's national health insurance initiative failed not because it was opposed by the medical industry and business, though such opposition was an important factor. Rather, it failed because it lost public support. As we have seen, Clinton's national health insurance plan commanded the support of an overwhelming majority of the public following the president's address to a joint session of Congress on September 22, 1993. However, public support for the Clinton plan declined dramatically during the months following the address. By July 1994, nearly half the public opposed the Clinton plan. Worse yet for Clinton, by August 1994 an overwhelming majority of the public believed that Congress should defer any action on health care reform until 1995, at the very earliest.

With public opposition to Clinton's national health insurance plan growing, and popular sentiment for immediate congressional action on health care reform waning, lawmakers saw no urgent and compelling need to pass legislation overhauling the medical system. When the 103rd Congress adjourned in October 1994 without taking any action on health care reform, lawmakers were only doing what their constituents wanted, which was to defer any action on health care reform until a later time. The 103rd Congress's decision not to take any action on health care reform was consistent with, rather than contrary to, the expressed will of the people, given the fact that every available poll taken on the issue during the summer of 1994 showed no popular enthusiasm for legislation to overhaul the medical system.[7]

Why did public support for Clinton's national health insurance plan collapse by the summer of 1994? Why had the public appetite for health care reform turned sour by the same time? The answer remains the massive and intense public relations campaign against the Clinton plan mounted by the Republican Party. Republicans convincingly argued that the Clinton plan would require middle-class, privately insured individuals to pay more for their coverage, with the added revenues devoted to providing coverage for the uninsured. At the same time, middle-class, privately insured individuals would have less coverage, since health care would have to be stringently rationed to assure the economic and fiscal viability of the national health insurance program Clinton would have established.

Clinton's national health insurance plan would have required middle-class, privately insured individuals to pay more for less coverage. Once the people became aware of this, which they had by the summer of 1994, public opinion swung decisively against the Clinton plan. Polling data clearly show that the public was not convinced that the middle class would gain from national health insurance, contrary to the president's claims. During August 8–9, 1994, *USA Today*, CNN, and Gallup conducted a poll of 1,016 adults, who were asked which socioeconomic segment of society—the upper class, middle class, or poor—stood to gain and lose the most from health care reform. Thirty-six percent of those polled believed the poor stood to gain the most from health care reform. Only 16 percent thought the upper class would gain, and 15 percent the middle class. By contrast, 38 percent believed the middle class stood to lose the most from health care reform. Only 19 percent thought the upper class would lose, and 14 percent the poor.[8] The *USA Today*/CNN/Gallup poll shows that the greatest single share of the public believed that the middle class stood to lose the most from health care reform, with the smallest single percentage of the population thinking that the middle class had the most to gain from an overhaul of the medical system. The public believed that the middle class had the most to lose, and the least to gain, from health care reform.

Why did the public doubt that the middle class stood to gain from health care insurance? The answer is simple: Middle-class, privately insured individuals knew that national health insurance would result in higher taxes and health care rationing to accommodate the needs of the uninsured, forcing them to pay more for less coverage than is currently the case. Middle-class anxiety over health care reform was perhaps best summed up by Mollyanne Brodie and Robert J. Blendon:

By the end of this debate [on national health insurance], the middle class became more worried about the possible negative effects of health care reform than they were about the [medical crisis] itself. By June 1994, more Americans were worried that a health care reform bill would jeopardize quality and cost more (57 percent) than were worried that universal coverage and cost control would not be achieved (29 percent). . . . At the same time most Americans believed that under the Clinton plan their costs would increase, that they would have fewer choices of physicians, and that the quality of health care they received would decrease rather than improve. . . . The status quo seemed more desirable than any major reform. In fact almost one-half of the public said they were relieved that Congress did not enact any reform.[9]

As Brodie and Blendon suggest, middle-class, privately insured individuals feared the costs of national health insurance—higher taxes and health care rationing—more than they did the costs of not having the program, that is, the possibility of losing one's insurance with the loss of a job.

Since the middle class represents an overwhelming majority of the population, the public's belief that the middle class stood to lose more than it would gain from national health insurance meant that most people, who are middle-class, also believed that the program would leave them worse off than they are under the current voluntary, employment-based insurance system. This is revealed in the *USA Today*/CNN/Gallup poll, which asked its respondents which they feared more: "being worse off" under health care reform, or becoming uninsured in the absence of national health insurance. Fifty-four percent of those surveyed said that they feared "being worse off" under health care reform more; and 40 percent feared becoming uninsured in absence of national health insurance more.[10] The *USA Today*/CNN/Gallup poll clearly shows that the public viewed national health insurance, with the health care rationing the federal government would impose under the program, more unfavorably than they did the prospect of becoming uninsured under the current insurance system.

A major element in Clinton's campaign to mobilize public support for his national health insurance plan was his argument that the program was good for the middle class, since it would give them the health security they currently lack. However, the *USA Today*/CNN/Gallup poll clearly shows that the public found Clinton's argument unconvincing. Far from gaining anything from national health insurance, middle-class, privately insured individuals came to the conclusion that they would be no better off, and possibly worse off, under the program, and had no rational interest in its establishment. Middle-class opposition dealt a crippling blow to Clinton's campaign to establish national health insurance, since it deprived the president of the one potentially convincing argument he could have used to mobilize congressional support for the program: that it would benefit the middle class. With mounting middle-class opposition to national health insurance, Clinton could no longer credibly argue that the program was needed to help this segment of the public, despite whatever benefits middle-class individuals would have gained from health care reform.

Given the opposition against Clinton's national health insurance plan mounted by the health care industry and business, Congress was already disinclined to take action on medical reform. However, any chance for congressional action on health care reform vanished once public opinion turned against the Clinton plan. With a plurality of the public joining the health care industry and business in opposing the plan, Congress had no rational basis in taking action on health care reform. This was especially true given that only a fraction of the public believed that national health insurance would benefit the middle class. Since the middle class represents the overwhelming majority of the population, Congress is attentive to its needs and is unlikely to take any action which hurts this group. The fact that the overwhelming majority of the public, most of whom are middle-class, did not believe that the middle class had much, if anything, to gain from national health insurance deprived Congress of any rational interest in taking action on health care reform.

Passage of health care reform legislation would have antagonized the medical industry, business, and a plurality of the public, especially the middle class, all of whom had become adamantly opposed to any overhaul of the medical system by the summer of 1994. The health care industry, business, and the voters were sure to use their substantial political resources to target for defeat congressional Democrats who supported national health insurance, should the Democratic congressional leadership have succeeded in passing a health care reform bill in the 103rd Congress. Congressional Democrats were not about to expose themselves to the substantial political risk they would have faced had they passed a health care reform bill, which was sure to anger their constituents as well as key interest groups with a substantial financial stake in the medical system. Overwhelmed by mounting opposition from the health care industry, business, and the public as a whole, especially the middle class, Clinton's medical reform initiative understandably collapsed following the completion of the Senate debate on the Mitchell bill in August 1994.

The Division within the Democratic Party Over National Health Insurance

In addition to opposition from the health care industry, business, and a plurality of the public, Clinton's health care reform initiative was derailed by division within the Democratic Party over what kind of national health insurance program the United States should have: between liberals, who supported a single-payer plan; and moderates, led by Clinton, who favored building upon, rather than scrapping and replacing, the current insurance system with a government program. Single-payer insurance commanded support among dozens of House Democrats, who served as cosponsors of the Wellstone-McDermott bill, which would have scrapped and replaced the current insurance system with a universal, comprehensive government program. As a result, Clinton's national health insurance plan, the Health Security Act, stood no chance of passage without the united support of House Democratic cosponsors of the Wellstone-McDermott bill.

However, the Health Security Act succeeded in garnering the support of only half the House Democratic cosponsors of the Wellstone-McDermott bill. The lead cosponsor of the Wellstone-McDermott bill, Representative McDermott, denounced the Health Security Act for failing to rectify the inequities and in-efficiencies which pervade the current employment-based health insurance sys-tem. McDermott demanded instead nothing less than passage of a single-payer insurance bill, which he believed was the only means to establish an equitable and efficient insurance system. McDermott's intransigent opposition to any health care reform plan which fell short of single-payer insurance deprived Clin-ton of any hope of building a Democratic majority within the 103rd Congress behind his more modest and incremental national health insurance program. With half of all Democratic House cosponsors of the Wellstone-McDermott bill following McDermott's lead in refusing to support the Health Security Act, Clinton's national health insurance plan stood no chance of passage.

BILL CLINTON AND THE LESSONS OF HEALTH CARE REFORM

What lessons have we learned about the politics of health care reform as a result of the debate on national health insurance which occurred during 1993–1994? Perhaps the most important lesson is that a national health insurance program cannot be established unless the public believes that they will be better off under health care reform. Clinton's national health insurance plan ultimately failed because the public was convinced that they would not benefit, and might even lose, from the president's program.

In attempting to mobilize popular support for national health insurance, sup-porters of the program must recognize that health care reform presents the public with a major trade-off. National health insurance assures the public cradle-to-grave coverage; under the program, health care becomes a right of citizenship, not, as is currently the case, a privilege of employment and income. National health insurance guarantees all individuals coverage, regardless of their employ-ment and income status.

Without question, the most attractive feature of national health insurance is that it would guarantee the public the health security which is currently absent. Under national health insurance, the public would be secure in the knowledge that they would be covered, regardless of whether they lost their jobs or fell on hard times. As we saw in Chapter 1, an overwhelming majority of the public believe that the government should guarantee every individual coverage, clear evidence that the public values health security. The public clearly wants all individuals to be guaranteed coverage, regardless of their employment and in-come status, and does not believe that persons should have to risk losing their insurance should they lose their jobs or fall on hard times.

Given the existence of strong public support for universal, cradle-to-grave, government-guaranteed insurance coverage, it is easy to see why Clinton fo-cused on the issue of health security in seeking to mobilize popular backing for his national health insurance plan, which, after all, was entitled the Health Security Act. In his address to a joint session of Congress on September 22, 1993, he emphasized that the Health Security Act would guarantee "every American health security; health care that can never be taken away, health care that is always there."[11] In making the case for the need for health security, Clinton warned that "millions of Americans are just one pink slip away from losing their health insurance, and one serious illness away from losing all their savings."[12] By focusing on the most popular feature of national health insurance, health security, Clinton succeeded in mobilizing strong public support for his health care reform plan following his address to Congress.

Given the existence of strong popular support for universal, cradle-to-grave, government-guaranteed health insurance coverage, why did public opinion swing so decisively against Clinton's national health insurance plan during 1994? The answer remains that no national health insurance program can be established on an economically and fiscally viable basis without the imposition of stringent health care cost-containment measures, which results in medical rationing. The public initially supported the Clinton plan because they wanted the health security the president's program would have provided. However, the public soured on the plan once they came to realize that it would result in health care rationing, which the overwhelming majority of the population oppose, as we have seen.

National health insurance presents the public with a very difficult and painful trade-off. The public is guaranteed health security under national health insurance. However, the cost the public must pay for health security is health care rationing. No nation, not even the United States, has the resources to guarantee every individual access to all the available health care resources he or she may need. Every other advanced industrial democracy which has a national health insurance program rations health care; and the United States would have to do the same should this country ever decide to guarantee its people universal coverage.

The 85 percent of the public who are insured currently have access to all the available health care they may need. Should they develop a catastrophic or life-threatening illness, insured individuals need not worry that they might be denied access to life-sustaining medical technology because of a shortage of health care resources. The abundance of health care resources in the United States stands in sharp contrast to the severe shortages of medical facilities existing in the other advanced industrial democracies, which have national health insurance programs. This abundance of health care resources and the absence of any institutionalized policy of medical rationing are clearly the most attractive features of the American medical system. As we saw in the previous chapter, during the Senate debate on the Mitchell bill in August 1994, Republican lawmakers repeatedly pointed to the abundance of health care resources in the United States as evidence that this nation has the best health care system, which should not be subjected to any major overhaul.

The overwhelming majority of the public are currently insured through their employment. For individuals covered by employment-based insurance, there are both positive and negative features to the current health care financing system. Insured working families currently have access to all available health care they may need; however, should they lose their jobs and be unable to find an employer willing to provide them insurance, they will become uninsured, with little or no access to medical services.

The current employment-based health insurance system provides working families an abundance of health care benefits, but no real health security. Insured working families have access to all available health care, but that access is dependent upon their continued employment. Should they lose their jobs and the insurance which comes with their employment, those working families could very well find themselves with little or no access to health care. Given the existence of increasing job insecurity resulting from corporate and government downsizing and layoffs, all but the wealthiest individuals are currently at risk of losing their jobs and the insurance which comes with their employment.

If a national health insurance program is to be established, individuals covered by employment-based health insurance must be willing to give up some of the health care benefits they now have in order to gain the medical security which they currently lack. Working families must be willing to give up the employment-based insurance, which currently provides them access to all the available health care they may need. In exchange, they must be willing to participate in a national health insurance program, which would provide them cradle-to-grave, government-guaranteed access to only a restricted set of health care benefits.

National health insurance involves a difficult and painful trade-off in which individuals give up some health care benefits in exchange for health security. Under national health insurance, all individuals would be guaranteed access to health care, in contrast to the current system, in which medical benefits are linked to employment. However, under national health insurance, health care would be stringently rationed, in contrast to the current medical financing system, in which insured individuals have access to all the available health care they may need.

Clinton's health care reform initiative failed precisely because the president could and would not convince middle-class, privately insured individuals to give up some of their medical benefits in order to gain health security that they currently lack. Insured individuals did not want to give up the right they currently have to all the available health care they need and be forced into a national health insurance program in which medical services would be stringently rationed. Insured working families wanted to preserve the current health insurance system, even at the risk of losing their coverage and access to health care, should they lose their jobs and become uninsured. This was a risk insured working families were willing to take in order to preserve the current insurance system, which guarantees them access to all the available health care they may need.

Clinton himself was unwilling to honestly confront the sacrifices the public would have to make to establish a national health insurance program. Throughout his campaign to establish national health insurance during 1993–1994, he repeatedly emphasized the benefits of the program—health security guaranteed by the federal government to every citizen and legal resident from cradle to grave. However, Clinton never once mentioned in public the cost of national health insurance—the imposition of federal limits on health care costs, which would inevitably result in health care rationing.

True, Clinton did publicly acknowledge that his national health insurance plan would impose limits on total health care spending. However, he unconvincingly argued that his national health insurance plan would reduce health care costs by squeezing out the waste, extravagance, administrative inefficiency, fraud, and abuse pervading the medical system. Clinton never once acknowledged that the limits his national health insurance plan would impose on total health care spending would inevitably result in medical rationing. Nevertheless, despite Clinton's insincerity, the public fully understood that the establishment of a national health insurance program would result in health care rationing, as the 1994 *Newsweek* poll cited in the previous chapter shows. The public fully understood the costs of national health insurance, despite Clinton's refusal to acknowledge those costs up front.

In the final analysis, the 85 percent of the public who are insured fear health care rationing more than they do losing their coverage. Insured families do not want to participate in a national health insurance program in which their health care will be stringently rationed. Rather, insured families want to preserve the current insurance system, which guarantees them access to all the health care they may need, even at the risk that they might lose their jobs and the coverage which comes with their employment, and become uninsured.

Why did Clinton's health care reform initiative, which began with such high hopes, ultimately end in such abysmal failure? Because the insured public fears health care rationing more than they do the possibility of becoming uninsured. The public finds government-imposed health care rationing to be more objectionable than the fact that 41 million individuals, representing 15 percent of the population, are currently uninsured. The current health care system is exactly the kind of system the public wants: a system which provides those who have insurance access to the best and most abundant health care services in the world, while leaving 41 million individuals with little or no access to medical care. As long as the public flatly rejects government-imposed health care rationing, and demands that the insured have access to all the available medical services they may need; as long as the public continues to turn a blind eye to the plight of the uninsured, no national health insurance program will be possible.

During the debate on health care reform, Clinton and congressional Democrats recited countless stories of uninsured sick individuals being literally left to die because they did not have access to life-sustaining medical services. However, those heart-wrenching stories never registered with the public. Instead, the public responded to the bleak image of health care rationing—of catastrophically and terminally ill individuals having to wait in long lines to gain access to the life-sustaining medical technology they needed, or being denied such access altogether. As we saw in the previous chapters, the Republican Party was quick to exploit public distaste for and fear of health care rationing in order to mobilize popular opposition to Clinton's national health insurance plan. The specter of health care rationing haunted the debate on medical reform during 1993–1994. Despite their attraction to the ideal of health security, the public ultimately flinched from their initial embrace of the Clinton plan when it became clear that health care rationing would be the inevitable result of the president's program.

Clinton's health care reform initiative failed because the insured public fears medical rationing more than they do the possibility of becoming uninsured. National health insurance will only become possible once the insured public fears the risk of becoming uninsured more than they do the certainty of health care rationing. That is the ultimate lesson of the collapse of Clinton's health care reform initiative supporters of national health insurance must bear in mind the next time they launch a campaign to establish the program.

Notes

PREFACE

1. *The President's Health Security Plan: The Complete Draft and Final Reports of the White House Domestic Policy Council* (New York: Times Books, 1993), pp. 104, 108.

2. William J. Clinton, *Public Papers of the Presidents of the United States 1993* (Washington, D.C.: United States Government Printing Office, 1994), p. 1831.

3. For an analysis of Truman's campaign to establish national health insurance, see Monte M. Poen, *Harry S. Truman Versus the Medical Lobby: The Genesis of Medicare* (Columbia: University of Missouri Press, 1979). For an examination of Carter's drive to institute the program, see Nicholas Laham, *Why the United States Lacks a National Insurance Program* (Westport, Conn.: Praeger Publishers, 1993), Part II.

4. William J. Clinton, *Public Papers of the Presidents of the United States 1994.* (Washington, D.C.: United States Government Printing Office, 1995), p. 131. Clinton's claim that President Franklin D. Roosevelt attempted to "reform health care" is historically incorrect. True, influential members of the Roosevelt administration recommended two separate national health insurance bills in 1935 and 1938, respectively. However, Roosevelt himself, bowing to AMA opposition, refused to endorse either bill. For an assessment of the politics of national health insurance during the Roosevelt administration, see David Hirshfield, *The Lost Reform: The Campaign for Compulsory Health Insurance from 1932 to 1943* (Cambridge: Harvard University Press, 1970).

5. Carter coupled his message to Congress with remarks to the media outlining his national health insurance plan. However, Carter delivered his remarks outside prime time, and they received little public attention. For texts containing the message to Congress delivered by Truman, Nixon, and Carter urging the establishment of national health insurance and Carter's remarks to the media outlining his health care reform plan, see Harry S. Truman, *Public Papers of the Presidents of the United States 1945* (Washington, D.C.: United States Government Printing Office, 1961), pp. 475–91; Harry S. Truman, *Public Papers of the Presidents of the United States 1947* (Washington, D.C.: United

States Government Printing Office, 1963), pp. 250–52; Harry S. Truman, *Public Papers of the Presidents of the United States 1949* (Washington, D.C.: United States Government Printing Office, 1964), pp. 226–30; Richard Nixon, *Public Papers of the Presidents of the United States 1971* (Washington, D.C.: United States Government Printing Office, 1972), pp. 170–86; Richard Nixon, *Public Papers of the Presidents of the United States 1974*, pp. 132–40; and Jimmy Carter, *Public Papers of the Presidents of the United States 1979* (Washington, D.C.: United States Government Printing Office, 1980), pp. 1024–31.

6. The Clinton Administration's case for health care reform is contained in The White House Domestic Policy Council, *Health Security: The President's Report to the American People* (New York: Touchstone, 1993). The administration's national health insurance plan is summarized in The White House Domestic Policy Council, *The President's Health Security Plan: The Clinton Blueprint* (New York: Times Books, 1993). Those two books have been combined into a single volume entitled *The President's Health Security Plan: The Complete Draft and Final Reports of the White House Domestic Policy Council* (New York: Times Books, 1993).

CHAPTER 1

1. Julie Rovner, "Democrats Take Two Paths to System Overhaul," *Congressional Quarterly Weekly Report*, July 4, 1992, p. 1966.

2. For a historical account of the AMA's campaign against national health insurance, see Paul Starr, *The Social Transformation of American Medicine* (New York: Basic Books, 1982), Book 2, Chapter 1.

3. For an analysis of the campaign to establish national health insurance during the early 1990s, see Nicholas Laham, *Why the United States Lacks a National Health Insurance Program* (Westport, Conn.: Praeger Publishers, 1993), Part III.

4. Richard Benedetto, "Democrats Hope 'the Bottom Has Been Reached'," *USA Today*, September 9, 1994, p. 8A. Fifty-seven percent of those polled approved of Clinton's handling of foreign policy, 54 percent of crime, and 52 percent of the economy. Forty-two percent disapproved of Clinton's handling of crime and the economy, respectively, and 34 percent of foreign policy.

5. Richard Benedetto, " 'Reservations' Aside, Voters Standing by GOP," *USA Today*, March 31, 1995, p. 8A. Forty-nine percent of those polled favored Republican congressional leaders on the deficit, 48 percent on the economy and taxes, respectively, and 46 percent on welfare and foreign policy, respectively. Forty-four percent perferred Clinton on welfare, 43 percent on foreign policy, 41 percent on the economy, 38 percent on taxes, and 37 percent on the deficit.

6. Richard Benedetto, "Clinton's Forte Is Issues; Dole's Is Character," *USA Today*, January 19, 1996, p. 9A. Fifty-four percent of those polled approved of Clinton's handling of education, 48 percent foreign affairs, 47 percent Medicare, 44 percent the economy and crime, respectively, 41 percent taxes, 40 percent welfare, and 35 percent the federal budget deficit. Forty percent approved of Dole's handling of foreign affairs, 38 percent the economy, 37 percent welfare, 36 percent the federal budget deficit and taxes, respectively, 35 percent education and crime, respectively, and 33 percent Medicare.

7. Ronald Brownstein, "Dissatisfied Americans May Spell Democratic Losses," *Los Angeles Times*, July 28, 1994, p. A19. Twenty-six percent of Clinton supporters said that

they backed the President because "he's trying" do a good job but "needs more time," 9 percent because he "cares about people like me," and 8 percent because "he's done well so far." Twelve percent of those who disapproved of Clinton did so because they believed he "lacks integrity" and "don't trust him," 11 percent because they felt that he was "not fulfilling his campaign promises," and 10 percent because they viewed him as "a weak leader" who was "indecisive."

8. James Carney, "Going Flat Out," *Time*, August 1, 1994, p. 17.

9. Edwin Chen, "Cost May Be Key to Whether Health Reforms Win Support," *Los Angeles Times*, October 3, 1993, pp. A22–23.

10. David Lauter, "Americans Sending Mixed Messages on Health Reform," *Los Angeles Times*, July 29, 1994, pp. A14–15.

11. For an analysis of the role the deterioration in America's employment-based health insurance system had in fueling rising public support for national health insurance during the early 1990s, see Laham, *Why the United States Lacks a National Health Insurance Program*, Chapters 6 and 8.

CHAPTER 2

1. *The President's Health Security Plan: The Complete Draft and Final Reports of the White House Domestic Policy Council* (New York: Times Books, 1993), p. xvii.

2. Ibid., p. 104.

3. Ibid.

4. William J. Clinton, *Public Papers of the Presidents of the United States 1993* (Washington, D.C.: United States Government Printing Office, 1994), p. 116.

5. Richard M. Coughlin, *Ideology, Public Opinion & Welfare Policy: Attitudes Toward Taxes and Spending in Industrialized Societies* (Berkeley: University of California, 1980), p. 82.

6. Henry J. Aaron, Barry P. Bosworth, and Gary Burtless, *Can America Afford to Grow Old? Paying for Social Security* (Washington, D.C.: The Brookings Institution, 1989), p. 25; John Holahan, Colin Winterbottom, and Shruti Rajan, *The Changing Composition of Health Insurance Coverage in the United States* (Washington, D.C.: The Urban Institute, January 1995); Ross Perot, *Intensive Care: We Must Save Medicare and Medicaid Now* (New York: Harper Perennial, 1995), p. 65.

7. David Lauter, "Americans Sending Mixed Messages on Health Reform," *Los Angeles Times*, July 29, 1994, p. A15.

8. George J. Church, "Are We Better Off?," *Time*, January 29, 1996, p. 36. Fifty-six percent of those polled said that they and their families were better off in the quality of products on the market, 46 percent in their standard of living, 34 percent in the amount of leisure time available, 31 percent in the quality of local public schools, and 17 percent in their safety from being the victim of a crime. Fifty-nine percent said that they and their families were worse off in their safety from being the victim of a crime, 43 percent in the quality of their local public schools, 42 percent in the amount of leisure time available, 21 percent in the quality of products on the market, and 20 percent in their standard of living.

9. Jon D. Hull, "Anger From the Grass Roots," *Time*, August 29, 1994, p. 39. In September 1993 16 percent of those polled said that unemployment was America's most important problem, 14 percent crime, 9 percent the economy, 8 percent the federal budget

deficit and lack of morals, respectively, and 5 percent politicians and government. In August 1994 27 percent said that crime was America's most important problem, 16 percent politicians and government, 9 percent the lack of morals, 6 percent the economy, 5 percent unemployment, and 3 percent the federal budget deficit.

10. U.S. Department of Health and Human Services, *Your Medicare Handbook 1995*, p. 1.

11. Henry J. Aaron, *Serious and Unstable Condition: Financing America's Health Care* (Washington, D.C.: The Brookings Institution, 1991), pp. 64–65.

12. Diane Rowland, *Directions for Health Reform: Testimony Before the Committee on Labor and Human Resources*, United States Senate, March 15, 1995, p. 6.

13. Robert Pear, "Health Advisers Plan Exemption for Big Business," *The New York Times*, April 26, 1993, p. A10.

14. Henry J. Kaiser Family Foundation, *Uninsured in America: Straight Facts on Health Reform*, April 1994.

15. "2.2 Million Americans Lose Insurance Monthly—Report," *USA Today*, September 16, 1993, p. 4A.

16. Rowland, *Directions for Health Reform*.

17. Aaron, *Serious and Unstable Condition*, p. 74; Sam Fulwood III and Melissa Healy, "1.3 Million More Drop Into Poverty," *Los Angeles Times*, October 7, 1994, p. A22.

18. Rowland, *Directions for Health Reform*.

19. Aaron, Bosworth, and Burtless, *Can America Afford to Grow Old?*, p. 25; Holahan, Winterbottom, and Rajan, *The Changing Composition of Health Insurance Coverage in the United States*; Ross Perot, *Intensive Care*, p. 65.

20. Theodore Marmor and Jerry Mashaw, "Health Care Reform: Rumor Is Scarier Than Reality," *Los Angeles Times*, July 6, 1993, p. B5. Of the 76 percent of the cost of health care which was financed by third-party payers in 1991, 35 percent was funded by private health insurance, 17 percent by Medicare, 11 percent by Medicaid, and the remaining 13 percent by other government programs. Of the 41 percent of the cost of health care which was financed by the government, 26 percent was funded by the federal government and 15 percent by state and local governments.

21. Diane Rowland, *Uninsured in America: Testimony Before the Committee on Finance, United States Senate*, February 10, 1994.

22. Fulwood and Healy, "1.3 Million More Drop Into Poverty."

23. Aaron, *Serious and Unstable Condition*, p. 74.

24. Ibid., pp. 42–45.

25. Henry J. Aaron, "Health Care Financing," in Henry J. Aaron and Charles L. Schultze, eds., *Setting Domestic Priorities: What Can Government Do?* (Washington, D.C.: The Brookings Institution, 1992), p. 36.

26. Aaron, *Serious and Unstable Condition*, pp. 48–49.

27. Sara Collins, "A Checkup for Health Care Costs," *U.S. News & World Report*, June 13, 1994, p. 63; Dianna Chapman Walsh and Richard Egdahl, *Payer, Provider, Consumer: Industry Confronts Health Care Costs* (New York: Springer-Verlag, 1977), p. 4.

28. Aaron, *Serious and Unstable Condition*, p. 39.

29. Beth Belton, "Consumer Price Growth at 7-Year Low," *USA Today*, January 14, 1994, pp. B1–2; Beth Belton, "Runaway Medical Costs Hit a Wall," *USA Today*, July 15, 1992, p. B1; Beth Belton, "Threat to Recovery Minimized," *USA Today*, January

18, 1993, p. B-2; Charles L. Schultze, "Paying the Bills," in Aaron and Schultze, *Setting Domestic Priorities*, p. 299.

30. Michael Wolff, Peter Rutten, and Albert Bayers III, *Where We Stand: Can America Make It in the Global Race for Wealth, Health, and Happiness?* (New York: Bantam Books, 1992), p. 136.

31. Ibid., p. 126.

32. Donald L. Bartlett and James B. Steele, *America: What Went Wrong?* (Kansas City, Mo.: Andrews and McMeel, 1992), pp. 125–26.

33. "Medical Bills to Double, Group Warns," *USA Today*, November 23, 1993, p. 4A.

34. *Congressional Record*, 103rd Congress, 2nd Session, p. S10259; "Medical Bills to Double, Group Warns."

35. "Medical Bills to Double, Group Warns."

36. *Congressional Record*, 103rd Congress, 2nd Session, p. S11033; "Medical Bills to Double, Group Warns."

37. *Congressional Record*, 103rd Congress, 2nd Session, p. S11005.

38. Don L. Boroughs, David Fischer, Monika Guttman, Scott McMurray, and Maria Mallory, "Winter of Discontent," *U.S. News & World Report*, January 22, 1996, p. 51; *Congressional Record*, 103rd Congress, 2nd Session, p. S11005.

39. *Congressional Record*, 103rd Congress, 2nd Session, p. S11005.

40. *The President's Health Security Plan*, p. 11.

41. Lauter, "Americans Sending Mixed Messages on Health Reform," p. A15.

42. Dorian Friedman, Stephen V. Roberts, Jonathan Sapers, Deborah A. Schwartz, and Jill Jordan Sieder, "Workers Take It On the Chin," *U.S. News & World Report*, January 22, 1996, p. 46. Twenty-four percent of those polled said that the federal government could "help average families the most" by providing a middle-class tax cut, and 23 percent stated that the same could be done through a balanced federal budget.

43. Rashi Fein, *Medical Care, Medical Costs: The Search for a Health Insurance Policy* (Cambridge: Harvard University Press, 1989), p. 69; Perot, *Intensive Care*, p. 54.

44. Robert J. Myers, *Social Security* (Homewood, Ill.: Richard D. Irwin, 1985), pp. 522, 552, 570; *Your Medicare Handbook 1995*, pp. 1, 5, 14.

45. *Your Medicare Handbook 1995*, p. 7.

46. Jonathan Peterson, "Given Facts, Cause to Slash Medicaid Not So Clear-Cut," *Los Angeles Times*, April 16, 1995, p. A13.

47. Peter Kerr, "Elderly Care: The Insurers' Role," *New York Times*, March 16, 1993, p. C6.

48. Kathy M. Kristof, "Long-Term Care Insurance Now Better Than Ever," *Los Angeles Times*, July 19, 1993, p. D6.

49. Kevin Anderson, "Health Care Still Too Costly to Seniors," *USA Today*, February 26, 1992, p. 1A.

50. Jann Wenner and William Greider, "President Clinton," *Rolling Stone*, December 9, 1993, p. 80.

51. Perot, *Intensive Care*, p. 124.

52. Robert H. Blank, *Rationing Medicine* (New York: Columbia University Press, 1988), p. 14; Perot, *Intensive Care*, p. 124.

53. Ronald Brownstein, "States' Medicaid Costs Top Higher Education Outlays," *Los Angeles Times*, July 27, 1993, p. A11.

54. Clinton, *Public Papers of the Presidents of the United States 1993*, p. 1383.

55. Members of the President's Task Force on National Health Reform included Secretary of Defense Les Aspin, Secretary of the Treasury Lloyd Bentsen, Secretary of Veterans Affairs Jesse Brown, Secretary of Commerce Ronald H. Brown, Secretary of Labor Robert B. Reich, Secretary of Health and Human Services Donna Shalala, and Leon E. Panetta, director of the Office of Management and Budget.

56. Clinton, *Public Papers of the Presidents of the United States 1993*, p. 14.

57. For an analysis of the role Clinton's deficit-reduction plan played in delaying the introduction of his national health insurance program, see Bob Woodward, *The Agenda: Inside the Clinton White House* (New York: Pocket Books, 1995).

58. For a text of Clinton's address to a joint session of Congress introducing his national health insurance plan, see *The President's Health Security Plan*, pp. 103–26.

59. For a summary of Clinton's national health insurance plan, see *The President's Health Security Plan*.

60. For a text of Clinton's remarks to congressional leaders introducing the Health Security Act, see Clinton, *Public Papers of the Presidents of the United States 1993*, pp. 1830–34.

61. *The President's Health Security Plan*, pp. 17–18.

62. Ibid., p. 15.

63. Ibid., Chapter 4.

64. Ibid., p. 53.

65. Ibid., p. 15.

66. Ibid., pp. 66, 73.

67. Ibid., pp. 229–30.

68. Ibid., pp. 216–17.

69. Ibid., pp. 81–82.

70. Ibid., p. 130.

71. Ibid., pp. 48, 266.

72. Ibid., pp. 257–58.

73. Ibid., pp. 221–22.

74. Ibid., pp. 170–73.

75. Ibid., pp. 279–80.

76. Ibid., p. 103.

77. Ibid., pp. 44–46.

78. Ibid., pp. 104–6.

79. Ibid., p. 66.

80. Ibid., p. 284.

81. Ibid., p. 280.

82. *Uninsured in America*.

83. *The President's Health Security Plan*, p. 30.

84. Ibid., p. 68.

85. Ibid., p. 113.

86. Ibid., p. 53.

87. Ibid., p. 267.

CHAPTER 3

1. Joseph A. Califano, Jr., *Radical Surgery: What's Next for America's Health Care* (New York: Times Books, 1994), p. 246.

2. Jill Abramson, "Lobbyists Threaten to Use Leverage to Protect a Very Special Interest: Their Prized Tax Break," *Wall Street Journal*, July 19, 1993, p. A16; Carol Greenwald, *Group Power: Lobbying and Public Policy* (New York: Praeger Publishers, 1977), p. 156; Ronald J. Hrebenar and Ruth K. Scott, *Interest Group Politics in America* (Englewood Cliffs, N.J.: Prentice-Hall, 1982), pp. 76, 135–36; Judith Robinson, "American Medical Political Action Committee," in Judith G. Robinson, ed., *Power Brokers: People, Organization, Money and Power* (New York: Liveright, 1972), p. 80; Philip Stern, *The Best Congress Money Can Buy* (New York: Pantheon Books, 1988), pp. 196, 277.

3. Califano, *Radical Surgery*, p. 252.

4. *Congressional Record*, 103rd Congress, 2nd Session, p. S11845.

5. Viki Kemper and Viveca Novak, "What's Blocking Health Care Reform?" in Nancy F. McKenzie, ed., *Beyond Crisis: Confronting Health Care in the United States* (New York: Meridian Books, 1994), pp. 594.

6. Kemper and Novak, "What's Blocking Health Care Reform?" p. 595; Navarro, *Dangerous To Your Health: Capitalism in Health Care*, p. 32.

7. In 1992 88 percent of House members and 86 percent of Senators who sought reelection won their races.

8. Jeanne Kassler, *Bitter Medicine: Greed and Chaos in American Health Care* (New York: Birch Lane Press, 1994), p. 143.

9. Julie Rovner, "Mitchell: New Priority," *Congressional Quarterly Weekly Report*, February 16, 1991, p. 421.

10. For the text of Mitchell's speech on the Senate floor introducing the Health-America Act, see *Congressional Record*, 102nd Congress, 1st Session, pp. S7175–77.

11. Robert Pear, "The Democrats Offer Wide Health Plan," *New York Times*, June 6, 1991, p. A22.

12. Julie Rovner, " 'Play or Pay' Gains Momentum As Labor Panel Marks Up Bill," *Congressional Quarterly Weekly Report*, January 25, 1992, p. 172.

13. Michael Kramer, "The Voters' Latest Ailment: Health Care," *Time*, November 11, 1991, p. 51; Susan Mandel, "Pennsylvania's Harris Wofford: His Upset Victory Made Health Care a Big Issue," *Investor's Business Daily*, February 3, 1992, pp. 1–2.

14. Mandel, "Pennsylvania's Harris Wofford," p. 1.

15. Michael deCourcy Hinds, "Wofford Win Shows Voter Mood Swing," *New York Times*, November 7, 1991, p. A11.

16. Arnold Birenbaum, *Putting Health Care on the National Agenda* (Westport: Praeger Publishers, 1995), p. 3.

17. Michael deCourcy Hinds, "Senate Hopefuls Withhold Attacks," *New York Times*, November 5, 1991, p. A9; Robert Shogan, "Elections Today Air Themes Likely to Shape '92 Contests," *Los Angeles Times*, November 5, 1991, p. A23.

18. For an examination of the importance of national health insurance as an issue in the 1991 Pennsylvania Senate election, see Laham, *Why the United States Lacks a National Health Insurance Program*, pp. 127–28.

19. Gerald F. Seib, "Public Is Losing Faith in the Democrats' Ability to Run Economy and Foreign Affairs, Poll Finds," *The Wall Street Journal*, October 29, 1993, p. A14.

20. For an assessment of Bush's opposition to national health insurance, see Laham, *Why the United States Lacks a National Health Insurance Program*, pp. 140–47.

21. Bill Clinton and Al Gore, *Putting People First: How We Can All Change America* (New York: Times Books, 1992), p. 223.

22. For an evaluation of the importance of national health insurance as an issue in the

1992 presidential campaign, see Laham, *Why the United States Lacks a National Health Insurance Program*, pp. 147–50.

23. Susan Headden, Penny Loeb, David Bowermaster, and Edward T. Pound, "Money, Congress and Health Care, *U.S. News & World Report*, May 24, 1993, p. 29.

24. Ibid.

25. Judi Hasson, "Health Care Lobbying Kicks Into High Gear," *USA Today*, May 13, 1993, p. 2A.

26. Richard Benedetto, "Health PACs' Giving Rises," *USA Today*, March 12, 1993, p. 4A.

27. Hasson, "Health Care Lobbying Kicks Into High Gear."

28. Benedetto, "Health PACs' Giving Rises"; Navarro, *Dangerous To Your Health*, p. 34.

29. Hasson, "Health Care Lobbying Kicks Into High Gear."

30. Califano, *Radical Surgery*, p. 42.

31. U.S. Department of Health and Human Services, *The Medicare 1994 Handbook*, pp. 41–45.

32. Robert M. Brandon, Michael Podhorzer, and Thomas H. Pollack, "Premiums Without Benefits: Waste and Inefficiency in the Commercial Health Insurance Industry," in Vincente Navarro, ed., *Why the United States Does Not Have a National Health Program* (Amityville: Baywood Publishing, 1992), p. 76.

33. *The President's Health Security Plan: A Complete Draft and Final Reports of the White House Domestic Policy Council* (New York: Times Books, 1993), p. 68.

34. For a summary of the HealthAmerica Act, see *Congressional Record*, 102nd Congress, 1st Session, pp. S7214–16.

35. Julie Rovner, "Democrats Taking a Gamble on Health-Care Overhaul," *Congressional Quarterly Weekly Report*, June 8, 1991, p. 1507.

36. For an analysis of the effects the HealthAmerica Act would have on the private health insurance industry, see Laham, *Why the United States Lacks a National Health Insurance Program*, p. 115.

37. Kemper and Novak, "What's Blocking Health Care Reform?" p. 594.

38. Califano, *Radical Surgery*, p. 253.

39. Kemper and Novak, "What's Blocking Health Care Reform?" p. 594.

40. Katharine Q. Seelye, "Lobbyists Are the Loudest in the Health Care Debate," *New York Times*, August 16, 1994, p. A12.

41. Alissa J. Rubin, "With Health Care Overhaul on Stage, PACs Want Front Row Seat," *Congressional Quarterly Weekly Report*, July 31, 1993, pp. 2052–54.

42. Seelye, "Lobbyists Are the Loudest in the Health Care Debate," p. A12.

43. Califano, *Radical Surgery*, p. 253.

44. Rubin, "With Health Care Overhaul on Stage, PACs Want Front Row Seat," p. 2054.

45. Sven Steinmo and Jon Watts, "It's the Institutions, Stupid: Why Comprehensive National Health Insurance Always Fails in America," *Journal of Health Politics, Policy and Law*, Summer 1995, p. 364.

46. Seelye, "Lobbyists Are the Loudest in the Health Care Debate," p. A12.

47. Neil A. Lewis, "Lawmakers Sow Health Bills and Reap Big Donations," *New York Times*, May 23, 1994, p. A8.

48. Ibid.

49. Kemper and Novak, "What's Blocking Health Care Reform?" pp. 594–95.

50. Steinmo and Watts, "It's the Institutions, Stupid," p. 364.

51. Seelye, "Lobbyists Are the Loudest in the Health Care Debate," p. A1.

52. Ibid., p. A12.

53. Kassler, *Bitter Medicine*, p. 143.

54. Benedetto, "Health PACs' Giving Rises."

CHAPTER 4

1. Julie Kosterlitz, "Itching for a Fight?" *National Journal*, January 15, 1994, p. 198.

2. For an analysis of the AMA's campaign against national health insurance during the 1940s, see Monte M. Poen, *Harry S. Truman Versus the Medical Lobby: The Genesis of Medicare* (Columbia: University of Missouri Press, 1979).

3. For polling data measuring physician opinion on national health insurance during the 1940s, see Nicholas Laham, *Why the United States Lacks a National Health Insurance Program* (Westport, Conn.: Praeger Publishers, 1993), pp. 167–68.

4. For an analysis of AMPAC's role in the House's rejection of the Hospital Cost Containment Act, see Laham, *Why the United States Lacks a National Health Insurance Program*, pp. 65–68.

5. Robert Pear, "AMA to Seek Major Changes in Clinton Plan," *New York Times*, January 13, 1994, p. B8.

6. Sara Fritz, "AMA to Be Neutral on Health Plan," *Los Angeles Times*, September 30, 1993, p. A22.

7. Judy Keen and Judi Hasson, "Medical Groups Join Clintons for Health-Care Rally," *USA Today*, December 17, 1993, p. 4A.

8. "Ideas From Those Who Give Health Care and Those Who Need It," *New York Times*, March 30, 1993, p. A10.

9. Keen and Hasson, "Medical Groups Join Clintons for Health Care Rally."

10. Hilary Stout and Jeffrey H. Birnbaum, "Clinton Plan Backed by Doctor's Group; GOP Chairman Attacks Parts of Reform," *Wall Street Journal*, September 21, 1993, p. A3.

11. Keen and Hasson, "Medical Groups Join Clintons for Health Care Rally."

12. Marlene Cimons, "U.S. Incentives for More Family Doctors Weighed," *Los Angeles Times*, March 22, 1993, p. A14.

13. Marlene Cimons, "U.S. Needs More Family Doctors, Study Warns," *Los Angeles Times*, November 9, 1992, p. A18.

14. Mary Williams Walsh, "A Big Dose of Family Medicine," *Los Angeles Times*, July 16, 1992, p. A18.

15. Elisabeth Rosenthal, "Medicine Suffers As Fewer Family Doctors Join Front Lines," *New York Times*, May 24, 1993, p. A1.

16. *The President's Health Security Plan: The Complete Draft and Final Reports of the White House Domestic Policy Council* (New York: Times Books, 1993), p. 140.

17. Ibid., pp. 148–50.

18. There are two kinds of HMOs: the staff model HMO and the network model HMO. A staff model HMO provides services to its members through a staff of salaried doctors and hospitals, which are owned by the HMO. A network model HMO contracts with selected groups of private-practice doctors and independently-owned hospitals to

provide services to its members. Practically all HMOs operate through the network model. Accordingly, our explanation of how HMOs operate refers to the network model, which remains the predominant form of HMO.

19. Erik Larson, "The Soul of an HMO," *Time*, January 22, 1996, pp. 46–47.

20. Arnold Birenbaum, *Putting Health Care on the National Agenda* (Westport, Conn.: Praeger Publishers, 1995), p. 47.

21. Marcia Angell, "Delivery System Is Achilles' Heel of Health Plan," *USA Today*, September 29, 1993, p. 11A.

22. Tom Morganthau and Andrew Murr, "Inside the World of an HMO," *Newsweek*, April 5, 1993, p. 39.

23. Michael A. Hiltzik and David R. Olmos, "Do HMOs Ration Their Health Care?" *Los Angeles Times*, August 27, 1995, p. A14.

24. *The President's Health Security Plan*, p. 66.

25. Richard Wolf and Robert Davis, "On Capitol Hill, Physicians Carry a Big Stick," *USA Today*, October 22, 1993, p. 10A.

26. David Lauter, "First Lady Calls Health Insurers' Ads 'Great Lies,' " *Los Angeles Times*, November 2, 1993, p. A11.

27. Adam Clymer, Robert Pear, and Robin Toner, "For Health Care, Time Was a Killer," *New York Times*, August 29, 1994, p. A8.

28. Adam Clymer, "Hillary Clinton Accuses Insurers of Lying About Health Proposal," *New York Times*, November 2, 1993, p. B7.

29. Christina Del Valle, "Even Cheerleaders Get the Blues," *Business Week*, May 30, 1994, p. 60.

30. Coalition for Health Insurance Choices, December 9, 1993.

31. Clymer, "Hillary Clinton Accuses Insurers of Lying About Health Proposal," p. A1.

32. Aaron Bernstein, "Why Universal Health Care Is Smart Medicine," *Business Week*, March 28, 1994, p. 171; Joseph A. Califano, Jr., *Radical Surgery: What's Next for America's Health Care* (New York: Times Books, 1994), pp. 218–82.

33. Clymer, "Hillary Clinton Accuses Insurers of Lying About Health Proposal."

34. For an international comparative analysis of the health care cost-containment measures practiced in other advanced industrial democracies, see Janice Castro, *The American Way of Health: How Medicine Is Changing and What It Means to You* (Boston: Little, Brown, 1994), Chapter 12.

CHAPTER 5

1. Mike McNamee, "Health Reform: How the GOP Could Blow Its Chance," *Business Week*, July 5, 1993, p. 43.

2. Richard Benedetto, "The Early Line Puts Dole Atop GOP Ticket," *USA Today*, April 1, 1994, p. 10A.

3. Ronald Brownstein, "By 2–1 Margin, Public Backs Health Care Plan," *Los Angeles Times*, September 30, 1993, p. A22. Twenty-four percent of both Democrats and independents and 17 percent of Republicans polled had no opinion on the Clinton plan.

4. *Congressional Record*, 103rd Congress, 2nd Session, p. S11845.

5. Susan Headden, Penny Loeb, David Bowermaster, and Edward T. Pound,

"Money, Congress and Health Care," *U.S. News & World Report*, May 24, 1993, p. 34.

6. Julie Rovner, "Democrats Taking a Gamble on Health-Care Overhaul," *Congressional Quarterly Weekly Report*, June 8, 1991, pp. 1508–9.

7. For a summary and critique of Bush's health care reform plan, see Nicholas Laham, *Why the United States Lacks a National Health Insurance Program* (Westport, Conn.: Praeger Publishers, 1993), pp. 131–38.

8. *Congressional Record*, 102nd Congress, 2nd Session, p. S1177.

9. William J. Clinton, *Public Papers of the Presidents of the United States 1993* (Washington, D.C.: United States Government Printing Office, 1994), p. 1388.

10. Richard L. Berke, "Dole Is Cautious on Health Plans," *New York Times*, August 18, 1993, p. 14A.

11. United States Congress, House of Representatives, Committee on Ways and Means, *The President's Health Care Reform Proposals: Hearings Before the Committee on Ways and Means*, 103rd Congress, 1st Session, September 28, October 5, 1993 (Washington, D.C.: United States Government Printing Office, 1994), p. 46.

12. *The President's Health Security Plan: The Complete Draft and Final Reports of the White House Domestic Policy Council* (New York: Times Books, 1993), p. 123.

13. Marlene Cimons and Karen Tumulty, "Package Draws Words of Praise, Warning," *Los Angeles Times*, September 23, 1993, p. A12.

14. William J. Clinton, *Public Papers of the Presidents of the United States 1994* (Washington, D.C.: United States Government Printing Office, 1995), p. 1.

15. Paul Richter, "Clinton Calls for Action on Social Issues," *Los Angeles Times*, January 2, 1994, p. A1.

16. Adam Zagorin, "Crisis? What Crisis?" *Time*, January 24, 1994, p. 35.

17. *The President's Health Security Plan*, p. xiii.

18. Robert Kuttner, "Pay Moynihan's Blarney on Health Care," *Business Week*, February 14, 1994, p. 18.

19. Neil A. Lewis, "Lawmakers Sow Health Bills and Reap Big Donations," *New York Times*, May 23, 1994, p. A8.

20. Clinton, *Public Papers of the Presidents of the United States 1994*, p. 130.

21. Ibid.

22. "Excerpts From the Republicans' Response to the President's Message," *New York Times*, January 26, 1994, p. A9.

23. Clinton, *Public Papers of the Presidents of the United States 1994*, p. 1283.

24. Robert Shogan and David Lauter, "President Signals He Is Flexible on Health Coverage," *Los Angeles Times*, July 20, 1994, p. A9.

25. *Congressional Record*, 103rd Congress, 2nd Session, p. S11007.

26. Ibid., p. 11009.

27. Ibid., p. 11012.

28. Richard Benedetto, "A Tough State of the Union Message Pays Off," *USA Today*, February 1, 1994, p. 4A.

29. Brownstein, "By 2–1 Margin, Public Backs Health Care Plan."

30. Judy Keen, "Clinton Message Misses Its Mark," *USA Today*, August 11, 1994, p. 6A.

31. *Weekly Compilation of Presidential Documents*, August 8, 1994, pp. 1614–15.

32. *The President's Health Security Plan*, pp. 110, 112.

33. Tom Morganthau and Mary Hager, "The Clinton Cure," *Newsweek*, October 4, 1993, p. 39.

34. *Congressional Record*, 103rd Congress, 2nd Session, p. S11845.

35. Headden, Loeb, Bowermaster, and Pound, "Money, Congress, and Health Care," p. 34.

36. Robert Shogan, "GOP Hopefuls Court Conservatives," *Los Angeles Times*, February 12, 1995, p. A9.

37. James A. Barnes, "Two-Edged Sword," *National Journal*, April 8, 1995, pp. 854–55.

38. Richard Wolf, "Congress Gets Ready to Dig In, Do the Dirty Work," *USA Today*, September 23, 1993, p. 7A.

39. Michael Wines, "At Capitol, Selling Health Proposals as Cure-Alls," *New York Times*, October 28, 1993, p. A10.

40. Phil Gramm, "Ten Questions They Don't Ask," *Health Care News*, Spring/Summer 1994, p. 6.

41. Ibid.

42. Ibid., p. 8.

43. Ibid., p. 6.

44. "Phil Gramm: Leadership for America," p. 6.

45. Phil Gramm, "A Novel Idea: Pay-As-You-Go Health Care," *Los Angeles Times*, April 11, 1993, p. M5.

46. For a comparative analysis of health care spending among the advanced industrial democracies, see Laham, *Why the United States Lacks a National Health Insurance Program*, pp. 99–100.

47. Gramm, "A Novel Idea."

48. A key tactic the AMA used to publicly discredit Truman's campaign to establish national health insurance during the 1940s was to define the program as "socialized medicine." With the public opposed to any program which smacked of socialism, the AMA succeeded in mobilizing popular opposition to national health insurance. For an examination of the AMA's campaign against the program, see Laham, *Why the United States Lacks a National Health Insurance Program*, Chapter 2.

49. Robert Shogan, "Conservatives Gather, Target Clinton Policies for Counterattack," *Los Angeles Times*, February 13, 1994, p. A4.

50. Robert Shogan, "Five Potential GOP Rivals Slam Clinton," *Los Angeles Times*, May 1, 1994, p. A17.

51. *Congressional Record*, 103rd Congress, 2nd Session, p. 11196.

52. Ibid., p. 11197.

53. Ibid., p. 11198.

54. Robert L. Jackson, "Dole, Kemp Attack Clinton Health Plan," *Los Angeles Times*, January 23, 1994, p. A20.

55. Jack Kemp, "Forget Europe as a Model for Creating Jobs," *Los Angeles Times*, March 20, 1994, p. M5.

56. Ibid.

57. In 1993 Medicaid and Medicare reimbursements to hospitals equaled 93 percent and 89 percent, respectively, of the cost of treating beneficiaries of the two programs. Hospitals offset the financial losses they sustain in treating Medicare and Medicaid beneficiaries by raising their charges for privately-insured patients. In 1993 private health

insurance reimbursements to hospitals equaled 129 percent of the cost of treating privately-insured patients. Like hospitals, doctors offset the financial losses they sustain in treating Medicare and Medicaid beneficiaries by raising their charges for privately-insured patients. In 1994 reimbursements to doctors under Medicare and Medicaid were 64 percent and 47 percent, respectively, of those of private insurance for comparable services. For an analysis of the cost-shifting which occurs within the health care system, see Laham, *Why the United States Lacks a National Health Insurance Program*, pp. 64–65.

58. The Johnson Administration designed Medicare as a means of serving the financial interests of the health care industry in order to secure its support for the program. For an account of how this occurred from a key administration official, see Joseph A. Califano, Jr., *Radical Surgery: What's Next for America's Health Care* (New York: Times Books, 1994), pp. 8–10.

59. For an analysis of health care rationing in Britain, see Henry J. Aaron and William B. Schwartz, *The Painful Prescription: Rationing Hospital Care* (Washington, D.C.: The Brookings Institution, 1984). For an examination of health care rationing in Canada, see Robert G. Evans, "Canada: The Real Issues," in James A. Morone and Gary S. Belkin, eds., *The Politics of Health Care Reform: Lessons from the Past, Prospects for the Future* (Durham: Duke University Press, 1994), pp. 463–86.

60. George J. Church, "Oh Noooo!" *Time*, March 14, 1994, p. 35.

61. *The President's Health Security Plan*, p. 114.

62. Ibid., p. 116.

63. Ibid., p. 107.

64. Morganthau and Hager, "The Clinton Cure," p. 39.

65. James Carney, "Going Flat Out," p. 19.

66. George J. Church, " 'Please Help Us,' " *Time*, November 8, 1993, p. 38; George J. Church, "Oh Noooo!" *Time*, March 14, 1994, p. 35.

67. Brownstein, "By 2–1 Margin, Public Backs Health Care Plan."

68. George J. Church, " 'Please Help Us,' " *Time*, November 8, 1993, p. 38.

69. Robin Toner, "Poll on Changes in Health Care Finds Support Amid Skepticism," *New York Times*, September 22, 1993, p. A19.

70. Margaret Carlson, "At the Center of Power," *Time*, May 10, 1993, p. 35; David Van Biema, "Hitting the Great Divide," *Time*, July 25, 1994, p. 24. Five percent of those polled in April 1993 and July 1994, respectively, had no opinion on when health care reform should be achieved.

71. Robert J. Samuelson, "Will Reform Bankrupt Us?" *Newsweek*, August 15, 1994, p. 51.

72. *Congressional Record*, 103rd Congress, 2nd Session, p. S11010.

73. Ibid., p. S12178.

74. *The President's Health Security Plan*, p. 106.

75. Edwin Chen, "Cost May Be Key to Whether Health Reforms Win Support," *Los Angeles Times*, October 3, 1993, p. A22.

76. Richard Lacayo, "Off to the Races," *Time*, September 12, 1994, p. 39.

77. *Congressional Record*, 103rd Congress, 1st Session, p. S16937–38.

78. U.S. Department of Health and Human Services, *The Medicare 1993 Handbook*, p. 1.

79. *Congressional Record*, 103rd Congress, 1st Session, p. S16938.

80. David Lauter, "Budget Cutters Joining Battle Lines Around Medicare," *Los Angeles Times*, February 4, 1995, p. A19. Two percent of those polled aged eighteen to

sixty-four and 9 percent of those aged sixty-five or older had no opinion on whether Medicare premiums should be raised on elderly individuals with above-average incomes.

81. "Defenders of Medicare Warn of GOP Cuts," *Los Angeles Times*, April 8, 1995, p. A18.

82. Henry J. Aaron, "Health Care Financing," in Henry J. Aaron and Charles L. Schultze, eds., *Setting Domestic Priorities: What Can Government Do?* (Washington, D.C.: The Brookings Institution, 1992), p. 36.

83. *Congressional Record*, 103rd Congress, 1st Session, p. S16938.

84. *Congressional Record*, 103rd Congress, 2nd Session, p. S11006; Robert A. Rosenblatt, "A Costly Cure," *Los Angeles Times*, June 13, 1993, p. D1.

85. George J. Church, "Are You Ready for the Cure?" *Time*, May 24, 1993, p. 35. Among the health care measures the public favored, 82 percent of those polled supported "providing health insurance through large groups that could bargain with hospitals and doctors for better rates" and 15 percent opposed it. Eighty-one percent backed "limiting the prices that doctors, hospitals, and drug companies could charge" and 16 percent opposed it. Seventy-eight percent favored "requiring most employees to pay for the employees' basic health coverage" and 18 percent opposed it. Seventy-one percent supported "using government money to provide mental health care for all who need it" and 24 percent opposed it. Sixty-seven percent favored "requiring insurance companies to provide coverage for people who have been sick for a long time at the same price charged to healthy people" and 26 percent opposed it. In addition to opposing taxation of employer-paid health care benefits, 87 percent of those polled were against "allowing insurance companies to charge the elderly more than younger people" and 11 percent supported it.

86. Dan Goodgame, "This May Hurt a Bit," *Time*, May 16, 1994, p. 50.

87. Robert A. Rosenblatt and Edwin Chen, "Coalition to Fight Taxation of Benefits," *Los Angeles Times*, February 9, 1993, p. D1.

88. The Henry J. Kaiser Foundation, the League of Women Voters Education Fund, and the Robert Wood Johnson Foundation, *Critical Choices in Health Reform*, p. 3.

89. Michael Wolff, Peter Rutten, and Albert F. Bayers III, *Where We Stand: Can America Make It in the Global Race for Wealth, Health, and Happiness?* (New York: Bantam Books, 1992), pp. 134–35.

90. Robert H. Blank, *Rationing Medicine* (New York: Columbia University Press, 1988), pp. 138–140.

91. *Congressional Record*, 103rd Congress, 1st Session, p. S16938.

92. "Are Malpractice Awards the Demon of Health Care?" *USA Today*, May 5, 1993, p. 13A.

CHAPTER 6

1. "Mixed Reaction to Health Care Speech," *USA Today*, September 23, 1993, p. 2B.

2. Edwin Chen, "Payroll Levy Idea in Health Care Detailed," *Los Angeles Times*, May 7, 1993, p. A18.

3. Chen, "Payroll Levy Idea in Health Plan Detailed," p. A18; Theodore Marmor and Jerry Mashaw, "Health Care Reform Costs: Rumor Is Scarier Than Reality," *Los Angeles Times*, July 6, 1993, p. B5. Business, workers, and self-insured individuals fi-

nanced their share of the cost of health care through private health insurance premiums, the government did so through taxes and Medicare Part B premiums, and patients did so through out-of-pocket payments for their medical services.

4. Judi Hasson, "All Players Have Ideas to Overhaul Health Care," *USA Today*, January 27, 1993, p. 5A.

5. *Congressional Record*, 103rd Congress, 2nd Session, p. S11733; Marmor and Mashaw, "Health Care Reform Costs."

6. Robert A. Rosenblatt, "A Costly Cure," *Los Angeles Times*, June 13, 1993, p. D1.

7. Bill Montague, "UAW Clings to Rarity: Full Health Benefits," *USA Today*, September 17, 1993, p. 5B.

8. Edwin Chen, "Health Plan May Call for 12% Payroll Tax on Firms," *Los Angeles Times*, June 4, 1993, p. A30; Rosenblatt, "A Costly Cure."

9. Mike McNamee, Greg Bowens, Zachary Schiller, and Mark Maremont, "Health Care: Just Address the Bills to Corporate America," *Business Week*, March 29, 1993, p. 66; Micheline Maynard, "UAW Pact Bad for GM," *USA Today*, September 17, 1993, p. 1B.

10. McNamee, Bowens, Schiller, and Maremont, "Health Care," p. 66.

11. Ann Reilly Dowd, "Companies Hate the Health Plan," *Fortune*, November 29, 1993, p. 124.

12. *President Clinton's New Beginning: The Complete Text, With Illustrations, of the Historic Clinton-Gore Economic Conference in Little Rock, Arkansas, December 14–15, 1992* (New York: Donald I. Fine, 1992), p. 61.

13. Ibid., p. 64.

14. Ibid., p. 61.

15. Ibid., pp. 61–62.

16. Ibid., p. 62.

17. Ibid., p. 61.

18. Ibid., p. 64.

19. "Mixed Reaction to Health Care Speech."

20. Ibid.

21. Robert A. Rosenblatt and Karen Tumulty, "50 Firms Back Health Mandate; Democrats Meet," *Los Angeles Times*, July 22, 1994, p. A1.

22. Ibid., p. A19.

23. Edwin Chen, "Health Debate Heats Up: Jobs Lost or Gained?," *Los Angeles Times*, August 17, 1993, p. A12.

24. United States Congress, House of Representatives, Committee on Ways and Means, *The President's Health Care Reform Proposals: Hearings Before the Committee on Ways and Means*, 103rd Congress, 1st Session, September 28; October 5, 1993 (Washington, D.C.: U.S. Government Printing Office, 1994), pp. 37–38.

25. William J. Clinton, *Public Papers of the Presidents of the United States 1994* (Washington, D.C.: United States Government Printing Office, 1995), pp. 1106–07.

26. Richard Wolf and Judi Hasson, "Big, Small Businesses Reject Plan," *USA Today*, February 4, 1994, p. 4A.

27. Edwin Chen, "Chamber Drops Its Support for Key Parts of Health Plan," *Los Angeles Times*, March 1, 1994, p. A14.

28. Robert A. Rosenblatt, "Chamber's Shift: All Firms Should Insure Workers," *Los Angeles Times*, March 9, 1993, p. A1.

29. Chen, "Chamber Drops Its Support for Key Parts of Health Plan."

30. Wolf and Hasson, "Big, Small Businesses Reject Health Plan."

31. Suneel Ratan, "Why CEOs Aren't Buying the Plan," *Fortune*, October 18, 1993, p. 63.

32. Adam Clymer, Robert Pear, and Robin Toner, "For Health Care, Time Was a Killer," *New York Times*, August 29, 1994, p. A9.

33. Ratan, "Why CEOs Aren't Buying the Plan," p. 64.

34. Louis Uchitelle, "Executives Balking at Clinton Health Plan," *New York Times*, May 10, 1994, p. C1.

CHAPTER 7

1. *Congressional Record*, 103rd Congress, 1st Session, p. S14556.

2. United States Congress, House of Representatives, Committee on Ways and Means, *The President's Health Care Reform Proposals: Hearings Before the Committee on Ways and Means, 103rd Congress, 1st Session, September 28, October 5, 1993* (Washington, D.C.: United States Government Printing Office, 1994), p. 68.

3. Of this total, the *Washington Post* published 804 articles on health care reform, the *New York Times* 743, *USA Today* 575, the *Los Angeles Times* 552, and the *Wall Street Journal* 444.

4. Of this total, CNN broadcast 169 stories on health care reform on its news programs, ABC 166, CBS 149, NBC 139, and PBS 126.

5. The Times Center for the People and the Press, the Henry J. Kaiser Foundation, and *Columbia Journalism Review*, *Media Coverage of Health Care Reform: A Final Report*, March/April 1995, pp. 1–3.

6. The Henry J. Kaiser Foundation, *Health Reform Legislation: A Comparison of Committee Action*, July 1994, p. 1; Alissa Rubin, "Two Ideological Poles Frame Debate Over Reform," *Congressional Quarterly Weekly Report*, January 8, 1994, pp. 25–26.

7. Karen Tumulty, "White House Picks Up GOP Ally on Health Care Plan," *Los Angeles Times*, September 30, 1993, p. A22.

8. For a summary of the Wellstone-McDermott bill, see Ellen R. Shaffer and Paul D. Wellstone, "Providing Comprehensive Coverage," in Richard Caplan and John Feffer, eds., *State of the Union 1994: The Clinton Administration and the Nation in Profile* (Boulder, Colo.: Westview Press, 1994), pp. 161–63.

9. Rubin, "Two Ideological Poles Frame Debate Over Reform," p. 25.

10. For a comparative analysis between the American and Canadian health care systems, see Nicholas Laham, *Why the United States Lacks a National Health Insurance Program* (Westport, Conn.: Praeger Publishers, 1993), pp. 107–10.

11. Steffie Woolhandler and David U. Himmelstein, "The Deteriorating Administrative Efficiency of the U.S. Health Care System," *New England Journal of Medicine*, May 2, 1991, pp. 1255–56.

12. Ibid., p. 1256.

13. "GAO Report Hails Canada Health System," *Los Angeles Times*, June 4, 1991, p. A20.

14. Phil Kuntz, "Embattled GAO Fights Back; Bowsher Denies Any Bias," *Congressional Quarterly Weekly Report*, July 27, 1991, p. 2050.

15. Elizabeth Drew, *On the Edge: the Clinton Presidency* (New York: Simon and Schuster, 1994), p. 191.

16. Ibid., pp. 190–91.

17. William J. Clinton, *Public Papers of the Presidents of the United States 1993* (Washington, D.C.: United States Government Printing Office, 1994), p. 1385.

18. Ibid., p. 1386.

19. Ronald Brownstein, "Enthusiasm for Clinton's Health Reform Is Waning," *Los Angeles Times*, April 21, 1994, p. A20.

20. David Lauter, "Americans Sending Mixed Messages on Health Reform," *Los Angeles Times*, July 29, 1994, p. A14.

21. Maureen Dowd, "Strong Support for Health Plans," *New York Times*, July 20, 1994, p. A12.

22. Henry J. Aaron, *Serious and Unstable Condition: Financing America's Health Care* (Washington, D.C.: The Brookings Institution, 1991), pp. 48–49.

23. For an analysis of the Kennedy-Waxman bill, see Laham, *Why the United States Lacks a National Health Insurance Program*, pp. 74–78.

24. Rubin, "Two Ideological Poles Frame Debate Over Reform," p. 25.

25. Robert Scheer, "Henry Waxman," *Los Angeles Times*, October 10, 1993, p. M3.

26. Ibid.

27. Karen Tumulty, "Clinton's Handoff to Congress Finds Forces Eager to Pounce," *Los Angeles Times*, September 23, 1993, p. A7.

28. Karen Tumulty, "Clinton's Balancing Act Impresses Few," *Los Angeles Times*, October 28, 1993, p. A22.

29. Scheer, "Henry Waxman," p. M3.

30. House of Representatives, *The President's Health Care Reform Proposals*, pp. 68–69.

31. Ibid., p. 70.

32. Richard E. Cohen, "Ready, Aim, Reform," *National Journal*, October 30, 1993, p. 2585.

33. Tumulty, "Clinton's Balancing Act Impresses Few."

34. Rubin, "Two Ideological Poles Frame Debate," p. 26.

35. *Health Reform Legislation*, p. 1.

36. *The President's Health Security Plan: The Complete Draft and Final Reports of the White House Domestic Policy Council* (New York: Times Books, 1993), pp. 58–59.

37. House of Representatives, *The President's Health Care Reform Proposals*, p. 70.

38. Shaffer and Wellstone, "Providing Comprehensive Coverage," p. 161.

39. Ibid., p. 164.

40. Ibid., p. 162.

41. Ibid., p. 163.

42. *Congressional Record*, 103rd Congress, 2nd Session, p. S11686.

43. Ibid., p. S11688.

CHAPTER 8

1. *Congressional Record*, 103rd Congress, 2nd Session, p. S12179.

2. For an analysis of Congress's consideration of national health insurance since

1945, see Nicholas Laham, *Why the United States Lacks a National Health Insurance Program* (Westport, Conn.: Praeger Publishere, 1993).

3. Beth Donovan, ''Senate Labor First Out of the Gate With Approval of Overhaul Bill,'' *Congressional Quarterly Weekly Report*, June 11, 1994, p. 1523.

4. Elizabeth A. Palmer, ''First House Panel Finishes Work, Gains Leverage By Its Action,'' *Congressional Quarterly Weekly Report*, June 25, 1994, p. 1710.

5. David S. Cloud, ''Gibbons' Patched-Together Health Bill Now Faces Test on the Floor,'' *Congressional Quarterly Weekly Report*, July 2, 1994, p. 1793.

6. For a summary of the national health insurance bills approved by the Senate Labor and Human Resources and House Education and Labor and Ways and Means Committees, see The Henry J. Kaiser Family Foundation, *Health Reform Legislation: A Comparison of Committee Action*, July 1994.

7. Alissa J. Rubin, ''Leaders Using Fervent Approach to Convert Wavering Members,'' *Congressional Quarterly Weekly Report*, July 30, 1994, p. 2142.

8. For a summary of Gephardt's national health insurance bill, see The Henry J. Kaiser Family Foundation, *Health Reform Legislation: A Comparison of House and Senate Majority Leadership Bills*, August 1994.

9. Alissa J. Rubin and Beth Donovan, ''With Outcome Still Uncertain, Members Face Critical Vote,'' *Congressional Quarterly Weekly Report*, August 6, 1994, p. 2204.

10. Karen Tumulty and Edwin Chen, ''House Leaders Delay Action on Health Bill,'' *Los Angeles Times*, August 12, 1994, p. A1.

11. Alissa J. Rubin, ''Finance Chairman's Bill Outline Becomes Bipartisan Flash Point,'' *Congressional Quarterly Weekly Report*, June 11, 1994, p. 1525.

12. Alissa J. Rubin, ''Senate Finance Panel Deals Blow to Universal Coverage Proposal,'' *Congressional Quarterly Weekly Report*, July 2, 1994, p. 1798.

13. Alissa J. Rubin, ''Big Decisions Now on Shoulders of House, Senate Leaders,'' *Congressional Quarterly Weekly Report*, July 9, 1994, p. 1866.

14. For a summary of the Senate Finance Committee's health care reform bill, see The Henry J. Kaiser Family Foundation, *Health Reform Legislation: A Comparison of Committee Action*, July 1994.

15. William J. Clinton, *Public Papers of the Presidents of the United States 1994* (Washington, D.C.: United States Government Printing Office, 1995), p. 131.

16. *Weekly Compilation of Presidential Documents*, August 8, 1994, p. 1611.

17. *Congressional Record*, 103rd Congress, 2nd Session, p. S10261.

18. Ibid., p. S10263.

19. Ibid., p. S10266.

20. Ibid., pp. S10261–62.

21. Ibid., p. S11227.

22. Ibid., p. S11009.

23. Ibid., pp. S11012–14.

24. Ibid., p. S11018.

25. Ibid., p. S11682.

26. Henry J. Kaiser Foundation, *Uninsured in America: Straight Facts on Health Reform*, April 1994.

27. *Congressional Record*, 103rd Congress, 2nd Session, p. S11230; Diane Rowland, *Directions for Health Reform: Testimony Before the Committee on Labor and Human Resources, United States Senate*, March 15, 1995.

28. *Congressional Record*, 103rd Congress, 2nd Session, p. S11731.

29. The issue of health care reform did not completely die in the Republican 104th Congress. In 1995 Senate Labor and Human Resources Committee Chairwoman Nancy Kassebaum of Kansas and Senator Edward M. Kennedy of Massachusetts introduced the Health Insurance Reform Act. The bill would prohibit private plans from denying coverage to any individual due to chronic ailments. The bill was co-sponsored by a bipartisan group of fourty-four Senators. On August 2, 1995 the Senate Labor and Human Resources Committee approved the bill with unanimous support of the body's sixteen members. However, a major means in which private plans limit the growth in their premiums is by denying coverage to sick and older individuals who suffer from costly illnesses. This allows private plans to limit their financial liabilities, which assures lower insurance premiums. By requiring private plans to provide coverage to any individual willing to pay for their health care benefits, regardless of how sick or old they may be, the Kassebaum-Kennedy bill would result in a substantial increase in insurance premiums. As a result, the bill met stiff opposition from the HIAA, which feared that major increases in premiums would result in many insured individuals dropping their coverage, leading to a loss of business for the private insurance industry. Bowing to pressure from the HIAA, a number of Senate Republicans acted to prevent the bill from coming to the Senate floor, clouding chances for its passage in the 104th Congress.

30. *Congressional Record*, 103rd Congress, 2nd Session, p. S11728.

31. Ibid., pp. S11215–17, S11220–22.

32. Ibid., pp. S11225–26.

33. For a list of the eighteen taxes contained in Mitchell's health care reform bill, see *Congressional Record*, 103rd Congress, 2nd Session, pp. S11715–16.

34. *Congressional Record*, 103rd Congress, 2nd Session, pp. S11218–19, S11223–24.

35. Ibid., p. S11226.

36. Ibid., pp. S11218–19, S11223–24.

37. Ibid., p. S11727.

38. Clinton, *Public Papers of the Presidents of the United States 1994*, p. 1144.

39. *Congressional Record*, 103rd Congress, 2nd Session, p. S11097.

40. Ibid., p. S11825.

41. John Holahan, Colin Winterbottom, and Shruti Rajan, *The Changing Composition of Health Insurance Coverage in the United States* (Washington, D.C.: The Urban Institute, January 1995), p. 13.

42. For an international comparative analysis of health care systems in various advanced industrial democracies, see Janice Castro, *The American Way of Health: How Medicine Is Changing and What It Means to You* (Boston: Little, Brown, 1994), Chapter 12.

43. Elizabeth McCaughey, "No Exit," *The New Republic*, February 7, 1994, p. 25.

44. *Congressional Record*, 103rd Congress, 2nd Session, p. S11195.

45. Ibid., p. S11698.

46. Ibid., p. S11700.

47. "Lost Jobs, Lost Lives," *Health Care News*, Spring/Summer 1994, p. 7.

48. *Congressional Record*, 103rd Congress, 2nd Session, p. S11928.

49. Ibid., pp. S11473–74.

50. Ibid., p. S11722.

51. Ibid., p. S11673.

52. Ibid., p. S11675.

53. Ibid., p. S11849.

54. Ibid., pp. S1151–52.

55. Arnold Birenbaum, *Putting Health Care on the National Agenda* (Westport, Conn.: Praeger Publishers, 1995), p. 175.

56. Robert G. Evans, "Canada: The Real Issues," in James A. Morone and Gary S. Belkin, eds., *The Politics of Health Care Reform: Lessons from the Past, Prospects for the Future* (Durham, N.C.: Duke University Press, 1994), p. 464.

57. Ibid., p. 471.

58. Ibid., pp. 476–77.

59. Ibid., p. 478.

60. Ibid., p. 472.

61. Birenbaum, *Putting Health Care on the National Agenda*, p. 175.

62. Ibid., p. 179.

63. Ibid., p. 181.

64. Theodore R. Marmor, *Understanding Health Reform* (New Haven, Conn.: Yale University Press, 1984), p. 181.

65. Ibid., pp. 187–88.

66. Ibid., p. 188.

67. Michael Wolff, Peter Rutten, and Albert F. Bayers III, *Where We Stand: Can America Make It in the Global Race for Wealth, Health, and Happiness?* (New York: Bantam Books, 1992), p. 126.

68. Melinda Beck, "Rationing Health Care," *Newsweek*, June 27, 1994, p. 31.

69. *Congressional Record*, 103rd Congress, 2nd Session, p. S11227.

70. Beck, "Rationing Health Care," p. 34.

CHAPTER 9

1. Karen Tumulty and Edwin Chen, "Blame for Health Plan's Collapse Falls Everywhere," *Los Angeles Times*, August 28, 1994, p. A24.

2. Adam Clymer, Robert Pear, and Robin Toner, "For Health Care, Time Was a Killer," *New York Times*, August 29, 1994, p. A9.

3. Clinton's two prime-time television addresses on health care reform were his speech to a joint session of Congress on September 22, 1993, in which he introduced his national health insurance plan, and his 1994 State of the Union address, which was largely devoted to a presidential appeal for swift congressional action on health care reform.

4. William J. Clinton, *Public Papers of the Presidents of the United States 1994* (Washington, D.C.: United States Government Printing Office, 1995), pp. 2–3.

5. Henry J. Kaiser Family Foundation, *Uninsured in America: Straight Facts on Health Reform*, April 1994.

6. Joseph A. Califano, Jr., *Radical Surgery: What's Next for America's Health Care* (New York: Times Books, 1994), p. 263.

7. For an analysis of polling data detailing the collapse of public support for health care reform during 1993–1994, see Lawrence R. Jacobs and Robert Y. Shapiro, "Don't Blame the Public for Failed Health Care Reform," *Journal of Health Politics, Policy and Law*, Summer 1995, pp. 411–23.

8. Judy Keen, "Clinton Message Misses Its Mark," *USA Today*, August 11, 1994, p. 6A.

9. Mollyanne Brodie and Robert J. Blendon, ''The Public's Contribution to Congressional Gridlock on Health Care Reform,'' *Journal of Health Politics, Policy and Law*, Summer 1995, p. 406.

10. Judy Keen, ''Clinton Message Misses Its Mark,'' *USA Today*, August 11, 1994, p. A6.

11. *The President's Health Security Plan: The Complete Draft and Final Reports of the White House Domestic Policy Council* (New York: Times Books, 1993), p. 104.

12. Ibid., p. 106.

Select Bibliography

Aaron, Henry, J. *Serious and Unstable Condition: Financing America's Health Care.* Washington, D.C.: The Brookings Institution, 1991.

Aaron, Henry J., and William B. Schwartz. *The Painful Prescription: Rationing Hospital Care.* Washington, D.C.: The Brookings Institution, 1984.

Beauchamp, Dan. *The Health of the Republic: Epidemics, Medicine, and Moralism as Challenges to Democracy.* Philadelphia: Temple University Press, 1988.

Birenbaum, Arnold. *Putting Health Care on the National Agenda.* Westport, Conn.: Praeger Publishers, 1995.

Blank, Robert H. *Rationing Medicine.* New York: Columbia University Press, 1988.

Califano, Joseph A., Jr. *Radical Surgery: What's Next for America's Health Care.* New York: Times Books, 1994.

Castro, Janice. *The American Way of Health: How Medicine Is Changing and What It Means to You.* Boston: Little, Brown, 1994.

Eckholm, Erik, ed. *Solving America's Health Care Crisis: A Guide to Understanding the Greatest Threat to Your Family's Economic Security.* New York: Times Books, 1993.

Fein, Rashi. *Medical Care, Medical Costs: The Search for a Health Insurance Policy.* Cambridge: Harvard University Press, 1989.

Fox, Daniel M. *Power and Illness: The Failure and Future of American Health Policy.* Berkeley: University of California Press, 1993.

Fuchs, Victor R. *The Future of Health Policy.* Cambridge: Harvard University Press, 1993.

Ginzberg, Eli. *The Medical Triangle: Physicians, Politicians, and the Public.* Cambridge: Harvard University Press, 1990.

———, ed. *Health Services Research: Key to Health Policy.* Cambridge: Harvard University Press, 1991.

Gray, Bradford H. *The Profit Motive and Patient Care: The Changing Accountability of Doctors and Hospitals.* Cambridge: Harvard University Press, 1991.

Health Security: The President's Report to the American People. New York: Touchstone Books, 1993.

Jacobs, Lawrence R. *The Health of Nations: Public Opinion and the Making of American and British Health Policy.* Ithaca, N.Y.: Cornell University Press, 1993.

Kassler, Jeanne. *Bitter Medicine: Greed and Chaos in American Health Care.* New York: Birch Lane Press, 1994.

Kissick, William L. *Medicine's Dilemmas: Infinite Needs Versus Finite Resources.* New Haven, Conn.: Yale University Press, 1994.

Laham, Nicholas. *Why the United States Lacks a National Health Insurance Program.* Westport, Conn.: Praeger Publishers, 1993.

Lindorff, Dave. *Marketplace Medicine: The Rise of the For-Profit Hospital Chains.* New York: Bantam Books, 1992.

McKenzie, Nancy F., ed. *Beyond Crisis: Confronting Health Care in the United States.* New York: Meridian Books, 1994.

Marmor, Theodore R. *Understanding Health Care Reform.* New Haven, Conn.: Yale University Press, 1994.

Marone, James A., and Gary S. Belkin, eds. *The Politics of Health Care Reform: Lessons From the Past, Prospects for the Future.* Durham, N.C.: Duke University Press, 1994.

Navarro, Vincente. *Dangerous to Your Health: Capitalism in Health Care.* New York: Monthly Review Press, 1993.

———. *The Politics of Health Policy: The U.S. Reforms 1980–1994.* Cambridge: Blackwell Publishers, 1994.

———, ed. *Why the United States Does Not Have a National Health Program.* Amityville, N.Y.: Baywood Publishing, 1992.

Orient, Jane M. *Your Doctor Is Not In: Healthy Skepticism About National Health Care.* New York: Crown Publishers, 1994.

Perot, Ross. *Intensive Care: We Must Save Medicare and Medicaid Now.* New York: Harper Perennial, 1995.

The President's Health Security Plan: The Complete Draft and Final Reports of the White House Domestic Policy Council. New York: Times Books, 1993.

The President's Health Security Plan: The White House Domestic Policy Council. New York: Times Books, 1993.

Roberts, Marc. *Your Money or Your Life: The Health Care Crisis Explained.* New York: Doubleday, 1993.

Rodwin, Marc A. *Medicine, Money, and Morals: Physicians' Conflicts of Interest.* New York: Oxford University Press, 1993.

Starr, Paul. *The Social Transformation of American Medicine.* New York: Basic Books, 1982.

Stevens, Rosemary. *In Sickness and in Wealth: American Hospitals in the Twentieth Century.* New York: Basic Books, 1989.

Index

About the Author

NICHOLAS LAHAM holds a Ph.D. from the Claremont Graduate School in California and specializes in the study of American politics and public policy. He is the author of *Why the United States Lacks a National Health Insurance Program* (Praeger, 1993), which was selected by *Choice* as an Outstanding Academic Book for 1994.

ISBN 0-275-95611-3

90000>

EAN

9 780275 956110

HARDCOVER BAR CODE